WORLD POVERTY

A Reference Handbook

Other Titles in ABC-CLIO's
**CONTEMPORARY
WORLD ISSUES**
Series

Books in the Contemporary World Issues series address vital issues in today's society such as terrorism, sexual harassment, homelessness, AIDS, gambling, animal rights, and air pollution. Written by professional writers, scholars, and nonacademic experts, these books are authoritative, clearly written, up-to-date, and objective. They provide a good starting point for research by high school and college students, scholars, and general readers, as well as by legislators, businesspeople, activists, and others.

Each book, carefully organized and easy to use, contains an overview of the subject; a detailed chronology; biographical sketches; facts and data and/or documents and other primary-source material; a directory of organizations and agencies; annotated lists of print and nonprint resources; a glossary; and an index.

Readers of books in the Contemporary World Issues series will find the information they need in order to better understand the social, political, environmental, and economic issues facing the world today.

WORLD POVERTY

A Reference Handbook

Geoffrey Gilbert

**CONTEMPORARY
WORLD ISSUES**

A B C  C L I O

Santa Barbara, California • Denver, Colorado • Oxford, England

Library of Congress Cataloging-in-Publication Data
Gilbert, Geoffrey, 1948—
  World poverty : a reference handbook / Geoffrey Gilbert.
    p. cm. — (Contemporary world issues)
  Includes bibliographical references and index.
  ISBN 1-85109-552-7 (hardcover : alk. paper)
  ISBN 1-85109-557-8 (e-book) 1. Poverty—Developing countries.
2. Poverty—Developing countries—Prevention. I. Title. II. Series.

  HC59.72.P6G53 2004
  339.4'6'091724—dc22
                              2004017605

07   06   05   04   9   8   7   6   5   4   3   2   1

This book is also available on the World Wide Web as an eBook.
Visit www.abc-clio.com for details.

ABC-CLIO, Inc.
130 Cremona Drive, P.O. Box 1911
Santa Barbara, California 93116–1911

This book is printed on acid-free paper
Manufactured in the United States of America

*To my parents, Judith Lee Whitney
and Will Gilbert*

Contents

Preface

In September 2000, the United Nations convened a special session of the General Assembly to consider and debate a set of "Millennium Development Goals." It was already apparent by the time the delegates took their seats that a worldwide campaign (Jubilee 2000) to cancel the foreign debts of the world's poorest countries had fallen short of its goal. Undeterred, the delegates proceeded to give their unanimous approval to a Millennium Declaration calling for dramatic improvements in the economic, environmental, and social condition of the world's poor by 2015. It was the broadest, most ambitious commitment of its kind ever made by the global community. Whether all the goals can be reached by 2015 remains to be seen; progress in some areas has been lagging. What no one questions, however, is that a new sense of urgency has been brought to the issue of world poverty. It has a higher priority on the global agenda today than ever before.

This handbook is intended for anyone who wants to become better informed about world poverty, its causes and extent, the forms it takes, and the efforts being made by organizations big and small, public and private, to eliminate it. The book is meant to be a handy one-volume reference work that can answer some—perhaps *many*—of the questions a student or other interested person might have about poverty in the developing world. If the answer isn't here, it can probably be found in one of the many books, articles, websites, or videos that are referred to along the way. Every effort has been made to present this complex topic objectively. Because people hold strong and divergent views on the causes of world poverty, they differ in opinion as to what should be done about it. This volume will display some of the diversity of perspectives without promoting any particular view.

It should serve as a resource for anyone who feels a need for basic information, no matter what direction they want to go with it.

For someone with little previous exposure to the subject of world poverty, chapter 1 is the best starting point, offering a basic overview of issues, institutions, and terminology. It distinguishes economic from social indicators of poverty, identifies the high-poverty regions of the world, and highlights some of the nutritional, health, and educational problems experienced by the world's poor. There is also a preliminary discussion of how foreign aid can be useful in moving a poor economy forward. Chapter 2 explores in much more depth the question of what economic aid can and cannot do for a developing country. It considers, as well, some of the controversial aspects of the trade and external debt of the developing countries. Chapter 3 addresses a set of world-poverty issues of special relevance to Americans: Is the United States providing a level of economic assistance to poor countries consistent with its status as the world's wealthiest nation? Is it using immigration policy as the tool for poverty reduction that it has the potential to be? Have U.S. policies on drug pricing placed the interests of U.S. corporations ahead of the health of AIDS, TB, and malaria sufferers in the world's poorest countries? And is reducing poverty a reliable way to combat terrorism?

Chapter 4 presents a timeline of world poverty "milestones": significant international conferences, declarations, beginnings of programs or organizations, policy shifts, publication years of influential books, and so forth. It is a highly selective list, to be sure, but one that may provide a context for understanding how our views of poverty have evolved through time. Chapter 5 offers brief biographical sketches of twenty-seven individuals whose actions and/or writings have mattered in regard to world poverty. Some are household names; most are not. Roughly half are American. Nearly all are still living and quite active in their respective fields.

Chapter 6, Data and Documents, will probably be the main reason this volume gets pulled off a bookshelf and opened. It supplies up-to-date information on per capita income, the human development index, and other key indicators for all countries in the world, as well as excerpts from some of the most important international documents relating to poverty. Its graphs and tables constitute the statistical "core" of the book. In chapter 7 one can learn about some of the organizations that are engaged in efforts to combat and overcome poverty, whether at the global or local level. The focus is mainly, though not exclusively, on U.S. organizations and on multilateral institutions like the World Food Programme and UNICEF. A range of faith-based NGOs are included. Chapter 8, Print and Nonprint Resources, offers a selective list of books, videos, and websites that can extend in almost any direction the issues raised in the handbook. All the books reviewed are in print, all the videos fairly recently produced and available. The websites are valid for now and likely to be supported and updated in the future.

I am pleased to acknowledge the help of three fellow economists here at Hobart and William Smith Colleges in making this, or so I think, a better book. Feisal Khan gave me useful feedback on chapter 1, Alan Frishman gave the same chapter an extraordinarily close reading and made numerous suggestions for improvements, and Pat McGuire shared his expertise in computer graphing for chapter 6. Another colleague, Bill Atwell of our Asian Studies department, was kind enough to translate an excerpt from a Chinese poem for chapter 4. Finally, I would like to thank my editor, Mim Vasan, for suggesting that I undertake this project and for being a steady source of encouragement from start to finish.

1

Introduction and Overview

Poverty in all its forms has plagued humankind for as long as we can see into the past. Only during the last century have significant numbers of the world's people managed to escape the miseries of unsafe drinking water, cramped living quarters, lack of sanitation, illiteracy, periodic food shortages, epidemic diseases, and premature death. *For hundreds of millions, however, these remain the normal conditions of life.* National and international efforts have been under way for decades to try to combat global poverty, but the task is daunting. Around 2.8 billion people subsist on less than $2 a day, and well over a billion of them scrape by on less than $1 a day. About 40 percent of the people of sub-Saharan Africa lack safe water to drink. Malnutrition afflicts almost 800 million people worldwide. AIDS has become a global pandemic, and while it strikes both rich and poor, it has so far taken its heaviest toll on the world's poorest continent, Africa.

The grim statistics could be elaborated for pages—indeed, there is no way to avoid the recitation of fact and figure as we attempt to grasp the full dimensions of global poverty. But quantitative measures tell only part of the story. The world's poor are deprived of many things not easily measured. One is *security.* Too much rainfall, or too little, can put a rural family's entire cash crop in doubt. A sip of contaminated water or a mosquito bite can put a child's life at risk. A downward turn in prices on the world commodity market can rob thousands of agricultural workers of their main source of income. These and many other kinds of risk render life precarious for millions of families in Asia, Africa, and Latin America. A pervasive daily sense of vulnerability can sap

1

the confidence of the poor, who know well how little control they have over the circumstances of their lives. And it isn't only in regard to crop prices, weather, and disease that the poor feel powerless. They also tend to have little say in the political process, finding it hard to make themselves heard even on questions of vital concern to them. Most of the time their opinions are scorned—or ignored—by those in power. Critical decisions affecting their communities, their livelihoods, and their children's future are too often made by distant elites. Two landmark studies by D. Narayan and associates, entitled *Voices of the Poor*, have begun to lift the silence so long imposed on the world's impoverished. See Narayan (2000a) and (2000b).

Current demographic trends put the global poverty picture in another, and more worrisome, light. The world's population has grown dramatically over the past century. It will continue to grow through most of the twenty-first century, if current UN projections prove accurate. In the first quarter of the century there will be 2 billion additional people living on earth, 97 percent of whom will live in the developing world. One could call this "Malthus in reverse," with a nod to T. R. Malthus, the English clergyman and economist who theorized, in his 1798 population essay, that higher real income levels would spur faster growth in population. Malthus cited the North American colonies as the place where living conditions were most favorable, real wages highest, and population growth the most rapid in the world (see Malthus 1999). Most of the population increase occurring today, however, is not in countries that are rich and growing richer but in countries that are poor and, in many cases, growing poorer. The stark truth is that in the near future, many millions will be born in countries where the standard of living today is actually lower than it was in 1980 or 1970.

A growing imbalance between poor and rich populations, though worrisome, might concern us less if incomes in the poor countries were catching up with those in the rich ones. Unfortunately, exactly the opposite is happening, according to many observers. In a 1999 speech, former U.S. president Jimmy Carter said, "At the beginning of this century, the ten richest countries were nine times as rich as the ten poorest countries. In 1960, the ratio had increased to 30 to 1. Now the ratio is 65 to 1." ("Bridging the Chasm between the Rich and the Poor," in Nancy Bearg Dyke 2000, 83). Nothing has happened since Carter gave his speech to alter the picture. As the world economy becomes increasingly globalized, hundreds of millions are being left further and further behind. The reasons are varied and complex. The end result is a widening gulf between "haves" and "have-nots," North and South, the developed countries and the developing. How wide the gap in per capita incomes will get is unclear, as are the factors that might eventually halt or reverse the trend. What we *can* say is that the repercussions will be felt on all sides, whether in unplanned flows of migration, environmental impacts, the transmission of disease, or political instability. Whether we recognize it or not, world poverty affects us all.

Concepts of Income Poverty

Those who make a serious study of poverty draw a distinction between *relative* and *absolute* poverty. *Relative* poverty refers to those members of society who are positioned lowest in the income scale. If, for example, you were to rank all the families in the United States by income, from the highest-income family down through the broad middle classes to the lowest, you could define the "poor" as the bottom 15 percent of families (or whatever percentage seemed most appropriate). That is not the only relative poverty measure, but it is the simplest. For some circumstances and administrative purposes, it may be perfectly acceptable. But if used in any kind of global poverty analysis, it quickly leads to nonsensical conclusions. A 15 percent definition tells us that poverty is equally extensive in Belgium and Burundi—in both cases, 15 percent of the population—even though the most casual observer can see that the two countries are grossly unequal in their living standards. Clearly, Burundi's poverty is much deeper and more extensive than Belgium's.

Absolute poverty is the condition of people whose incomes are too low to satisfy their most basic needs. This is the concept used by the World Bank in computing its widely cited global poverty figures. One might suppose that it would be possible to specify the basic material needs of every family everywhere—for example, W square feet of housing space per family member, X calories per adult, Y calories per child, Z gallons of clean water daily, and so on. Yet because climates and cultures differ so much, it is hardly feasible to establish a set of subsistence requirements that will make sense everywhere. Many countries choose to draw their own (absolute) poverty lines according to their specific estimates of how much money it would take for a family within their borders to achieve its minimal food and non-food requirements. One such country is the United States, which established an absolute poverty line in the 1960s and continues to update it annually.

In preparing its 1990 *World Development Report*, the World Bank took a close look at the country-specific poverty lines used by a number of low-income countries during the 1980s, selected what it considered to be the most typical of those lines, and defined that as a new international poverty line. Thus was born the familiar $1-a-day, or $370-per-year, poverty line. Below that income a person was (and is) considered to be in extreme poverty. The U.S. dollar of 1985 purchasing power was the reference currency. An example may make all of this clearer. If a family of six in the African nation of Zambia currently consumes annual goods and services with a market value below what $2,220 (six times $370)—or its equivalent in Zambian kwacha—would have purchased in 1985, that family is judged to be in extreme poverty.

Do poverty experts apply the $1-a-day yardstick to countries like France, Norway, Singapore, and the United States? Definitely not. Cultural norms regarding the income level below which a person cannot meet basic needs show considerable variation from country to country. The richer the country, the higher it tends to draw its poverty line. An American man or woman in 1985 could have had an income far above $370 a year and still have been considered destitute by U.S. standards. To come at it another way, if the $1-a-day yardstick were applied to the United States today, almost no one would be counted as poor; the poverty rate would be close to *zero*. In reality, the official poverty rate, as estimated by the U.S. Census Bureau since the 1960s, has never dipped below 10 percent and often been much higher. The World Bank has decided that poverty lines higher than $1 a day are appropriate in some parts of the world. Thus the poverty line for middle-income countries, such as many in the Caribbean, Latin America, and East Asia, is set at $2 a day in 1985 dollars. For the industrialized countries (outside the former Soviet Union), the poverty line is drawn at $14.40 a day in 1985 dollars.

Measuring Income Poverty

When people are unable to satisfy their basic material needs, they are poor. As described above, levels of income have been defined to establish who is and is not "poor," with due regard to the current economic standing of each country or region. Once the poverty lines have been drawn, it would seem a simple task to determine the extent of poverty in each country. All that's needed is to find the number of people below the line—the so-called poverty headcount—and divide it by the total size of the population. If low-income country G, for example, has 3 million people living on less than $1 a day, out of a national population of 12 million, its poverty rate is 3/12, or 25 percent.

But matters are never that straightforward. In the first place, how does country G actually *know* how many of its citizens are below the poverty line? Poor countries often have cash-strapped governments that cannot afford to gather such economic information regularly. Most therefore rely on occasional surveys, using scientific sampling techniques to try to obtain an approximation of the true picture. Country G may choose to conduct a survey every four or five years, with one household per thousand randomly selected to respond to a questionnaire on its income and/or expenditures. If the selection of the sample, construction of the questionnaire, and tabulation of the results are done with skill, the resulting estimates can be very reliable. Many countries get technical assistance from the World Bank and other international experts to ensure that their survey results are as accurate as possible.

Household surveys can focus on either income or consumption (expenditure) to determine rates of poverty. Consumption data, where available, is preferred to income data, since poverty is really about consuming too little to meet basic needs. Besides, reported income figures can be misleading. Respondents may understate their income by failing to report nonmarket production that family members have engaged in. Or respondents may fear that reporting a high income will lead to a high tax bill, and "fudge the numbers" accordingly. Also, income and consumption do not always correlate closely. A family may experience a large deficiency in its cash income and yet be able, through various strategies, to cushion the impact on its consumption, at least for a time. (Pawning family jewelry is a common strategy for "smoothing consumption" in some low-income countries.) While there are good reasons to prefer consumption/expenditure estimates to income estimates when studying global poverty, in the end one has to work with whatever data one finds; hence both types of data are widely used.

The extent of a nation's poverty is only partially reflected in the "headcount" measure. What the headcount fails to reveal is the *depth* of poverty. If all the "poor" in a country were just below the poverty line, it would be quite different from—and less serious than—having all the poor *far* below the line. To get a fuller sense of the extent of deprivation, experts go beyond the poverty headcount and compute the "poverty gap." The poverty gap is the average shortfall of income among the poor as a percentage of the poverty line. For example, if the poverty line in country H is set at $500 per year, and incomes among the poor average only $350, or $150 below the poverty line, then the poverty gap is 150/500, or 30 percent. If country H now pursued a set of policies that raised average incomes of the poor to $400, thus shrinking the income shortfall from $150 to $100, its poverty gap would decrease from 30 to 20 percent.

The Map of World Poverty

A simple way to find the main locations of poverty around the world is to check per capita income levels, country by country. Those countries in which the income per person is quite low will be the ones, inescapably, in which the worst poverty exists. Economic logic dictates that this be so, since "poverty" is merely another name for inadequate income. The World Bank at present puts every country into one of four income categories, based on 2001 per capita gross national income: *low* ($745 or less), *lower middle* ($746–$2,975), *upper middle* ($2,976–$9,205), and *high* ($9,206 or more). The low-income countries are mainly in sub-Saharan Africa, south Asia, and Southeast Asia; a few are former Soviet republics. The only low-income countries in the Western Hemisphere are Haiti and Nicaragua. See chapter 6, table 1 for a full listing of the world's countries by income category, as presented in the authoritative *World Development Indicators 2003 (WDI)*. WDI is issued each year by the World Bank. (Statistical data in this chapter, unless otherwise noted, are taken from the 2003 *WDI*.)

For the sixty-six low-income countries, $1 of income per day is considered the appropriate standard for gauging the extent of poverty. As mentioned before, every country has the option to define its own national poverty line, and may draw it above, below, or right at $1 a day. But if we stick to the international benchmark, we can compare poverty rates across countries and regions.

Again the *WDI* volume provides the data, and it is presented in chapter 6, table 2. Three nations, Ethiopia, Nicaragua, and Uganda, have poverty rates in excess of 80 percent, meaning that only 20 percent of the people in those nations have $1 a day or more to live on. Two countries have poverty rates in the 70 percent range: Mali and Nigeria. Four have poverty rates in the 60 percent range: Burkina Faso, Central African Republic, Niger, and Zimbabwe. And three have poverty in the 50 percent range: Burundi, The Gambia, and Sierra Leone. Aside from crushing burdens of poverty, what nearly all the nations named above have in common is a location in sub-Saharan Africa. The exception, Nicaragua, has been staggered in recent years by weather (Hurricane Mitch, 1999) and plummeting international prices for its main export, coffee.

Outside Africa, the highest reported rates of extreme poverty in the world are found in south and Southeast Asia. India, the world's second most populous nation, has 35 percent living below $1 a day. Given India's recent crossing of the 1 billion population mark, this means 300 to 400 million Indians live in abject poverty—by far the largest total in any country. India's northeastern neighbors, Nepal and Bangladesh, have poverty rates very similar to India's. Extreme poverty is hardly unknown in the Western Hemisphere, as we saw with Nicaragua. The nation of Haiti is probably even more impoverished than Nicaragua, but, as with some other lower-income countries, it has not conducted any recent household surveys. Thus its poverty data are missing from the *WDI*. Applying its own national poverty line, however, Haiti reported about 65 percent poverty in 1987. Nicaragua reported about 50 percent below its poverty line in 1993. See *WDI*, 59.

If we shift our attention to the fifty-three lower-middle-income countries and territories that are located mainly in Latin America, northern Africa, Eastern Europe, and east Asia, we find that poverty rates rarely exceed 50 percent, using the $2-a-day standard considered appropriate to those countries. The rates *are* that high, however, in Ecuador and Namibia. A disparate group of nine countries, including the world's most populous one, report poverty in the 40 percent range on the $2-a-day standard: China, Egypt, El Salvador, Honduras, Paraguay, Peru, the Philippines, Sri Lanka, and Turkmenistan. Three countries have poverty in the 30 percent range: Bolivia, Guatemala, and Thailand. And four nations—Bulgaria, Colombia, Romania, and the Russian Federation—report poverty in the 20 percent range. The rest of the lower-middle-income countries either have poverty rates below 20 percent or have no data reported in the 2003 *WDI*. Note, however, that certain anomalies may be found in the *WDI* data—for example, the indicated poverty rate for Belarus is less than 2 percent, yet according to that country's own national poverty measure, its poverty rate is 42 percent. The likely explanation: Belarus sets its own poverty line far higher than $2 a day and thus counts many more poor people below its own line than below the $2 line.

The countries of Eastern Europe and central Asia with economies "in transition" are all over the map—literally, and in terms of their current income rankings and poverty profiles. At the lower end of the rankings, Armenia, Azerbaijan, Georgia, the Kyrgyz Republic, Moldova, Tajikistan, Ukraine, and Uzbekistan now appear in the World Bank's "low income" category, which they share mainly with the sub-Saharan African countries. In the next higher category, "lower middle income" countries, we find the Russian Federation and nine other nations whose economies were centrally planned before about 1990. Ascending another level, to the "upper middle income" category, we find former Soviet-dominated nations, including the Czech Republic, Estonia, Latvia, Lithuania, and Poland. Of the once centrally planned economies, only tiny Slovenia sits in the *upper income* category. Using the $2-a-day international poverty line, we find that six of the economies "in transition" have poverty rates in excess of 40 percent: Armenia, Moldova, Tajikistan, Turkmenistan, Ukraine, and Uzbekistan. By the $1-a-day standard, five of the six have *extreme* poverty affecting 10 percent or more of their populations.

Why is the world poverty count sometimes put at 1 billion and other times at 3 billion? The answer is simple: it depends on whether you are using the $1- or $2-a-day standard. Moving from the first to the second standard raises the count from 1.2 billion to 2.8 billion. In table 3 of chapter 6, we can see where the additional numbers of poor come from, by region. South Asia, with about half a billion poor under the $1-a-day standard, has more than *twice* that many poor under the $2-a-day standard. In sub-Saharan Africa, the number of poor rises from 300 million to almost 500 million. Indeed, four out of five people in south Asia and sub-Saharan Africa are poor according to the $2-a-day definition—a statistic unequaled anywhere else in the world. The Latin American/Caribbean number of poor more than doubles, from 77 million to 168 million, with a shift to the higher poverty line. For

Europe and central Asia, the relative increase is far larger, from about 18 million to 98 million. In the Middle East and northern Africa, the number leaps from 7 million to 87 million! China by itself adds 400 million to the world poverty total when the $2 standard rather than the $1 standard is used.

Other Poverty Indicators

In editorials, textbooks, official documents, and wherever global poverty is debated, it is *income poverty*, as measured by the $1-a-day and $2-a-day standards, that receives the most attention. Yet to be poor is to be deprived of much more than money. It can mean illiteracy, poor health, short life expectancy, lack of access to clean water and health care, and vulnerability. These dimensions of poverty do not correlate perfectly with income. Two countries, for example, may report identical poverty rates and yet be quite dissimilar in other dimensions of social well-being. India and Bangladesh have nearly identical rates of extreme poverty—about 36 percent—but adult male illiteracy is much higher in Bangladesh (50 percent) than in India (31 percent). Moreover, it is possible for a country to make significant improvements in the welfare of its citizens and yet see no change in its income poverty rate.

Given such limitations in the World Bank's $1- and $2-a-day measuring rods, various alternative social indicators have been proposed. In 1990 the United Nations Development Program created the Human Development Index (HDI), according to which all countries could be compared on the basis of a combination of welfare indicators. The HDI incorporates per capita income, life expectancy, and educational attainment into an overall "quality of life" index number for each country. The news media report the national rankings—or whatever they find most notable in the new rankings—each year as they are released. The HDI has some relevance for the study of international poverty. No one can doubt that the lowest-ranked countries in 2003, characterized as showing "low human development," are, in every sense of the word, *poor*. They range from Cameroon (142nd) through Sierra Leone (175th). Of the thirty-four countries in this category, only four lie outside Africa. Africa's dominance of the "low human development" category has been a feature of the HDI rankings since their first release. (The top five countries in 2003 are, of course, rich, First World, industrialized countries: Norway, Iceland, Sweden, Australia, and The Netherlands. The United States is ranked seventh.)

In 1997 the United Nations introduced a new index of impoverishment, rather similar to the HDI but focused more on *lack* of achievement than on positive achievement. Dubbed the Human Poverty Index (HPI), it captures the extent of deprivation for each country in the areas of longevity, knowledge, and decent standard of living. There are separate HPI series for developing countries and industrialized countries. The HPI-1, for developing countries, looks at the percentage of newborns not expected to reach the age of forty, the percentage of adults who are illiterate, lack of access to safe water and health services, and the percentage of children under age five who are below normal weight. The HPI-2, for industrialized countries, looks at the percentage of newborns not expected to reach the age of sixty, the percentage of functionally illiterate individuals in the population, the percentage of the labor force who are long-term unemployed, and the percentage who are relatively poor, as measured by having household income below one-half the national median. Like the HDI, the HPI table is released annually in the *Human Development Report;* the 2003 results are presented in chapter 6, table 4.

A skeptic might question the value of constructing an index like the HPI if the rankings turned out to match closely the rankings derived from the World Bank's income poverty lines ($1 and $2 a day). In that case, what new information would we be gaining from the HPI? As it turns out, however, the two ranking lists show considerable divergence. Some countries "outperform" on the HPI, that is, their citizens suffer less overall human deprivation than might have been expected on the basis of their income poverty rankings. Among the standouts in 2003 were Nicaragua, Nigeria, Uganda, and Paraguay. Less impressive were the countries that underperformed on the human poverty index, that is, demonstrated worse overall deprivation than might have been expected given their income levels. Those countries included Morocco, South Africa, Cote d'Ivoire, Algeria, and Tunisia.

Two other notes of interest regarding the Human Poverty Index: among the seventeen OECD nations (industrialized North American and European countries, plus Japan and Australia), the United States placed dead last in 2003. The high scorers were Sweden, Norway, and Finland. And if we shift our focus to the other end of the spectrum, the ninety-four developing countries for which an HPI-1 value was computed, we find that only a single sub-Saharan African country, Ghana, appeared in the top half of the list. Every other sub-Saharan state ranked in the bottom half. The dreary consistency with which those countries appear "worst off," whether on measures of per capita income, income poverty, human development, or human poverty, reinforces the sense that Africa is in terrible straits and falling further and further behind the rest of the world.

World Hunger

Can there be any more shocking scene on a television screen or the cover of a news magazine than the sight of starving human beings? This is poverty pushed beyond the limit. Since there is sufficient food in the world to feed everyone, it is appalling to think that people anywhere are allowed to lose their lives for lack of it. And yet in recent years there have been food shortages (and civil strife) so severe as to cause, or threaten, starvation in places as diverse as North Korea, Afghanistan, Tajikistan, Bangladesh, the Balkans, and large swaths of sub-Saharan Africa. It is difficult to estimate how many people actually die of hunger each year, but whatever the number, it is much lower than the number who are underfed. The Food and Agriculture Organization (FAO) of the United Nations issues a count of the global undernourished population each year, in a document entitled *The State of Food Insecurity in the World*. Their 2002 report placed the total number of malnourished people in 1998–2000 at 840 million, of whom 799 million were in developing countries, 11 million in industrialized countries, and 30 million in transitional economies (Eastern Europe and central Asia).

A matter of concern to policy-makers and the public alike is whether the developing countries are managing, over time, to cut the levels of malnutrition experienced by their citizens. The trend is in the right direction but glacially slow—the figure of 799 million undernourished in the developing world represents a reduction of a mere 20 million, or less than 2.5 percent, from the period 1990–1992. The long-term trend downward in the *proportion* of developing-country populations who are undernourished should also be noted. In 1969–1971 that proportion was 37 percent; in 1978–1981, 29 percent; in 1990–1992, 21 percent; and most recently (1998–2000), 17 percent (see FAO 2001).Given the growing size of the developing world's population, this kind of shrinkage in the proportion undernourished must be considered an impressive achievement.

Those who are more concerned about actual numbers of hungry people than about their *proportion* of the total population take less comfort in recent trends. The total underfed population in the developing world was 956 million in 1970. Thirty years later, the number remains just shy of 800 million. Many developing countries—in fact, the great majority—actually saw their malnourished populations increase during the 1990s. Because a few countries, such as Indonesia, Viet Nam, Thailand, and (especially) China, have recorded large decreases in their malnourished numbers, the worldwide total has gone down in spite of increases in dozens of other nations. The biggest increases in malnutrition in the 1990s were seen in central Africa and India.

When undernourished individuals do not starve—and most do not, even in the poorest countries—they are afflicted instead with a variety of debilitating health conditions. The bad effects of inadequate nourishment begin before birth, contribute to abnormally high death rates *at* birth for both babies and their mothers, and continue into childhood. Up to the age of five, children are particularly vulnerable to the effects of malnutrition. Protein-energy malnutrition (PEM), the result of a shortage of calories and protein in the diet, stunts the young both physically and mentally. It is widely prevalent in south Asia and sub-Saharan Africa. Even a diet with sufficient calories may lack critical micronutrients, such as iodine, vitamin A, and iron, with devastating consequences. Iodine deficiency affects more than 700 million people globally, with brain damage its worst result. An even more common micronutrient disorder is anemia, caused by iron deficiency. It can hinder physical activity and mental development in the young, and is thought to cause 20 percent of all maternal deaths. Vitamin A deficiency, affecting as many as 30 percent of children in Africa and south Asia, can lower resistance to disease, retard growth, and even cause blindness.

These nutritional problems need not persist if national and global efforts to address them are supported by enough resolve and resources. In 1996 the World Food Summit in Rome, attended by representatives from 186 nations, set a goal of reducing by half the number of undernourished in the developing world by the year 2015. The baseline selected was the 1990–1992 period, when the total malnourished population in the developing countries was 816 million. Sadly, during the 1990s the number of hungry people fell by only about 2.5 million annually, putting the world far behind schedule in meeting the 2015 goal. One thing the evidence makes clear is that poverty correlates strongly with hunger and malnutrition. The regions of the world in which poverty rates are highest are the ones with the highest rates of hunger. Likewise, those regions in which poverty has been reduced the most are the ones where malnutrition has been cut the most.

Poverty and Health

Good nutrition, a low incidence of communicable diseases, and long life expectancies are never encountered in the same places as extreme poverty. A well-known economist alluded to this fact recently when, advocating more health-related aid to the Third World, he observed that "millions of people . . . are dying from their poverty right now" (Jeffrey Sachs, quoted in "To Cure Poverty, Heal the Poor" [2002]). So how do rich and poor nations differ in terms of the preconditions for good health? We can start with access to clean water—an obvious necessity for the avoidance of all sorts of waterborne disease organisms. *World Development Indicators 2003* presents data on "access to an improved water source" for all countries individually and by broad income categories. For high-income countries, access is nearly universal; for low-income countries as a whole, one-quarter of the population lack access to an improved water source.

The rich-poor gap is much wider for sanitation facilities than it is for clean water. Sanitation here means access to suitable facilities for disposal of human waste. Such facilities can range from "simple but protected pit latrines to flush toilets with sewerage." (See World Bank 2001, 287, 321.) High-income countries take adequate sanitation virtually for granted, while among low-income populations around the world, only 44 percent have such access. There is a rich-poor gap in vaccination rates as well. The DPT infant vaccination rate is 94 percent among high-income nations, but only 61 percent among the low-income. For measles vaccinations, the respective rates are 90 percent and 60 percent.

Infectious disease rates are starkly different between poor and rich countries. In 2001, among adults age fifteen to twenty-four, the HIV prevalence rate in low-income countries was nearly seven times what it was in the high-income ones. In Botswana, almost 40 percent of adults are HIV infected; in neighboring Zimbabwe the infection rate may soon approach the same level. In more than a dozen African nations, the social support network is being strained by a huge number of AIDS orphans. Tuberculosis also preys disproportionately upon the poor. In 2001 the high-income countries recorded 18 new cases of TB per 100,000 people, compared to 233 per 100,000 among the low-income. The third great killer in the developing world, malaria, takes the lives mainly of children—largely in sub-Saharan Africa. Experts estimate the disease's annual death toll at between 1.5 and 2.7 million. When it doesn't kill, malaria renders adult victims anemic and less capable of work, placing a further burden on weak economies.

The two diseases that account for the most deaths in *high-income* countries, heart disease and cancer, are much less important in the world's poorer regions. That would be viewed as a blessing except for the fact that research on treatments and cures by the big pharmaceutical companies tends to be directed toward the diseases of rich countries, and not, for example, toward the tropical "poor man's diseases" such as malaria. Although it is true that research has produced fairly effective drug treatments for AIDS, their cost is far beyond the reach of most infected individuals outside the First World. Meanwhile, concerns are growing about the emergence of drug-resistant strains of TB and the declining effectiveness of the main antimalarial drug, chloroquine.

Not surprisingly, the mortality and longevity profile for poor countries is markedly different from what it is for rich ones. The infant mortality rate is 80 per 1,000 live births for low-income countries, and 5 per 1,000 for high-income. Under-five mortality is 121 per 1,000 for low-income countries, and 7 per 1,000 in high-income countries. Life expectancy at birth is currently fifty-nine in the low-income countries, seventy-eight in the high-income countries. Still, there has been definite progress in the past two decades: infant and below-five mortality rates have fallen substantially in the poorer countries, and life expectancy has risen by six years.

To better appreciate what health challenges an individual nation can face, consider the landlocked West African nation of Niger, a former French colony granted independence in 1960 (not to be confused with its more populous neighbor to the south, Nigeria). Only 59 percent of Nigeriens have access to an improved water source, and 20 percent to improved sanitation. Only 31 percent of infants receive DPT vaccinations, and 51 percent, measles vaccinations. Forty percent of children under five are underweight. The under-five mortality rate is 265 per 1,000—among the worst rates in the world but an improvement from 320 per 1,000 in 1980. Life expectancy in Niger is currently forty-six. With standard health indicators at these woeful levels, it is not surprising that Niger's per capita income is low enough to put 61 percent of its population in extreme poverty. Its Human Poverty Index and Human Development Index values are among the lowest in the world.

The kinds of inequality in health status that are found when comparing rich countries with poor ones also exist within the borders of most poor countries. This goes against a fairly common misperception that everyone in a low-income country must be equally poor and thus share the same deprivations to the same degree. Nothing could be further from the truth. Wealth and income inequalities within poor countries are, in general, just as pronounced as what we see in Western European and North American societies. All the social indicators, including health, show considerable variation in a poor country. One of the lowest-income nations in Latin America, a continent known for marked disparities in income, is Bolivia. If we compare the poorest quintile (one-fifth) of the Bolivian population with the richest, we find that infant mortality is about four times higher and child malnutrition more than five times higher in the poorest quintile. The richest quintile is about five times as likely as the poorest to have a medically trained person in attendance at childbirth. Similar patterns of uneven health status prevail throughout the Third World.

Poverty and Education

An educated labor force can contribute more to the process of economic development—and poverty reduction—than an uneducated one. A more educated population can better understand and put into practice recommendations on good health and nutrition than a less educated one. A nation of literate, well-educated citizens is more likely to demand good government and democracy than a nation of unschooled illiterates. These are relatively uncontroversial assertions. The existence of a rich-poor, or North-South, gap in education is also beyond dispute. While primary and secondary school enrollment is nearly universal in the rich nations, it is far less so among poor nations. And the rich countries spend far more on each primary- and secondary-school student: an average of $4,636 per pupil in 1995, compared with a mere $165 per pupil in developing countries. In sub-Saharan Africa the per pupil figure was $49 (Watkins 2000, 125). Desks, blackboards, books, paper, and pencils are normally available in the schools of the high-income countries. Conditions at the other end of the spectrum are well depicted in *The Oxfam Education Report:* "In much of the developing world, 'school' is often a dilapidated mud building with crumbling walls. More than 80 children, many of them undernourished, might be crammed into a classroom, sitting on the floor with scarcely a book, pencil, or notepad to share. Their teachers, most of them untrained, may have second jobs to make ends meet" (ibid., 123).

A key educational outcome and an absolute requirement for a modern, technology-receptive workforce is the ability to read and write. In the low-income countries, adult female literacy wasn't much above 50 percent in 2001; for males, the figure was 72 percent. These statistics represent an improvement over 1990, but illiteracy continues to plague a number of the world's poorest countries. In India more than half of adult women and one-third of men are illiterate. The picture is even worse in parts of Africa. The *WDI* provides the information in table 1.1 on six African countries in which male illiteracy tops 50 percent. *Female* illiteracy rates in these six nations were *15 to 20 percent higher* than male rates.

There are obvious problems with the schooling systems of countries where such high proportions of adults remain illiterate. The problems begin when large numbers of children who are the right age to enter the first grade of primary school do *not* enter. Delayed school entry is common in poor countries; whenever and for whatever reason it happens, it is an educational setback. In Ethiopia only 27 percent of boys and 24 percent of girls enter

Table 1.1
Adult Male Literacy Rates in Selected African Countries, 1999 and 2001

Country	Illiteracy Rate	
	1990	2001
Burkina Faso	75	65
Ethiopia	63	52
The Gambia	68	55
Mali	72	63
Niger	82	76
Senegal	62	52

Source: World Bank. 2003. *World Development Indicators 2003.* Washington, DC: World Bank.

grade 1 at the age-appropriate time; in Burkina Faso, only 25 percent of boys and 17 percent of girls; in Mozambique, 22 and 21; in Tanzania, 12 and 14. Among the low-income countries, these are fairly typical numbers for the "net intake rate in grade 1."

Once children begin primary school, whether at the "right" age or later, there are a host of pitfalls along the way to completion of that stage of their education. Many never make it. Dropout rates are high in poor countries. There are various reasons for this, one being that financial setbacks to poor families can quickly result in the withdrawal of a child from school in order to save costs or, in some cases, put the child to work. Girls can be withdrawn even from *primary* school because of pregnancy or because their family wants to get them married. For low-income countries as a group, the primary completion rate in 1992–2000 was only 69 percent. For some individual countries, the completion rate was much lower: Benin, 39 percent; Burkina Faso, 25 percent; Cote d'Ivoire, 40 percent; Ethiopia, 24 percent; Mozambique, 36 percent; Senegal, 41 percent; and Sudan, 35 percent. For all of sub-Saharan Africa, the completion rate was 53 percent.

As with health care, there are tremendous class disparities in educational access and achievement within each low-income country. Research by Deon Filmer of the World Bank and Lant Pritchett of Harvard University has enabled them to draw the clearest picture yet of such class (and gender) disparities in education (see Filmer and Pritchett 1999). The wealthiest families are by far the most likely to have their children attend school right through the university level. Consider India, where the average fifteen- to nineteen-year-old from the richest quintile of families has completed ten years of schooling, whereas the average youth from the poorest 40 percent of families has completed *zero* years of schooling. Filmer and Pritchett have found that there are distinct patterns of enrollment and dropping out of school according to the region observed. For example, in south Asia and western and central Africa, one finds a high percentage of youth who never enroll at all. In south Asia, however, the dropout rate is low for those who actually do enroll in school. In Latin America, the initial enrollment rate is high but so is the dropout rate.

It is often asserted that the poor countries of the world need to invest more in education. The trouble is that education comes with a price tag, like everything else. If the government of a low-income country wants to devote more resources to education, it must decide where to make cuts elsewhere in its budget. Even within the "social spending" part of a national budget, priorities other than education may be compelling. Expenditures on family planning, for example, can lead to slower population growth, thereby easing pressures on school and other social service budgets within a short time. Increased spending on nutrition (beginning with pregnant women) can lead to improved physical and mental development of children, getting them readier to learn in the classroom. The point is this: direct investment in education is not necessarily more valuable than every other kind of investment a government or multilateral donor organization might make in a poor country.

When it comes to deciding where the marginal dollar of investment in education should go—to primary or higher levels of schooling—the answer for most poor countries seems to be the former. The return on investment to higher-than-primary levels of education in a developing country can be problematic. Why? Because university-trained microbiologists, computer engineers, or physicists in a poor country may find suitable jobs scarce or nonexistent. Their best option may be to relocate to North America or Europe, where of course salaries will be much higher than at home. The "brain drain" is an aptly named and continuing phenomenon.

Where Does Poverty Come from?

If we ask why some countries are rich and others poor, we echo a question asked in one form or another by some of the greatest thinkers of the past three centuries. No consensus has yet emerged on the right answer. One idea that has been quite influential in Western thinking about economic development since the eighteenth century is that all societies pass through distinct stages, where each stage is defined by the manner in which people produce the goods they need for subsistence. The earliest stage is hunting and gathering, followed by nomadic livestock-herding, then settled agriculture (crop-cultivation), and finally a mixed system of agriculture, industry, and trade. Some societies pass through the stages of development ahead of others, achieving wealth sooner, but all can expect to reach the highest stage eventually. By this way of thinking, today's impoverished societies are simply passing through an early stage of development, one traversed earlier in history by the now developed societies.

But why, if this theory has any truth to it, do some countries get a head start in their development, leaving others behind? Various answers have been put forward, involving cultural values, religion, climate, geography, politics, and institutional frameworks, but history seems to provide one of the most persuasive, if disconcerting answers—sheer good luck. Great Britain happened to be an island nation with an outward-looking, trading orientation, a merchant class bent on acquiring wealth, and a dwindling timber supply offset by ample deposits of coal. This fortuitous combination of natural and social endowments could not have set the stage better for a rapid exploitation of the key inventions of the industrial revolution, especially the coal-fired steam engine, the spinning jenny, and the power-loom. The added contribution made by colonial raw-material supplies and assured colonial markets for British manufactures must also be factored in. Once economic growth got underway in Britain, it became self-sustaining. The same held true of most Western European economies, as well as the United States, by the mid-nineteenth century.

In his 1776 masterwork *The Wealth of Nations*, Adam Smith stressed the advantages of favorable geography—specifically, locations near navigable waterways and coastal ports—for holding down the shipping costs of producers and thus widening their access to domestic and foreign markets. As Smith saw it, large markets permitted economies of scale in production, specialization of labor, cost reductions, and a resulting stream of profits from which additional investments could be financed. Recently, Smith's insights about favorable geography have been incorporated into a cogent explanation of where the world's rich and poor presently live (Sachs, Mellinger, and Gallup 2001). If one divides the world into four climate zones—tropical, desert, highland, and temperate—and makes a further division between locations *near* to, and *far* from, the ocean, one gets eight combinations of climate and geography. Out of these eight, one in particular is far more favorable to development than any other: a temperate climate with access to the seacoast. Although only 8.4 percent of the earth's land surface fits that category, it accounts for about 23 percent of the world's population, and a whopping 53 percent of the world's total GNP. That is where high per capita incomes are found. No other combination of climate and location is nearly as advantageous. The world's poorest people, on the other hand, live in tropical areas without easy access to ocean transport.

Geography-based limitations take several forms, according to Sachs, Mellinger, and Gallup. First, there is the "Adam Smith effect": businesses in hinterland locations, lacking access to ocean transport, find costs raised at times prohibitively high. The markets in which they might compete are therefore sharply limited. Second, certain diseases are climate-specific. Malaria, in particular, is rarely seen outside the tropics. It is a chronic, recurring malady that saps workers' energy and productivity. It also causes high infant mortality, hence high fertility rates (to ensure surviving children). Women end up spending much of their lives not in the workforce but bearing and rearing children. Third, geography affects food production. Of the world's three great staple grains—wheat, maize, and rice—the first grows only in temperate climates, while the other two tend to grow better there. Furthermore, the production techniques developed for temperate-zone farming are difficult to transfer to the tropics. It is a daunting set of challenges, indeed, that geography poses for the world's poor nations.

For those who find geography too deterministic an explanation of poverty's location and persistence, there are alternatives. One that found considerable favor during the 1970s and still claims a large following, especially among Western academics, is dependency theory. This theory points to the fact that the world's poorest regions tend to be former colonial areas. All have long since achieved formal independence, but their economic dependence on, and domination by, their former colonial rulers continues. Power resides in the "center," that is, in Europe and the United States. Nations at the "periphery"—whether in Africa, Asia, or Latin America—have no autonomy. They are limited to their age-old role in the world capitalist system, which is to supply raw materials to the industrial center in exchange for its manufactures and services. Such trading is unbalanced, with disproportionate gains going to the center. Why do the poor nations not throw off this exploitative system? Because they are governed by "neocolonial" elites who benefit, in wealth, status, and power, from the perpetuation of the status quo.

Poverty in Neoclassical Perspective

The 1980s and 1990s saw a waning of dependency theory's influence, not because its analysis of global economic realities was faulty, but because countries that adopted its policy prescriptions

for gaining more economic self-reliance, such as price controls, restrictions on international trade, and support for state over private enterprise, did not enjoy much economic success. Many observers concluded that for the world's poor to be lifted up, what
was needed most was a single-minded focus on economic
growth. Standard economic theory, sometimes called neoclassical
theory, had its own analysis of the problem. Low incomes resulted from low labor *productivity* (output per worker-hour). Economic growth would raise productivity and per capita incomes.
If the poorer countries grew at a faster pace than the richer ones,
they would gradually catch up in their standard of living. The
key to economic growth was *investment*. Investment would build
up the physical and human capital of poor nations, just as it had
done for the now rich nations in the past.

Investment can be funded either by the government or the
private sector. Private individuals and companies need to receive
high enough returns to cover their cost of capital, or they will not
invest. For example, if potential investors in a new port facility
cannot see any way to get enough revenues from the project to
cover the cost of the capital used, they will not go forward, even
though such a facility might create enormous indirect benefits for
the economy as a whole. Many projects of social and physical infrastructure are like that. They promise to generate much higher
total returns to society than to the investor. Economic theory says
that those are the kinds of investment that justify, and even require, public funding. Unfortunately, governments of poor nations are usually too revenue starved to invest in all the projects
promising healthy rates of social return. Thus public-type investments tend to be underfunded. Grants and subsidized loans from
international agencies and donor nations, however, can offer a
valuable augmentation of national funding.

The neoclassical take on private investment is that developing countries offer attractive opportunities for investment. Past
poverty ensures that capital is scarce, as compared with more advanced economies. Its very scarcity means that additions to the
capital stock should earn attractive returns. But investment can
come only from surplus income, that is, income that people do
not require for their immediate subsistence. In a poor country,
such surpluses are neither large nor dependable, hence the importance of *foreign* sources of investment funds. If poor countries
can tap into foreign capital markets, they will have one of the
keys to economic growth.

The other key lies in openness to foreign trade. Countries with low per capita incomes and often small populations—the legacy of colonial empire-carving—typically do not offer a large enough national market to justify building the kind of large manufacturing plants that keep production costs low. Thus it is essential for these countries to look beyond the local market. They cannot overcome the constraints of their small market size except by competing in regional or world markets. Not only must they aim to export; they must also lift protective duties on their imports. Why? Because protective duties have two market-distorting effects: they raise the cost of inputs to domestic manufacturers, making it that much harder for them to produce goods at low enough cost to compete in world markets, and they cause resources to be allocated into inefficient areas of production. (On the second point, Adam Smith was quite lucid as early as 1776.) Perhaps a simple example can illustrate the issue. A small, poor nation can try building an automobile company, but the cars it produces will have little chance of competing in the world market against those coming from high-volume, low-cost assembly plants abroad. The locally produced cars may generate some sales in the local market, but only if heavy taxes (tariffs) or quotas are placed on imported cars. Result: an inefficient use of the country's capital and labor resources.

So how does neoclassical theory explain poverty? Its adherents, who incidentally wield great influence in such places as the World Bank, the International Monetary Fund, the U.S. Treasury Department, and the Federal Reserve, point to bad economic policies pursued in the less developed nations. Those policies have restricted trade, misallocated resources, reduced human and physical capital formation, and thereby limited economic growth. In the neoclassical perspective, there is not much chance that poverty can be reduced under policies that hinder the workings of a flexible, unfettered market.

The Washington Consensus

Neoclassical economics with a strong infusion of supply-side, free-market ideology lay behind what came to be known in the 1990s as the "Washington Consensus." The phrase came from a 1990 essay by John Williamson: "What Washington Means by Policy Reform." In this piece Williamson listed a set of policy reforms that he thought were supported by key financial entities in Washington, D.C.—the IMF, the World Bank, and the U.S. Treasury Department—for improving economic performance in Latin America. The term's range of application quickly expanded beyond Latin America (see Williamson 1990).

Washington Consensus was the shorthand term for a whole package of promarket policies (also known as "structural adjustment programs," or SAPs) that were pressed upon poor nations whenever they applied for assistance from the IMF or the World Bank. Some of the policies had long been urged, or enforced, by the IMF when it came to the aid of countries experiencing foreign exchange crises. "Fiscal discipline," for example, was regularly preached to such countries when they received loans from the IMF. They were asked to rein in government spending, improve tax collections, and shrink their budget deficits as ways of combating inflation. Borrowing nations were also expected to set more realistic exchange rates for their currencies. In theory, depreciation would bring exports and imports into balance. Exports, becoming less expensive in foreign markets, would increase; imports, becoming more expensive at home, would decrease. The net result would be an improved balance of payments. Import duties were also to be lowered as part of the "trade liberalization" envisioned by the Washington Consensus.

A further aspect of the Washington Consensus push toward more "open" economies was the call for fewer restrictions on direct foreign investment. If a country was too poor to generate enough savings to finance its own private investment and economic growth, it should open the door to foreign investors to fill the gap with *their* investment capital. But this did not go down well with skeptics in the developing countries (and elsewhere) who had long argued that direct foreign investment led to an erosion of sovereignty and the entrenchment of a development pattern based solely on commodity exports. The Washington Consensus call for lower trade barriers and freer flows of international capital clearly ran counter to the policies espoused by dependency theorists, policies aimed at promoting more self-reliance and self-determination for developing countries.

The other elements of the Washington Consensus were directed at increasing overall economic efficiency within poor countries through various legal and institutional changes. Recommended policies included lowering marginal tax rates, broadening the tax base, lifting interest rate ceilings, privatizing state enterprises, deregulating industries to make them more competitive, and enacting legal reforms to make property rights more secure. The program, taken as a whole, could be seen as placing a heavy wager on the superiority of free markets over regulated ones. Indeed, a country that followed each and every recommendation of the Washington Consensus could have been held up as a paragon of textbook neoclassical capitalism. But in the Asian debt crisis of 1997–1998, some of the countries most frequently praised as Consensus success stories—Korea, Indonesia, Singapore, Malaysia—went into a painful economic tailspin. Today, one hears less about the Washington Consensus. Yet it remains an unusually clear statement of the principles and priorities that inform much of the policy-making by Western, industrialized nations toward the developing world.

International Borrowing

Where do low-income countries go when they need loans or grants to assist in their development? *Grants,* which do not entail any kind of repayment, are generally received only from official, public entities, such as governments or multilateral institutions, not from private sources like commercial banks. Banks do not give away money! *Loans* may be sought from all kinds of sources: governments; multilateral agencies like the IMF, the World Bank, the African Development Bank, the Asian Development Bank, and the Inter-American Development Bank; nongovernmental organizations (NGOs); and private commercial banks. The bookkeeping entries can get complicated, especially when one is trying to identify the amount of "foreign aid" that has gone from one country or group of countries to another. What's clear is that, over the years, a huge amount of capital has flowed from the rich nations to the poor, some of which has been economically productive, much of which has not. The recipient nations have repaid enormous sums of principal and interest that they owed, yet they remain deeply in debt. For a fuller discussion of the debt issue, see chapter 2.

Pride of place among the international financial institutions to which poor nations apply for loans or grants goes to the World Bank. Officially titled the International Bank for Reconstruction and Development, it was founded in 1945 as part of the postwar financial architecture set in place by the Bretton Woods conference of the previous year. In its first decade, the World Bank's main function was to assist in the recovery of the war-torn economies of Europe. The 1960s and 1970s brought a big change in policy emphasis, however, as the Bank directed more and more attention to the less developed countries, especially under the leadership of Robert S. McNamara (1968–1981). Today the World Bank claims that its main function is to alleviate poverty world-wide. It can lend to poor countries on favorable (low-interest) terms because its own credit rating is AAA, allowing it to raise funds more cheaply in the capital markets than any developing nation could. Like most banks the World Bank has shareholders, but unlike other banks, its shareholders are sovereign nations. Its purpose is not to make profits but to assist borrowing nations in their economic and social development.

The World Bank is sometimes attacked as a "tool" of the U.S. government or of the industrialized countries generally. Whatever the merits of that charge, it has some basis in the way the World Bank is governed. All of the 184 member, or "shareholder," countries in the Bank are required to contribute capital to the institution. When it comes to voting on policy issues, voting power is proportional to the amount of capital each country has contributed. Since the United States is the largest contributor, it has the most votes—about 17 percent. Other wealthy "shareholders," such as Japan, Germany, and Great Britain, wield a similar influence because of their large subscriptions to the Bank's capital. Thus it is certainly the case that if the high-income countries join together, they can and do determine what World Bank policy will be. The same is true at the IMF, and for the same reasons.

Aid with Strings Attached

As just noted, the World Bank has been criticized as an undemocratic institution; the same has been said of the IMF. When one considers the essentially unequal dealings that borrowing nations have with the "Bretton Woods institutions," with one side needing funds badly and often urgently, and the other providing those funds only on certain conditions, it comes as no surprise that a great deal of friction has been generated. During the 1980s and 1990s, dozens of countries around the world—middle-income as well as low-income countries—found themselves needing loans from the World Bank and the IMF. When the loans were granted, it was normally on condition that the borrower undergo a structural adjustment program. Typically this required the borrowing government to take action against inflation, adjust its official exchange rate to more realistic levels, and take steps to privatize state-owned enterprises. Borrowers, in other words, were expected to adopt Washington Consensus policies even in the years before a handy label could be attached to such policies. Sometimes the policies solved short-term problems. But often the structural adjustments brought additional economic pain to families already struggling with poverty—a fact widely reported and complained of by Third World nations.

At the annual meeting of the World Bank and the IMF in September 1999, a new approach was announced: Henceforth, the two institutions would pay more attention to social conditions within the nations borrowing from them. There would be less emphasis on macroeconomic policy targets, more on the strengthening of safety net programs and the alleviation of poverty. Every borrower would be asked, as part of its application for a loan or grant, to submit a Poverty Reduction Strategy Paper (PRSP). The PRSP was to be drafted not just by teams of government ministers and economic advisors but also with the active participation of members of "civil society," that is, representatives of labor groups, religious groups, educators, environmentalists, NGOs, and others. The consultative nature of the drafting process was intended to ensure national "ownership" of the PRSP. Loans would still come with strings attached, but the strings would include "social conditionality," with attention paid to how the adjustment program might affect poverty, income inequality, education, health, and other social variables.

Dissatisfaction with the harsh impact of earlier adjustment programs on the most vulnerable members of society was not the only factor behind the PRSP approach. In 1999, with a new millennium about to dawn, a worldwide movement to forgive the foreign debts of the world's poorest countries was gathering steam. Known as Jubilee 2000, the campaign was supported by activists (rock star Bono, for example), the pope, NGOs, the less developed countries themselves, and many others who considered this the right moment for a generous gesture toward the world's most impoverished nations. As discussed in the next section, there was also an evolving consensus at the United Nations to set ambitious "millennial goals" for the developing world. Thus the PRSP approach was introduced in a period when the international community seemed headed toward a renewed commitment to combat global poverty. It remains an open question whether PRSPs have a significant role to play in that effort.

Millennium Development Goals

At the so-called Millennium Summit of the UN General Assembly, held in September of 2000, delegates adopted an ambitious set of goals for progress against global poverty, ignorance, and misery over the next decade and a half. Some of the goals had been proposed at earlier summits devoted to specific social problems, such as health and education, but never before had the United Nations backed such a comprehensive antipoverty agenda. The seven substantive goals call for: (1) Halving the proportion of people who live in extreme poverty and the proportion of people in hunger, over the period 1990–2015; (2) Achieving universal primary education for both boys and girls by 2015; (3) Promoting gender equality and the empowerment of women; (4) Reducing child (under-five) mortality by two-thirds between 1990 and 2015; (5) Reducing maternal mortality by three-quarters between 1990 and 2015; (6) Halting and beginning to reverse the spread of HIV/AIDS, malaria, and other major diseases by 2015; and (7) Integrating environmental-sustainability principles into national development programs. (One of the best discussions of the Millennium Goals will be found in the *Human Development Report 2002*, 16–33.)

The assembled UN delegates were as aware as the journalists and other observers at the millennium session that good intentions alone would do little to alleviate poverty. For that reason, they specified numerical targets to be met under each of the seven headings and gave considerable thought to the monitoring of progress toward meeting the goals.

It was equally clear to the delegates that achieving the Millennium Development Goals (MDGs) would not be inexpensive. Hence an eighth goal was also adopted: building a "global partnership" for development. The rich nations were asked to increase their assistance to the poor nations through an expansion of financial aid, debt relief, and a reduction of the trade barriers that developing countries face when exporting to the industrialized world. On the other side of the partnership, it was expected that poor countries would adopt appropriate policies for maximizing the benefits of new aid and trade provisions. That meant reforms in their financial sectors, more macroeconomic discipline, and efforts to reduce corruption. (The term "good governance" is appearing more and more frequently in policy documents of international institutions—a clear indication of concern that bribery and other corrupt practices at all levels of government are jeopardizing the prospects for economic advancement in the developing world.)

How much would it cost to achieve the Millennium Development Goals? Perhaps the most widely publicized estimate is that offered in the Zedillo Report (Zedillo Report 2001). Cutting poverty in half, it argues, would cost about $20 billion annually. Halving hunger would involve no added costs if the poverty goal were met. Getting to universal primary education would cost $9 billion annually. Halving and reversing HIV/AIDS would be another $7–$10 billion. For some of the MDGs, no cost estimates were offered. Altogether, the Zedillo Report put the annual cost of achieving the Millennium Goals at approximately $50 billion. That would represent roughly a doubling of the current flow of aid to the developing countries.

Room for Hope

The glass is half empty. Severe poverty afflicts well over 1 billion people around the globe, and for many there is scant hope of seeing any change for the better in their lifetimes. HIV/AIDS is nearly out of control in many poverty-stricken areas, especially in sub-Saharan Africa. Life expectancies there have been dropping—by eight years in Burkina Faso, seventeen years in Kenya, and as much as thirty-four years in Botswana. Globally, upward of 20 million people have died of AIDS so far. Less life-threatening but surely life-impairing are the many other diseases to which humankind are subject in every continent. Many of the world's people, especially children, are at present virtually defenseless against them. Each year, for example, between 170 and 400 million children are infected with intestinal parasites. Iodine deficiency, one of the least expensive dietary deficiencies to correct, causes 120,000 children every year to be born with mental retardation; it causes one person in ten around the world to be affected by goiter. The number of people malnourished in the world exceeds the combined populations of forty-two European countries. And in fifteen countries, mainly in Africa, malnutrition got worse during the 1990s.

Behind the global aggregate picture of poverty and disease, a further cause of concern has arisen in the past decade. We now see not only sub-Saharan Africa moving backward on a wide range of poverty indicators but also a new geographic area that the United Nations refers to as "Central and Eastern Europe and the Commonwealth of Independent States (CIS)." These are the countries whose economies are making a transition from central planning to some form of market system. The absolute degree of human poverty in this newly designated region is far less than what Africa is experiencing. Still, it is disconcerting to have so many countries in one region moving to lower levels of per capita income, lagging badly in trying to reduce child mortality, going backward in life expectancy, and experiencing sharply increased rates of HIV infection.

Every half-empty glass is also half full, and in the case of world poverty, one may be tempted to say *more* than half full. Solid progress has been made in reducing poverty. In 1999, 23 percent of the world's population lived in extreme poverty, down significantly from 30 percent in 1990. China's enormous strides have been a major factor behind the global improvement; indeed, China as a nation has already met the UN goal of cutting 1990 poverty levels in half by 2015! World hunger is also on the decrease, though not nearly fast enough to reach the goal, by 2015, of halving the number of people suffering from hunger worldwide. Fifty-one countries were on track in 2002 to achieve the goal of universal primary education by 2015, and ninety countries looked likely to meet the goal of gender equality in education. Child mortality is always tragic, especially with so much of it preventable, but the long-term trend is now moving in the right direction: from 1970 to 2000, the global under-five mortality rate fell from 96 to 56 per 1,000 live births, a 42 percent decrease.

Since 1990, three-quarters of a billion people have gained access to improved sanitation, and even more have gained access to improved water supplies. In September 2002, the World Summit on Sustainable Development, held in Johannesburg, South Africa, took the important step of adopting an additional Millennial Goal to be met by 2015: reducing by half the proportion of people lacking sanitation. These kinds of public health advances, as humdrum as they may sound to residents of industrialized nations (who take such amenities for granted), can make a world of difference in the daily lives and health of poor people. The only optimism that can be mustered on the issue of HIV/AIDS, on the other hand, comes from the realization that knowledge, resources, and determined leadership can make a real dent in the course of the epidemic. The nation of Uganda has become an example of doing what's right to turn the tide. Its preventive measures enabled that impoverished country to reduce its HIV prevalence rate from 14 percent in the early 1990s to 5 percent by the end of 2001. What Uganda has accomplished, other countries can accomplish.

Global poverty poses far too complex a challenge to have any easy solution. Around the world, various programs are either in place or in preparation to ease the burdens of ill health, inadequate education, malnutrition, and all the other manifestations of poverty. And we are learning from them. Valuable, life-enhancing work is being done by individuals and organizations of every description. The events of September 11, 2001, rocked the international community and, by some early estimates, did more economic harm to the world's poorest than to anyone else. It appears unlikely, however, that the attacks weakened the international will to reduce poverty. Indeed, from the statements, resolutions, and pledges of aid coming out of international development meetings since 9/11, it seems that there is a strengthened resolve to address the needs of the world's poor.

References and Further Reading

Birdsall, Nancy, and John Williamson. 2002. *Delivering on Debt Relief: From IMF Gold to a New Aid Architecture*. Washington, DC: Center for Global Development.

Dyke, Nancy Bearg, ed. 2000. *The International Poverty Gap: Investing in People & Technology to Build Sustainable Pathways Out*. Washington, DC: Aspen Institute.

Easterly, William. 2001. *The Elusive Quest for Growth: Economists' Adventures and Misadventures in the Tropics*. Cambridge: MIT Press.

Filmer, Deon, and Lant Pritchett. 1999. "The Effect of Household Wealth on Educational Attainment." *Population and Development Review* 25, 1 (March): 85–120.

Food and Agriculture Organization of the UN (FAO). 2001. *The State of Food Insecurity in the World 2001*. Rome: FAO.

———. 2002. *The State of Food Insecurity in the World 2002*. Rome: FAO.

Malthus, Thomas Robert. 1999. *An Essay on the Principle of Population (1798)*. Edited by Geoffrey Gilbert for Oxford World's Classics. New York: Oxford University Press.

McGovern, George. 2001. *The Third Freedom: Ending Hunger in Our Time*. New York: Simon and Schuster.

Narayan, Deepa, et al. 2000a. *Voices of the Poor: Can Anyone Hear Us?* New York: Oxford University Press.

———. 2000b. *Voices of the Poor: Crying Out for Change*. New York: Oxford University Press.

Sachs, J. D., A. D. Mellinger, and J. L. Gallup. 2001. "The Geography of Poverty and Wealth." *Scientific American* 284, 3 (March): 70–75.

"To Cure Poverty, Heal the Poor." 2002. *Africa Recovery* 16, 1 (April).

Todaro, Michael P. 2002. *Economic Development*. 8th ed. New York: Addison-Wesley.

United Nations Development Program. 2003. *Human Development Report 2003: Millennium Development Goals: A Compact among Nations to End Human Poverty*. New York: Oxford University Press.

Watkins, Kevin. 2000. *The Oxfam Education Report*. Oxford: Oxfam Publications.

Williamson, John. 1990. "What Washington Means by Policy Reform," in J. Williamson, ed. *Latin American Adjustment: How Much Has Happened?* Washington, DC: Center for Global Development, chapter 2.

World Bank. 2001. *World Development Report 2000/2001: Attacking Poverty*. Washington, DC: World Bank.

———. 2003. *World Development Indicators 2003*. Washington, DC: World Bank.

Zedillo Report. 2001. *Report of the High-Level Panel on Financing for Development*. New York: United Nations.

2

Aid, Trade, Debt, and the World's Poor: Some Key Controversies

You don't need a Ph.D. in ethics to know that the world's poorest people deserve much better lives than they now have. The impoverished South African mother of five whose husband has died of AIDS, and who is now dying of the same disease herself, deserves much better. The rural families of Malawi subsisting on a single daily meal of corn porridge as they try to hang on through the "hungry months" until the next harvest deserve much better. And the eight-year-old child abandoned to the streets of Rio de Janeiro by a family that can no longer afford to support him deserves much better. To actually make life better for the world's poor, as they so clearly deserve, is the hard work of economic and social development. Moral philosophers can awaken our consciences, reminding us of our obligations toward the world's least fortunate, and delegates to international conferences can make ringing declarations of what *should* be done for our global neighbors living in misery and degradation. But at the end of the day, policy-makers must identify, and governments implement, the policies that stand the best chance of bringing about the changes that all agree are needed.

This chapter will put the spotlight on some current policy issues relating to global poverty. As noted in chapter 1, economic growth is the key to major, long-term reductions in poverty. Some of the questions relating to poverty and growth that have sparked controversy in recent years are: How effective is foreign aid, if at all, in boosting a poor country's economic growth? Do the billions of dollars of aid make a positive difference, or is it just "money down a rat hole," as former Senator Jesse Helms used to say? Is export trade the key to growth for the developing countries? If so, are the industrialized countries doing enough to open up their own markets to the products that the developing nations are trying to export? What about debt? Is there a case to be made for forgiving some or all of the huge debt incurred by the world's poorest countries? Is debt relief an effective way to promote economic development?

These questions are posed and discussed in fairly general terms below. In chapter 3, we take a much more concrete look at how the United States is affected by world poverty and what it could do to reduce such poverty. In particular, we will consider the U.S. foreign aid budget, U.S. immigration policy, drug-pricing policies, and the connection between international poverty and terrorism.

Before continuing, a few simple points need to be made about economic growth and the poor. Growth can be defined as rising per capita GDP (gross domestic product). In itself, growth is no guarantee of poverty reduction. If the gains from a growing economy were unevenly shared, with the middle and upper classes getting the most, the poor might get little or nothing. The pie could be growing yet the slices served to the poor remain as small as ever. In reality, however, the news about growth is much more encouraging than that. The main empirical study on this topic (Ravallion and Chen 1997) strongly suggests that growth and poverty reduction in the developing countries go hand in hand. In the 1980s and early 1990s, the countries clocking the fastest economic growth were the ones experiencing the largest reductions in poverty. On the flip side of the coin, the countries that saw big *increases* in poverty were the ones suffering large economic contractions, or negative growth. In sum, the global evidence supports the notion that economic growth is an engine of poverty reduction.

But growth isn't the only mechanism for reducing poverty. *Redistribution* of a country's existing wealth can also reduce the poverty of the low-income classes—at the expense of the higher-income classes. With economic growth, the whole pie gets larger. With redistribution, the pie stays the same size, but the slices going to the poor get bigger. History offers many examples of wealth redistributions: confiscation of landholdings and other properties of the rich, the imposition of extra-high tax rates on large incomes, and other tax and subsidy measures. Needless to say, these steps are not popular with those who stand to lose wealth. Forced redistributions are resisted by economic elites, sometimes violently. Even the hint of a possible rich-to-poor redistribution can be enough to trigger "capital flight" from a developing country, draining it of the little wealth it may previously have had. And in many of the world's poorest countries there is not much wealth to reallocate. The pie is so small to begin with that reslicing it won't make the portions for the poor much bigger than they were before.

These are a few of the reasons why wholesale income and wealth redistributions within developing countries are not currently on the policy agenda of the World Bank, the UN Development Programme, or any other international bodies. Two other approaches to poverty reduction are preferred. The first is pro-poor growth policies. As noted above, research tells us that economic growth is likely to be pro-poor in any case. But if governments can devise and implement policies that simultaneously speed up growth and put more of the gains from that growth into the pockets of the poor, so much the better. The second preferred approach is redistribution not *within* but *between* countries, that is, redistribution on an international scale. Think foreign aid and debt relief. In principle, these represent shifts of resources from the rich nations to the poor, made in the hope that they will promote economic development, self-reliance, and a gradual lessening of the need for such transfers in the future. And that brings us to the first area of controversy, foreign aid.

The Effectiveness of Aid

Does foreign aid help a poor country grow faster, economically? In theory, it could. To put matters as simply as possible, poor countries tend to be capital-deficient. They have plentiful labor and often plentiful natural resources but usually they lack sufficient capital—factories, equipment, computers, road and rail networks, port facilities—for their workforces to achieve high levels of productivity. That puts a lid on wages and the standard of living. The scarcity of capital, if caused by the simple inability of low-income people to do much saving, can be remedied by an inflow of foreign investment. On average, these funds should earn an attractive rate of return. But foreign aid funds do not (necessarily) flow according to the same logic as investment funds. Aid dollars come from government agencies and multilateral organizations, not commercial banks and investors. These dollars may be targeted to much-needed physical and social infrastructure, in which case they will be every bit as productive as—and conceivably *more* productive than—dollars of private investment. But if the aid funds end up going to more dubious purposes (or down Senator Helms's rat hole), they will surely not boost economic growth.

There is no simple answer to the question, Has aid made a positive difference? Aid supporters say it has; aid skeptics say it has not. The skeptics have been on the offensive in recent years, and their arguments have shifted from "rat holes" to econometric equations. Critics have always been able to point to specific countries where aid has made no apparent contribution to the reduction of poverty. A front-page *New York Times* article (Gonzalez) on July 30, 2002, described the sorry record of aid to Haiti, the poorest country in the Western Hemisphere. It noted that "official corruption and mismanagement, regardless of who was in power, has given pause to many international aid officials." And it cited a recent World Bank study that found that 15 years of aid to Haiti had had "no discernible impact in reducing poverty, since projects were carried out haphazardly and government officials did not sustain improvements."

Leading the aid skeptics is William Easterly, an economist who worked for many years at the World Bank before leaving the Bank for a position at New York University. His 2001 book *The Elusive Quest for Growth: Economists' Adventures and Misadventures in the Tropics,* written while he was still employed at the World Bank, leveled a powerful blast at the theories underpinning the aid programs of the past fifty years. Donor agencies have proceeded on the mistaken assumption that directing their assistance toward one area or another—whether roads, family planning, health, or education—would put the recipient country on a secure path of economic growth. Time and again the assumption has been proven wrong. Since the 1960s, Easterly notes, assistance from the donor countries has totaled 1 trillion dollars, and yet the growth rate of per capita income for the average developing country over the past two decades has been zero! For some countries, the record has been far worse. Zambia, for example, received $2 billion in aid, yet its living standards today are 40 percent *lower* than they were when the country declared its independence in 1964.

Defenders of aid cite counterexamples of countries that have made large economic strides due, in part, to foreign aid. South Korea, Thailand, and Chile were poor countries in the 1960s. All received significant amounts of aid. Today South Korea is a high-income country; Chile is an upper-middle-income country; and Thailand, though still in the lower-middle-income category, has cut its rate of severe poverty to less than 1 percent. Two more recent examples of aid success have received a lot of attention: Uganda and Mozambique. Uganda spent the 1960s and 1970s under brutal dictatorships, and in the 1980s and 1990s it was ravaged by HIV/AIDS. Yet from the mid-1980s onward, strong reformist leadership and some healthy doses of foreign assistance enabled it to reduce the HIV infection rate among pregnant women by 80 percent, cut poverty by 35 percent, double the number of children in school, and reduce the annual inflation rate from 200 to 2 percent. Its economic growth rate has been close to 7 percent for the past decade. Developments in Mozambique have been just as dramatic. Mozambique was a ruined nation in 1992 at the end of a long and disastrous civil war. But the United Nations, the World Bank, and other international agencies moved in quickly with assistance, and a decade later the picture was far different. New schools and clinics had been built, a new financial system set up, refugees resettled, and price controls dismantled. Economic growth in Mozambique was very rapid by the end of the 1990s.

Statistics Don't Lie (Do They?)

So proponents of foreign aid celebrate the Ugandas and the Mozambiques, skeptics cite the Haitis and the Zambias, and everyone else is left wondering where the truth lies—and how we will ever manage to discover it. One reasonable strategy for cutting through the clutter is to study a large number of countries, using advanced statistical techniques, and see whether foreign aid emerges as a significant variable in accounting for different rates of economic growth. That is exactly what Craig Burnside and David Dollar, two World Bank economists, did in an article published in the *American Economic Review* in 2000. It turned out to be one of the most influential pieces of economic research in recent years, frequently cited by the press and by international agencies, and even alluded to by the president of the United States in a speech on March 16, 2002, announcing a significant increase in the U.S. foreign aid budget. By crunching data on fifty-six countries between 1970 and 1993 through an econometric model of the growth process, Burnside and Dollar were able to reach a telling conclusion: foreign aid has no significant impact on the growth rate of countries with "average" policies, but *aid has a positive impact on countries that have good policy environments.*

Why was this an important and even exciting result? It was exciting because, as much as policymakers wanted to believe in aid's effectiveness, they hadn't found much support for it in previous statistical studies. In general, those studies had offered very little basis for thinking that aid could lift growth rates (and thus lower poverty rates) in the long run. The Burnside-Dollar result was important because it gave the rich nations a "scientific" basis for increasing their foreign aid budgets, as long as the recipient countries were maintaining suitable political and economic conditions for development. For the purposes of their study, Burnside and Dollar defined a "good" economic environment as one in which the government budget deficit, the inflation rate, and the tariff rate on imported goods were all kept low. This turned out to be just the formula the Bush administration was looking for in the spring of 2002, with the summit on development (to be held in Monterrey, Mexico) fast approaching. The message of Burnside-Dollar was clear: aid could be effective, and more aid could be justified, but only if donors directed their assistance to countries that sustained the right, development-friendly policies.

Alas, nothing is ever proven beyond question in the social sciences. Just when the Burnside-Dollar finding was becoming part of the conventional wisdom in development circles, it came under serious attack by the aid skeptics. William Easterly and two colleagues decided to update the Burnside-Dollar study with more recent data (through 1997) and a larger sample of countries. Strictly duplicating the methodology of Burnside and Dollar, deviating only by the addition of new, more complete data, they discovered that they could not confirm the finding that foreign aid boosts growth in a good policy environment. The data no longer point that way. Since the Burnside-Dollar paper concluded that aid is effective *only* in the right policy environment, and now even that result appears invalid, it seems that the aid skeptics have won the day. At any rate, they have won the most recent round.

(Debates like this can rage on for a long time!) Aid supporters are now forced once again to argue their case mainly on the basis of individual success stories, such as Uganda, Mozambique, and Vietnam, with assertions rather than proof that benefits can be expected to flow from aid if it is put to good use.

Some Aid Realities

No one expects miracles from foreign aid, but it does strike many observers that the payoff for U.S. and other Western aid has been, at the very least, disappointing. Why has that been so? Where have all those billions of dollars gone, anyway?

The first reality to be confronted is that aid is not universally allocated to the countries in the most desperate need of it. If it were allocated on that principle, it would be hard to understand why Hungary, with per capita income estimated at $4,830, and Malawi, with per capita income estimated at $160, received roughly the same amount of official aid from donors, about $400 million, in 2001 (World Bank 2003). Indeed, if aid were directed only or mainly to the world's poorest people, it would be hard to fathom why Hungary should have received any aid at all, since it is on the World Bank's list of upper-middle-income countries. And it is by no means the only country in that category currently receiving aid. In fact, two countries on the "high income" list, Slovenia and Israel, received significant amounts of assistance in 2001. (Recall that per capita incomes must be over $9,200 per year for a country to be considered *high* income.)

The mention of Israel leads us to the next point: countries give aid to other countries partly for humanitarian reasons but mainly for other reasons. Aid is usually considered a means of advancing the commercial, political, and strategic interests of the donor. U.S. economic aid to Israel, for example, is intended to support and reward a geopolitical ally; the same holds true of Egypt, the second-largest recipient of U.S. economic aid. (These two countries are the signatories to the Camp David peace accord of 1978, a cornerstone of U.S. diplomacy in the Middle East.) Other big industrialized countries behave like the United States in this regard. One can easily detect strategic, diplomatic, and commercial motives in the very substantial aid France delivers to its former colonies in Africa, such as Algeria, Cote d'Ivoire, Cameroon, and Senegal. The same goes for the bilateral aid from

Great Britain to its former colonies in Asia and Africa, as well as Japan's concentration on aid to trading partners in Asia.

The economic motive behind a lot of aid becomes much clearer when we look at something called *tied aid*. That is the term used to describe the policy under which a donor country grants aid to a recipient country on condition that some percentage (up to 100 percent) of the aid be spent on goods and services produced by the donor. At first glance this might seem reasonable, until one realizes that oftentimes the tying requirement forces the recipient to buy at a much higher price from the donor than from a lower cost source. When that happens, the true value of the aid is overstated by the difference in cost. By one estimate, the value of aid is reduced by 15 to 30 percent when it is tied. (World Bank 2001, 200). As much as one-quarter of official development assistance is tied.

Another foreign aid reality is corruption. There is no getting around the unpleasant fact that much of the aid funding designated for development projects over the years has wound up in the pockets of government officials. Corruption is a sensitive issue for all concerned because it can bring embarrassment (or worse) to the multinational corporations that offer the kickbacks and bribes, the Third World government officials who accept them, and the international lending agencies that finance the projects. When corruption reaches a truly grand scale, we call it *kleptocracy*. (For numerous examples, do an Internet search.) The problem is that kickbacks and payoffs "grease the wheels" when it comes to awarding contracts for big aid projects such as dams, bridges, and power plants. In some countries—*not* the United States—bribes paid to foreign officials are considered a normal, and even deductible, cost of doing business! The worst kinds of graft appear to be diminishing, however. The end of the Cold War reduced the flow of "aid" to governments whose main claim to such funds was their reliability as anticommunist allies. The growth of democracy, rising demands for institutional transparency, and tougher attitudes on the part of donors have also played a part in creating a "cleaner" environment for aid.

A New Aid Challenge: Aging

It is well known that the populations of the industrialized nations are getting older. People are marrying later, having fewer children, and living longer. One result is a looming crisis for the pension systems of Europe and the United States; another is rapidly rising costs for medical and institutional care for the growing numbers of elderly. Hardly anyone seems to have noticed yet, but the same trends are underway in the developing world as well. This will have profound implications for the way in which these societies function—and for the way in which economic assistance is directed to them.

In an important *Foreign Affairs* article in the spring of 2003, Susan Raymond laid out some of the issues at stake. Over the next two decades, demographic changes will work to the advantage of the developing countries: their birth rates will continue to fall, their working-age populations will keep expanding, and their numbers of older people will increase, though not too rapidly. With dependents, young and old, declining as a share of total population, the resources available to society for saving and investment should be more plentiful. That will create favorable conditions for economic growth. By 2025, however, the demographic "window of opportunity" will be closing. The continuing growth of the elderly population will reimpose a heavy dependency burden, and the poorest nations may not be prepared for it. (Even the richest nations will have serious difficulties, experts believe.)

Adjusting to these changing demographic facts will be a challenge for aid policy. The health component of bilateral and multilateral assistance will need to be reoriented from child-centered aid, such as vaccinations, child nutrition, and education, toward the management of chronic conditions such as heart disease, diabetes, and Alzheimer's disease. And as if this were not challenging enough, it appears that working-age men and women in low-income regions are developing chronic health problems like circulatory disease and diabetes *earlier* in their lives than their counterparts in high-income regions. Caring for growing numbers of adults with these conditions (not to mention AIDS) will be costly. Urbanization in the developing world is bringing more people within visiting distance of hospitals and clinics, which is a plus, but it is also "modernizing" their diets and activity patterns in ways that tend to worsen health rather than improve it.

Finally, a demographic issue virtually no one has yet addressed is the changing ratio of populations in the developing versus developed worlds as it relates to foreign aid. Today, there are approximately 4.25 people in the poor countries for every one in the rich. By 2050, because of divergent rates of population growth, the ratio will be 6.3 to 1 (Population Reference Bureau 2003). If aid still flows from rich to poor nations in 2050—it has been in decline from a peak in 1992—the aid dollars will be spread much more thinly than they are today. Policymakers need to be thinking ahead of the curve on all these issues.

Poverty and Trade

Walk through the clothing aisles of Wal-Mart, the Gap, or Old Navy, and check the labels to see where the garments were produced. You will find the names of countries like Indonesia, Belarus, Bangladesh, Myanmar, Peru, El Salvador, Botswana, and a great many other places from which the United States rarely imported clothes a few decades ago. The increasing importance of trade among all nations, rich and poor, is a defining feature of *globalization*. This is not the place to explore in depth the nature of that complex phenomenon, but there are several basic questions relating to trade and poverty that need to be considered: Is trade helping to reduce poverty among developing countries? Could the United States and other wealthy, industrialized countries be doing more to facilitate trade with the low-income countries? If they could, what is keeping them from doing so?

Economists have spent two centuries or more explaining how, in theory, trade works to the advantage of all who participate in it. Each country can find some products or services that it is relatively efficient at producing. If it specializes in producing those things, and produces a large enough quantity to supply its own needs, with a surplus for trading, it can export the surplus to other countries in exchange for items that it wants but cannot produce cheaply itself. In this way all countries can put their resources to best use, maximizing their real incomes and consumption levels. It's a nice theory, and one that has led the great majority of economists to be squarely in favor of free trade. But there have always been dissenters, and during the 1950s and 1960s, many developing countries took the path of dissent, rejecting the whole theory of free trade. They chose instead to consciously direct their resources into various industries in which they did not have any sort of cost advantage over foreign producers. The strategy required that they impose high protective tariffs on imports of manufactures.

The *import-substitution* strategy seemed to work initially, but as time went on it became more and more evident that nations actively participating in international trade—such as South Korea, Taiwan, Singapore, and Mauritius—were growing faster than those pursuing an inward-looking strategy of development behind tariff walls. Openness to the world market, including openness to foreign investment, came to be seen as a dependable route to rapid growth. A much-cited 1995 study by Jeffrey Sachs and Andrew Warner concluded that open economies tend to have growth rates 2 percent above those of closed economies.

The contribution that economic growth can make to poverty reduction has also become clearer in recent years. Growth fueled by exports certainly appears to be a major factor in the massive reduction of poverty in China over the past decade and a half. Dollar and Kray (2001b) find that China, India, and twenty-two other "post-1980 globalizers"—their term for nations that significantly increased their trade as a percentage of GDP—on average reduced their tariffs and increased their growth rates from the 1970s to the 1990s. Forty-eight other developing countries, called "nonglobalizers," cut their tariffs much less and experienced a *slowdown* in growth from the 1970s to the 1990s. The overall conclusion of Dollar and Kray is that for poor countries, more trade means faster economic growth and sharper reductions in poverty.

It is easy to get caught up in generalizations on poverty and trade, and therefore important to remember that developing countries are highly diverse in terms of how they participate in the world economy. The United Nations has placed forty-nine countries in a special category called "least developed countries" (LDCs) on the basis of income, literacy, and economic vulnerability. Economic success for these countries depends greatly on what kind of exporting they do. A small group of them (Angola, Equatorial Guinea, Sudan, and Yemen) export mainly oil. A much larger group of LDCs export commodities other than oil. And one-third of the group chiefly export manufactured goods or services. The total value of exports from the first group rose by over 90 percent from 1997 to 2000; exports from the second group fell by about 8 percent; and exports from the third group rose by some 46 percent. Poor countries that depend on commodity exports prosper or suffer according to the world price of their products. Unfortunately, recent price trends have been harshly unfavorable. For example, copper, cotton, and coffee prices fell between 1997 and 2001 by 27 percent, 39 percent, and 66 percent, respectively (UNCTAD 2002).

The Damage from Agricultural Subsidies

The need for poor nations to integrate more fully into the world economy in order to speed growth and lessen the burden of poverty is no longer debated. The real problem, many believe, is that poor nations trying to do more trade are running up against major hurdles imposed on them by the developed nations. Those hurdles come in two forms: agricultural subsidies and high tariffs. For many years, the nations of the South, particularly in Africa and Latin America, have criticized those of the North for hypocritically proclaiming the advantages of trade liberalization while not living up to its requirements themselves. They have a point.

Agricultural subsidy programs have existed for decades in both the United States and the countries of the European Union (EU). How do they work? In the United States, the government makes promises to growers of a particular product, say cotton, that they can count on a minimum price for their output even if they can't find anyone but the government itself willing to buy at that price. Since the support price is often above what the free market would have determined, growers respond in a very natural way: they grow more cotton than they would have grown in the absence of the program. The net result is a larger cotton harvest in the United States—and millions of dollars paid to cotton growers by the government (ultimately, by taxpayers). Because the total output of cotton exceeds what the private market demands at the support price, the excess cotton must go somewhere. Most gets shipped into the world cotton market, where it tends to depress the world price.

Cotton is the primary export of some of the world's poorest countries, including several in sub-Saharan Africa. It accounts for 22 percent of exports from Benin, 40 percent of exports from Tanzania, and as much as 60 percent of exports from Burkina Faso. These countries and many others suffer an indirect, yet very real, financial loss when world prices are lowered as a result of U.S. dumping of its surplus cotton into the world market. A World Bank study places the total annual loss for West African cotton farmers at $250 million. An Oxfam report puts that cost into context: U.S. cotton subsidies, through their price-depressing effect, impose a 1 percent loss of GDP to the countries of Benin, Burkina Faso, and Mali. Remarkably, this same report finds that the U.S. government spends three times as much on subsidies for 25,000

American cotton growers as it does *on all foreign* aid to Africa's 500 million people each year!

Mexico's corn (or maize) growers have also been undercut by U.S. farm subsidies, though in a somewhat different way. NAFTA, the North American Free Trade Agreement, took effect in 1994. Within a year, imports of U.S. corn into Mexico had doubled, and that inflow continued to grow in subsequent years. Thanks to subsidies, U.S. corn could be sold in Mexico at 20 percent below its actual cost of production. Mexican farmers found it nearly impossible to compete with efficient—and subsidized—Kansas and Nebraska growers. By one estimate, half a million were driven from the land into Mexico's cities or to the United States as migrants. Those who remained, of course, faced the prospect of sharply lower crop revenues.

Corn and cotton are only two of the many agricultural commodities being subsidized by the U.S. government with harmful consequences for developing countries. Most analysts view Europe as an even heavier subsidizer of *its farmers.* Oxfam estimates that the Common Agricultural Policy, or CAP, operated by the EU provides the dairy industry with an annual subsidy of about 16 billion euros (roughly $16 billion). Those subsidies have the expected effect of generating large dairy surpluses, and the surpluses are directed—or dumped—into the world market. Nicholas Stern, chief economist at the World Bank, makes an interesting point: cows in Europe receive a daily subsidy of about $2.50; cows in Japan get a daily subsidy of about $7. Three-quarters of the people in Africa live on less than $2 a day! In places as distant from Europe as Jamaica and Kenya, local dairymen are struggling to compete against imported, CAP-subsidized dairy products.

It is the same with sugar production in Europe. With the encouragement of generous government subsidies, European farmers are producing far more sugar (from sugar beets) than can possibly be consumed in Europe. The excess is dumped into world markets, driving down the price. Sugar producers in developing countries around the world, from Guatemala and Brazil to Mozambique, suffer the consequences. They are penalized not because of their inefficiency but because of the unwillingness of the EU to discontinue subsidies to its farmers.

The U.S. Congress over the years has debated various proposals to revamp the U.S. farm subsidy program. The impetus behind reform proposals has never been a desire to give Third World farmers a break. Rather, it has been to save taxpayer dollars and to increase the overall efficiency of the economy. The simple goal of most proposals has been to eliminate price supports over some period of time. When Congress revised the program in 2002 (by no coincidence, an election year), the "reform" that emerged took almost everybody by surprise. Rather than cut agricultural subsidies, Congress *increased* them by a total of between $80 billion and $180 billion over the next ten years. This will almost certainly lead to further increases in U.S. farm surpluses, more dumping of those surpluses into the global market, and further downward pressure on prices—very bad news for small farmers in developing nations.

Defending Agricultural Subsidies

If helping low-income nations reduce their poverty through wider participation in the world economy is a goal of the United States and other industrialized countries, what can possibly explain the continuation of farm subsidies that have the opposite effect? When the question is put that way, there is hardly any rational answer. One occasionally finds an argument that makes some sense in a very limited context. For example, it has been argued that the flooding of the Mexican corn market with cheap (subsidized) U.S. corn worked to the benefit of the Mexican chicken and pork industries, for which corn is a major input. No doubt those industries did reap some economic gains. It could also be said that lower corn prices made it possible to produce cheaper tortillas, thus helping Mexico's poor, for whom tortillas are a staple food. The problem with that argument is that Mexico eliminated price controls on tortillas at about the same time that cheaper corn began flooding into the country, so in fact tortillas did *not* become cheaper for consumers.

Staying with Mexico, it could also be argued that the thousands of corn farmers who were unable to withstand the competition of cheap (subsidized) U.S. corn imports were inefficient campesinos who were barely making a living anyway. Being forced off the land and into the towns and cities was a harsh yet perhaps unavoidable part of the modernization of the Mexican economy. There may be some truth in this. No one has ever claimed that economic development is painless. It also may be the case that the opening of the Mexican market under NAFTA rules is more to blame than U.S. farm subsidies for the hardships experienced by Mexico's indigent maize farmers during the past decade. The adjustment pains would have been less, however, if corn imports had not been priced artificially low.

In Europe, the defense of farm subsidies—whatever the collateral damage to Third World agriculture—is often grounded in a belief that rural values must be preserved. Without subsidies, it is said, many farmers would fail and the fabric of rural life unravel. In the United States, similar claims are made for the importance of the "family farm" by those defending crop subsidies. It should be noted, however, that roughly two-thirds of total U.S. subsidies go to the top 10 percent of producers, who are better described as corporate farmers or agribusinesses than family farmers. European crop subsidies are similarly skewed toward the large-scale producers.

If the subsidy issue comes down to rich-country farmers versus poor-country farmers, it is unlikely that the political process will offer a way forward. American farmers and their representatives will not accept the proposition that economic uplift in low-income countries should come at their expense, any more than American teachers or truck drivers would accept such a proposition. But if other good reasons are given for cutting back on farm subsidies—the saving of taxpayer dollars and the weaning of farmers from continuous dependence on government checks—it could certainly be considered a welcome bonus that the well-being of poor farmers abroad would be boosted in the bargain. If farm subsidies ever *are* reduced, it will surely be done in a gradual way, so that farmers have enough time to adapt to a new and less distorted price structure.

Trade Restrictions on Poor Countries

Not only do rich countries flood the international markets with subsidized farm products, putting the squeeze on poor-country agricultural exports, but they also tend to impose restrictions on certain goods that developing countries would like to send into their own markets. The restrictions take two basic forms: tariffs and quotas. Tariffs, or import taxes, reduce the demand for imports by causing the price of the foreign-produced item to be pushed above the price of the domestically produced equivalent. Quotas are a cruder device for limiting imports; they set quantitative limits on the importation of designated products. Either method can have the effect of discouraging the flow of goods from developing countries into high-income markets.

The kinds of exports the developing countries have typically had the best chance of selling to the industrialized world are agricultural goods and textiles. These can often be produced relatively cheaply by developing countries. But in the United States, Europe, and Japan, textile producers and farmers lean on their governments to erect import barriers, so that they can stay in business (or preserve their profit margins). Some developing countries put barriers on the importation of these goods from other developing countries. The net result is less export volume and lower productivity for poor countries—and higher prices at the checkout line for consumers in rich countries.

The developed countries are selective about the tariffs and quotas they impose on developing countries. They don't attempt to restrict the import of cocoa beans, coffee beans, and bananas, for example, since they have no farmers who would need protection from such products. The story is quite different, however, when it comes to *processed* agricultural items. Ghana can export its cocoa beans duty free to Europe. If it were to export chocolate or cocoa butter to Europe, however, protective tariffs would be applied. Likewise, a number of developing countries are permitted to ship raw sugar into the EU duty free, but not candy, the processed product from sugar. In fact, African countries like Swaziland have found their own candy industries crippled by imports from Europe, where companies receiving heavy government subsidies can set export prices artificially low. Some of the North-South trade patterns seen today conform remarkably well to the classic idea of colonial empire, with the (former) colonies sending raw materials to Europe and taking, in return, the manufactures of Europe. But that pattern is not the "natural" outgrowth of a free market; rather, it is, to a considerable degree, the product of trade restrictions insisted upon by the North.

Because the types of goods exported from poor countries to rich ones tend to be subject to much higher tax rates, one can find some troubling, if not bizarre, quirks in the trade statistics. For example, far more U.S. customs revenue is collected from Vietnamese goods than from Dutch goods, even though the Netherlands is a bigger U.S. trading partner and, obviously, a country with far less poverty than Vietnam. Another example: Since most Bangladeshi exports to the United States are textiles, and textiles are subject to high tariffs, the average tariff rate faced by

Bangladesh exporters to the United States is fourteen times higher than the average tariff rate faced by French exporters. These anomalies suggest that if trade were made freer—more liberalized—the potential gains for developing nations would be quite large. A World Bank simulation of the impact from full trade liberalization puts the overall income gains for the developing nations at $500 billion!

The term "fair trade" is often used to capture the concerns of poor countries about tariffs, quotas, and subsidies. These countries view the high tariffs and strict quotas imposed on their goods upon entry into rich-country markets as anything *but* fair. They also challenge the fairness of the huge subsidies that rich countries continue to grant their farmers, resulting in the dumping of farm output onto world markets. These issues, particularly the $300 billion of annual farm subsidies, have become increasingly contentious. In September 2003, trade talks among the member states of the World Trade Organization (WTO) held in Cancun, Mexico, collapsed when the rich and poor nations could not resolve their differences on these questions. It was a major setback for the "development round" of trade negotiations that had been initiated at a WTO ministerial conference in Doha, Qatar, in 2001. It now looks unlikely that this round of negotiations can be concluded on schedule, on January 1, 2005.

The Debt Issue

In the 1990s, with the new millennium fast approaching, voices were raised around the world in support of a general forgiveness of the foreign debt of poor nations. It was not only those nations themselves who were pushing for debt relief. Many activists, clergy, academics, celebrities, and NGOs in the developed world also joined the "Jubilee 2000" campaign. The Jubilee movement did not produce a blanket cancellation of the debt, but it had an impact. In late 1996 the IMF and World Bank, feeling the heat of Jubilee rhetoric, initiated a Highly Indebted Poor Countries (HIPC) program that promised to deliver debt relief to countries that (a) were demonstrably in need of help and (b) were able to undertake internal reforms aimed at reducing poverty. Three years later an *enhanced* HIPC program was approved by the IMF and World Bank, and it remains in effect today, with features to be discussed below.

Why does foreign debt pose such a problem for low-income countries? After all, there is nothing intrinsically wrong with a country borrowing money and going into debt, as long as it makes effective use of the funds. When countries put borrowed capital to good use, they build up their economies in ways that make possible the repayment of the loans, plus interest. At the end of the nineteenth century, following decades of public and private borrowing abroad, the United States was the world's most indebted country. Much of the borrowed money had been sunk into canal and railroad construction, thus helping build up America's infrastructure and ensuring its future capacity for debt repayment. But many of the world's poorest countries today have foreign debt on their books that is not reflected in physical infrastructure, well-educated populations, or anything else that might enable them to pay off the debt in coming years. Merely *servicing* the debt—making the interest payments each year—places a tremendous burden on these countries. For some, debt service exceeds all spending on social programs!

The debt situation of the developing countries has grown to such proportions that its handling has become controversial in several ways. Some observers have argued that the debt, or a good part of it, was not incurred legitimately, and therefore poor countries have no obligation to repay it. The HIPC debt-relief program, while welcomed by some, has been criticized by others as insufficient to meet the needs of the nations it was meant to help. And the whole idea of debt relief has been sharply questioned by one prominent economist, who argues that it doesn't have the effects that its supporters think it does. We will take up these points in turn.

Odious Debt

If the ruthless dictator of a poor country borrows billions of dollars overseas in order to pad the Swiss bank accounts of his cronies and himself, is a successor government obliged to repay those loans? Not according to the "odious debt" doctrine. Debt is defined as odious if it was incurred by an undemocratic government and used for purposes contrary to the interests of the people. Both these conditions must be met for the debt to be odious.

This doctrine did not spring from the inventive mind of a latter-day legal scholar. Its roots lie deep in U.S. and Russian historical experience. In 1898 the United States went to war with Spain, won a quick victory, and evicted the Spanish from their long-time colony of Cuba. As rulers of the island, the Spanish authorities had borrowed heavily over the years, resulting in a mountain of debt, which, Spain insisted, now belonged to the new Cuban government. The United States disagreed, arguing that Cuba's colonial rulers had borrowed mainly for the purpose of repressing the people. Since the people had not authorized or approved of such borrowing, nor benefited from the loans, their new, independent government was absolved of any duty to repay the debt. That is how the matter eventually was resolved: the debt was repudiated. A few decades later, in the 1920s, a Russian legal theorist named Alexander Sack set forth the formal doctrine of odious debt to cover the case of debt incurred by a despotic regime for its own ends, rather than for the good of the nation. He had in mind the foreign debts of the czarist regime, now replaced by the Soviets. According to Sack, the debts of the former regime were nullified upon its removal from power. (Czarist debt was indeed repudiated by the Soviets.)

Although it has not achieved acceptance in international law, the odious debt idea has been raised in support of efforts to lighten or eliminate the debt burden on the world's poorest countries. It came to public awareness during the Jubilee 2000 campaign (later renamed Drop the Debt). Several countries offer plausible examples of places to which the idea would seem to pertain. South Africa's people now bear the burden of debt incurred by the former apartheid regime; many, including the archbishop of Cape Town, believe this debt should be repudiated. Nicaragua threatened to repudiate the debt run up by its pre-1979 dictator, Somoza, but then thought better of it (on advice from Cuba). The former Zaire, under the rule of Mobutu Sese Seko, built up foreign debts of about $12 billion; one-third of the funds apparently ended up in Mobutu's *kleptocratic* hands. Much the same is true of Ferdinand Marcos of the Philippines, who reportedly accumulated a vast fortune while his country accumulated vast debts. Currently there is debate over whether the debts of post-Saddam Iraq, estimated at over $100 billion, can be viewed as "odious." The *Wall Street Journal*, never mistaken for a radical newspaper, offered some support for that proposition in an editorial on April 30, 2003.

Could the idea of odious debt ever become a practical reality? Two scholars have argued that it could. Michael Kremer, a

Harvard economist, and Seema Jayachandran, a graduate student at Harvard, have proposed the creation of an international judicial body with powers to declare a regime "odious." Such a declaration would be made before, not after, any questionable loans had been made. It would do little good, from a policy point of view, to declare odiousness after the fact. By then, it would be too late to hold lending institutions responsible for exercising proper caution in extending credit to an unsavory regime. But if the "odious" label were attached to all *future* loans from a certain date, lending institutions (and their stockholders) would be put on fair notice that any new loans would very likely not be repaid under future governments. The hoped-for result: less odious debt placed on the backs of impoverished people.

Objections to "Odious Debt"

The Kremer-Jayachandran proposal has not met with universal enthusiasm. One objection, which they have anticipated, is that the international body charged with making judgments of odium would be biased toward developing-country debtors and against the lending agencies in the rich nations. It might be too quick to judge regimes odious, thereby preventing countries from getting the advantages of foreign capital. Kremer and Jayachandran reject this argument. They believe that the individuals making the judgments, while sympathetic toward people in borrowing countries, would appreciate the fact that declaring odiousness without sufficient cause would not be in the long-term best interests of those people. Contrariwise, *not* declaring a corrupt, self-serving regime to be odious would hurt the citizens of a poor country by saddling them with unjustified debt burdens. All in all, the incentives would be on making an impartial assessment of odium.

Another objection to the implementation of the odious debt doctrine is that, in the larger scheme of things, it would reward the worst kinds of corrupt and unjust behavior. Declaring a country's debts, or part of its debts, "odious" would free the country from the obligation of repayment. That would amount to debt relief in the form of a special dispensation available only to countries that had been seriously misruled and plundered—not to countries that had been honestly governed but perhaps had faced unexpected hurdles in their development. Economists call this an example of perverse incentives.

Finally, there is a whole grab-bag of practical and political difficulties in the way of an odious-debt system. Consider the case of a country whose regime, and future foreign debts, are declared odious by the international body. Suppose the regime remains in power for another decade and then is replaced by a new regime. Are any loans obtained by the new regime automatically legitimate, or does the international body have to issue a reversal of its earlier finding? How will it decide that a government is sufficiently new and reformed? On the basis of what track record? New regimes are rarely total and complete departures from their predecessors, so the odious/nonodious judgment would be fraught with uncertainty. William Easterly says that this raises the dread specter of "conditionality." Developing countries today receive some loans and grants from the wealthier nations only on certain conditions, having to do with the economic policies followed by their governments. An odious-debt system would add a *political* layer of conditionality to economic conditionality. It isn't easy to see how this could be made workable.

The HIPC Initiatives, 1996 and 1999

The world's poorest countries, mainly in Africa, piled up a mountain of foreign debt in the last decades of the twentieth century. Their debt levels grew so large that even "servicing" the debt—paying interest on it each year—became extremely burdensome. In late 1996, following a series of earlier, more modest efforts to deal with the problem, the World Bank and IMF jointly created the HIPC program of debt relief for forty countries that met certain criteria. The main qualification for inclusion, aside from very low levels of income, was a total debt more than twice the amount of the country's annual exports. This was a level of debt experts considered "unsustainable," one that justified relief measures.

Three years later, Uganda was the only HIPC that had reached the "completion point" at which debt would actually be reduced under the program, and a mere handful of nations had reached the "decision point" that made them *candidates* for eventual debt relief. Everyone agreed that things were moving too slowly. The general dissatisfaction felt within the donor and debtor communities, combined with growing pressures from the Jubilee 2000 movement, led the G-7 group of industrialized nations, at their 1999 summit in Cologne, Germany, to approve an "enhanced" HIPC program. Many features of the initial program were modified. The details need not detain us, but the overall impact can be summarized briefly: Debt relief was made broader—more countries could qualify; it was made deeper—the amount of possible debt relief was increased; and it was made faster—countries could start getting help on their debt service at the "decision point" rather than waiting until they reached the "completion point." In addition, an explicit linkage was made between debt relief and poverty reduction. In other words, countries were expected to apply the savings they reaped from debt relief to policies and programs aimed at cutting poverty.

There are currently forty-two HIPCs. The list includes a few Asian countries (Myanmar, Vietnam, the Lao PDR) and four Latin American countries (Bolivia, Guyana, Honduras, and Nicaragua), but the great majority of HIPCs are in sub-Saharan Africa. By the end of July 2003, twenty-seven HIPCs had reached their decision points and begun to receive debt relief, a much quicker pace than had been seen under the earlier program. Eight countries have reached not only the decision point but also the completion point in the HIPC process: Benin, Bolivia, Burkina Faso, Mauritania, Mali, Mozambique, Tanzania, and Uganda. The total amount of debt relief, when all the countries have reached their completion points, is expected to be about $40 billion. Roughly two-thirds of the foreign debt that once burdened these countries is set to be canceled under the program.

Problems with HIPC

The strongest complaint made against the HIPC program is that it does not go far enough in easing the burden of debt on some extremely poor nations. An Oxfam report in 2001 noted that a number of countries receiving HIPC debt relief were, in spite of that relief, still badly overburdened by their debt obligations. The report cited Niger, where more than one-quarter of the government's revenues were being spent on debt repayment, and Zambia, where one-fifth of government revenues were committed to debt service. These desperately poor countries, and many others, find themselves in the position of spending more on debt than on basic education or health care. Some countries have had notable success in using debt relief to improve social services to their people, according to Oxfam. Uganda, for example, used such relief to help pay for free primary education, and Tanzania looks likely to do the same. But when debt totals are very large, the help provided to HIPCs simply isn't adequate to the needs of the recipient countries.

Is there light at the end of the debt tunnel? Is there a realistic prospect that many or most of the poor countries that have begun to receive relief will be able to stay on a sustainable path of economic growth, with debt levels they can manage? In its *Least Developed Countries Report 2002*, UNCTAD looked at seventeen LDCs that are also HIPCs and had reached the decision point by April 2001. It found that the IMF/World Bank scenario for these countries' economic performance in the decade 2000–2010 was highly optimistic. It assumed, for example, that fifteen of the seventeen would experience faster economic growth in 2000–2010 than in 1990–1999. It also projected faster export growth for fourteen out of the seventeen, and less new borrowing from foreign sources by thirteen out of the seventeen, than in 1990–1999. Even if the first years of the 2000–2010 decade had not been marred by a global economic slowdown, these would have been tough goals to achieve. If, as now seems likely, they cannot be met, impoverished countries may find themselves forced once more to go so deeply into debt that the servicing of that debt will divert resources from more socially valuable ends, such as health and education.

One other way to gauge the adequacy of the HIPC initiative is to juxtapose it with the Millennium Development Goals (MDGs) discussed in chapter 1. HIPC was approved in 1999 and the MDGs in 2000. The most widely quoted "price tag" placed on the MDGs is $50 billion annually—over and above current levels of aid from the rich to the poor countries. Birdsall and Williamson (2002) suggest that the cost of meeting the development goals in the HIPCs will be on the order of $25 billion annually. One might reasonably ask how much of that figure could be covered by savings from debt relief. Depending on how one measures debt "relief," the annual savings for the HIPCs when they have been given the full scheduled amount of debt reduction will be between $1 billion and $4 billion. Clearly, debt relief under the enhanced HIPC program goes only a *very* small way toward paying for the MDGs.

Is Debt Relief Useless?

It's difficult to believe that anyone could be against forgiving the debt of the world's lowest-income countries, but for various reasons that is the case. In trying to understand why, it helps if we realize that debt relief is quite similar to foreign aid—indeed it *is* foreign aid by another name. Writing off Country X's obligation to make $100 million of annual debt service payments is tantamount to giving Country X an extra $100 million of foreign aid each year. That means most of the arguments that are made against foreign aid can also be made against debt relief. If one believes additional foreign aid would be wasted, one probably expects the same result from a dose of debt relief.

With either form of assistance, foreign aid or debt relief, the funds becoming available to the poor country are fungible. Fungibility is economic jargon for the fact that money can be shifted from one use to another, defeating efforts to channel funds into specified uses. If the United States sends $20 million of aid to Country Y to be used for the construction of new schools, and if Country Y's government would prefer to spend any fresh funds it receives on military adventures in neighboring countries, it can quietly shift $20 million from its education budget to its military budget and replace the lost education funds with the new U.S. aid dollars. Superficially, it will look as if the United States is paying for school buildings, but in reality the United States is paying for weapons, ammunition, and soldier's pay. Without ironclad mechanisms for monitoring funds, this could be the fate of any type of financial assistance to a poor country, including debt relief.

Those who question the effectiveness of debt relief can point to a long history of debt forgiveness preceding the HIPC initiatives. For more than two decades, the rich countries have been lightening the debt burdens of the developing countries. How? They have lengthened the grace periods during which no interest need be paid on loans; they have recategorized loans as "concessional" (eligible for lower or zero interest rates); they have substituted outright grants for loans; and they have straightforwardly forgiven some loans. In spite of all this, the debt service burdens of the poor nations have steadily increased for many years, so that skeptics feel justified in doubting whether HIPC, Jubilee, Drop the Debt, or any other mass debt-relief program will truly alter the debt tendencies of those nations.

Some critics of debt relief make an argument based on equity—not equity between rich and poor countries but between some poor countries and others. It is based on the notion that there is only so much assistance the donor countries are willing to offer, whether in the form of grants, concessional loans, or debt relief. Therefore, if they offer a debt amnesty to one set of poor countries, as the debt campaigners have been urging for years, they may balance that aid boost with a *reduction* of aid to the rest of the recipient countries. It is not at all clear that this would be equitable. The countries with the most debt are not always the countries with the most impoverished populations. Nor is it clear that the most indebted countries are the ones that could make the best use of additional aid from donor countries. (It may be the opposite: the most indebted countries may have gotten so deeply in debt from having the most corrupt or ineffective leaders, and debt forgiveness isn't likely to change those leaders' behavior.) The premise of this argument—that donors have only so much money they are willing to provide—looks plausible. It may even be too optimistic. In recent years, the amount of official development assistance (ODA) going from the richest countries to the least developed ones has actually declined.

The most hard-nosed critics of debt relief object to it on the grounds that contracts are sacred. They cannot be torn up with impunity. When countries borrow money and their finance officials sign loan agreements, it is important that the terms of the agreements be honored. If not, the future creditworthiness of the country is put in doubt. Those who take this line tend to oppose not just debt relief but foreign aid in general. They believe the best way to get the world's poor countries growing faster is to reform their institutions. State-owned enterprises must be sold off. Laws must be passed—and enforced—that guarantee property rights and permit markets to function efficiently. Government officials must be accountable to the law and to voters. If these changes are made, private investment will flow into the economy, making all forms of foreign aid unnecessary. It's an interesting point of view, but perhaps too rigid. One response might be that financial assistance from donor countries, though not a panacea, could be a useful "carrot" in getting countries to adopt good-governance practices. It might also be said that when developing countries are moving in the right direction, achieving economic gains and reducing poverty, they do not need aid. But if they are hit by unanticipated events—a hurricane or an AIDS epidemic—they may require aid, even debt relief, to get back on track.

References and Further Reading

Foreign Aid and Poverty

Burnside, Craig, and David Dollar. 2000. "Aid, Policies, and Growth." *American Economic Review* 90, 4: 289–329.

Dixit, Kunda. 1995. "Kleptocrats and Development Aid." *Oxfam Horizons* (April).

Easterly, William. 2001. *The Elusive Quest for Growth: Economists' Adventures and Misadventures in the Tropics.* Cambridge, MA: MIT Press.

Easterly, William, Ross Levine, and David Roodman. 2003. "New Data, New Doubts: A Comment on Burnside and Dollar's 'Aid, Policies, and Growth' (2000)." Forthcoming in *American Economic Review.*

Gonzalez, David. 2002. "Eight Years after U.S. Invasion, Haitians' Squalor Worsens." *New York Times,* July 30, A1–A8.

Mallaby, Sebastian. 2002. "Poor-Mouthing Aid: The Truth Is, It Works." *Washington Post,* March 4, A19.

Population Reference Bureau. 2003. *World Population Data Sheet 2003.* Washington: Population Reference Bureau.

Ravallion, Martin, and Shaohua Chen. 1997. "What Can New Survey Data Tell Us about Recent Changes in Distribution and Poverty?" *World Bank Economic Review* 11, 2 (May), 357–382.

Raymond, Susan. 2003. "Foreign Assistance in an Aging World." *Foreign Affairs* 82, 2 (March/April), 91–105.

Weinstein, Michael M. 2002. "The Aid Debate: Helping Hand, or Hardly Helping?" *New York Times,* May 26.

World Bank. 2001. *World Development Report 2000/2001.* New York: Oxford University Press.

———. 2003. *World Development Indicators 2003.* Washington, DC: World Bank.

Trade and Poverty

Dollar, David, and Aart Kraay. 2001a. "Growth Is Good for the Poor." *World Bank Policy Research Department Working Paper No. 2587.* Available at http://econ.worldbank.org/files/1696_wps2587.pdf.

———. 2001b. "Trade, Growth, and Poverty." *World Bank Policy Research Department Working Paper No. 2615.* Available at http://econ.worldbank. org/files/2207_wps2615.pdf.

Oxfam. 2002a. "Cultivating Poverty: The Impact of US Cotton Subsidies on Africa." *Oxfam Briefing Papers* 30, September.

———. 2002b. "Milking the CAP: How Europe's Dairy Regime Is Devastating Livelihoods in the Developing World." *Oxfam Briefing Paper* 34 (December).

———. 2003. "Dumping without Borders: How US Agricultural Policies Are Destroying the Livelihoods of Mexican Corn Farmers." *Oxfam Briefing Paper* 50 (August).

Sachs, Jeffrey, and Andrew Warner. 1995. "Economic Reform and the Process of Global Integration." *Brookings Papers on Economic Activity* 1.

UNCTAD. 2002. *The Least Developed Countries Report 2002.* New York and Geneva: United Nations.

Debt and Poverty

Birdsall, Nancy, and John Williamson. 2002. *Delivering on Debt Relief: From IMF Gold to a New Aid Architecture.* Washington, DC: Center for Global Development and Institute for International Economics.

Easterly, William. 2001. "Think Again: Debt Relief." *Foreign Policy* 127 (November–December), 20–26.

Kremer, Michael, and Seema Jayachandran. 2003. "Odious Debt: When Dictators Borrow, Who Repays the Loan?" *Brookings Review* 21, 2, (spring), 32–35.

Oxfam International. 2001. "Debt Relief: Still Failing the Poor." *Oxfam Research Reports* (April).

3

Special U.S. Issues

Although it has its own poverty problems—some quite persistent—the United States is a rich nation by almost any measure. It boasts the world's largest economy, and its per capita national income is surpassed by only a handful of other countries. Its child and maternal mortality rates are very low; U.S. boys and girls have equal access to primary and secondary school and enroll at high rates; the major communicable diseases are firmly in check; and U.S. life expectancy, at seventy-seven, is close to the highest anywhere. These favorable facts do not—and *should* not— lead Americans to believe they can remove themselves from engagement with people and countries that are less privileged. The world has become highly interdependent. Isolation is not an option (and never really has been). In this chapter, therefore, we take a closer look at some U.S. policies and actions that relate to world poverty. The issues of concern are foreign aid, immigration, drug pricing, and the link between poverty and terrorism. In each case, we will see that what the United States does can have a significant impact on poverty in distant places.

The Right Amount of Foreign Aid

How much of a rich country's national income should it pledge to the cause of helping poor countries overcome economic stagnation and human misery? Does the United States, the world's wealthiest nation, give enough? Without an answer to the first question it is impossible to answer the second. No one has ever

Figure 3.1 Official Development Assistance As Percentage of Gross National Income

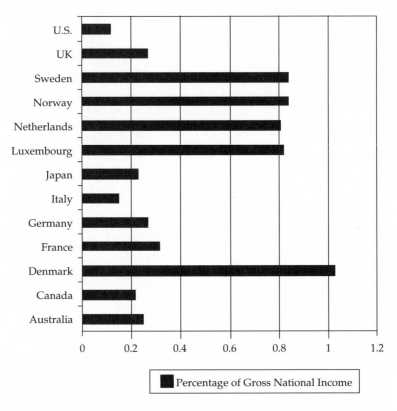

Source: World Bank. *World Development Indicators 2003.* Washington, DC: World Bank. p. 336.

defined a universally accepted minimum level of aid. For thirty-five years, however, the figure of 0.7 percent of GNP has been held out as an ideal or target for developed countries to aim at in setting their aid budgets. It was first put forward by the Pearson Commission, headed by former Canadian prime minister (and Nobel Peace Prize winner) Lester Pearson, in its 1969 report "Partners in Development." What the commission actually urged was that rich, or First World, countries try to achieve the 0.7 percent level of assistance to the Third World by 1975. Though widely applauded, that goal was not met.

In fact, overall aid levels drifted *downward* for many years after the Pearson Commission made its recommendation. Figure 3.1 shows wide variations in official development assistance (ODA) for a selection of high-income countries in 2001. Five small countries met and surpassed the 0.7 percent target: Denmark, Luxembourg, The Netherlands, Norway, and Sweden. The United States, on the other hand, devoted only 0.11 percent of its gross national income (GNI) to foreign aid in 2001, well below its 0.24 percent level of the mid-1980s. This low figure is scheduled to rise, to perhaps 0.16 percent by 2006, under the Bush administration's Millennium Challenge and AIDS programs. But it will not *begin* to approach the level promoted by the Pearson Commission and reaffirmed at several international conferences over the past few years.

While the United States lags far behind most other industrialized nations in the percentage of its GNI committed to foreign aid, it remains the biggest single donor in the world. In 2001 its total ODA was $11.4 billion. Only one other country came close to that total—Japan spent $9.8 billion. It should perhaps also be noted that between 1996 and 2001, when total ODA flows from rich to poor countries *declined* by more than $3 billion, the United States increased its own aid by over $2 billion (World Bank 2003, 336). One student of international aid flows, Carole Adelman, has recently argued that foreign aid budgets do not accurately convey the extent of a nation's "largesse," and we will examine her case later.

Does the Public Support Foreign Aid?

There has been fairly extensive public-opinion polling to try to gauge U.S. attitudes toward foreign aid. Some of the results could have been predicted; others are quite surprising. Traditionally Americans have opposed "handouts" to the poor, particularly when they come from the "hand" of government. The self-sufficient individualism characteristic of Anglo-Americans is often contrasted with Continental European attitudes, which tend to support the idea of collective responsibility. Such generalizations notwithstanding, there is solid support among Americans for the principle of foreign aid. About eight out of ten agree that "the United States should be willing to share at least a small portion of its wealth with those in the world who are in great need." Over half of those polled explicitly disagree with the contention that "helping people in foreign countries is not the proper role for the US government" (Program on International Policy Attitudes 2001).

Despite their basic support for the principle of foreign aid, Americans have often expressed the view that aid should be reduced from its current levels. In the mid-1990s that was the view of roughly two-thirds of the public. More recently, however, trim-the-aid attitudes have subsided; in polls taken in 1998 and 2000, the proportion favoring cuts in aid has fallen into the 40 percent range.

Where is the consistency, one might ask, between accepting the principle of foreign aid on the one hand, and wanting to reduce aid, as many Americans still do, on the other? One plausible explanation lies in misperceptions about the size of the foreign aid budget. Americans, for some reason, have a greatly exaggerated notion of how much money goes to foreign aid. When respondents to a Program on International Policy Attitudes (PIPA) survey in 2000 were asked to give an estimate of how much of the federal budget went to foreign aid, the median response was 20 percent. The true figure was, and is, less than 1 percent! In a Pew survey done in 1997, people were asked this question: "As far as you know, is more of the federal budget now spent on Medicare or is more spent on foreign aid?" An astounding 63 percent thought more was spent on foreign aid; only 27 percent thought more was spent on Medicare. In reality, Medicare spending in 1997 was about *ten times* the spending on foreign aid. If Americans have such a grossly inflated sense of the amount of money being spent on foreign aid, it should come as no surprise that significant numbers of them want to see that spending reduced.

Who Gets U.S. Foreign Aid?

To which countries does the United States send the largest amounts of foreign aid? The answer varies from year to year. In 2001, as table 3.1 indicates, the biggest recipient of U.S. bilateral aid was Russia. It was one of six "lower middle income" countries, as defined by the World Bank, in the top ten list. Three "low income" countries also made the list: Pakistan, Ukraine, and Indonesia. Israel, a "high income" country, ranked third among U.S. aid recipients. Notably absent from the list is any country in sub-Saharan Africa. The per capita incomes (PPP) of Russia, Egypt, and Israel, as reported in the *World Development Indicators* of 2003,

Table 3.1
Top Ten Recipients of Gross ODA/OA* in Millions of Dollars, 2001

1	Russia	834
2	Egypt	808
3	Israel	568
4	Pakistan	438
5	Ukraine	246
6	Colombia	228
7	Jordan	173
8	Former Republic of Yugoslavia	159
9	Peru	158
10	Indonesia	158

*ODA/OA stands for official development assistance/official aid and is a close approximation to what most people think of as foreign aid.

Source: OECD, Development Assistance Committee. "Aid at a Glance" Accessed at http://www.oecd.org/dataoecd/42/30/1860571.gif.

are $6,880, $3,560, and $19,630, respectively. By contrast, per capita incomes for the sub-Saharan region as a whole average $1,750 a year.

The conclusion some might draw is that U.S. aid, aside from being inadequate to the global need, is incorrectly targeted. Why should *any* assistance be earmarked for a high-income country like Israel, or even a lower-middle-income country, when there are so many *low*-income countries whose populations live in much greater poverty? It's a good question, well worth asking, but it is also naive. For the United States, bilateral aid has never been entirely, or even mainly, about reducing the sum total of human misery in the rest of the world. Rather, it has been about advancing U.S. national interests. The fact that Russia and Ukraine are among the top five recipients of U.S. aid is partly explained by the judgment of the U.S. government that it serves the interests of the United States and its allies to see those former communist lands stabilized economically (and their stockpiles of nuclear weapons safeguarded). Similarly, the United States has allocated generous economic and military aid to Israel and Egypt for decades in the belief that such aid helps preserve peace in a troubled region of great strategic importance. Substantial aid to Colombia is related to a U.S. desire to see that country defeat a guerrilla movement that appears to facilitate narcotics-trafficking to the United States. One could go down the list in this way and uncover a great many political and security reasons why the U.S. aid budget is structured the way it is.

The U.S. government, then, much like the governments of France, Great Britain, and Japan, has long considered its foreign aid budget to be an instrument for advancing its own geopolitical and commercial interests. That's how aid is viewed by those who appropriate the funds and by those who administer them. Does this mean that humanitarian motives never come into play? Not quite. Some of the funds that the United States directs to foreign aid are indeed intended primarily for the relief and eradication of global poverty. But such funds tend to be delivered first to an international agency like the United Nations or World Bank and only then to recipient countries. The United States in 2000 devoted about one-quarter of its ODA to multilateral aid. Development experts strongly favor the multilateral over the bilateral approach. There is much to be said for having institutions like the World Bank raise funds from the developed countries, weigh the competing needs of developing countries, and then, with the least possible reference to political agendas, make whatever loans and grants promise to do the most good in combating poverty.

The Bigger Picture

The charge that the United States does not "step up to the plate" when it comes to foreign aid has been made so often that certain responses to it have become familiar by repetition. First, as noted above, *total* U.S. foreign aid exceeds that of any other country. (For a time during the 1990s, Japan claimed that honor, despite a much smaller economy and population than the United States.) Second, it can be argued that if the United States tried to meet the Pearson standard by committing a full 0.7 percent of its GNP to foreign aid, it would produce such an avalanche of aid money that developing countries would not be able to absorb it all. This is a complicated issue that we will not try to resolve here. Third, it can be said—or at least it often *is* said—that the United States shoulders the heaviest burden of any industrialized nation in regard to defense spending, and that such spending, while it does not directly promote economic development or poverty reduction, helps to create a security environment in which those things are more likely to occur. Again, this is a complex and controversial position that would best be addressed elsewhere. There remains an interesting fourth response to the charge of U.S. foreign-aid stinginess—namely, that the United States delivers generous help to other countries in a variety of unofficial forms.

Carole C. Adelman, a senior fellow at the Hudson Institute, contends that U.S. generosity toward the developing world is mismeasured, and greatly understated, by official aid figures. (See her article in the November/December 2003 issue of *Foreign Affairs* and the USAID report to which she contributed, both listed in *Further Reading* below.) In the bigger picture described by Adelman, private giving by Americans now vastly exceeds public giving. Private giving takes many forms. U.S. foundations, like the Bill and Melinda Gates Foundation and the David and Lucille Packard Foundation, have become "megadonors" to the developing nations, with total grants on the order of $3 billion annually. Private voluntary organizations, such as the American Red Cross and Catholic Relief Services, also consistently give billions each year—about $7 billion in 2000. Charitable giving by U.S. corporations in the same year totaled nearly $3 billion, and a conservative estimate of the contributions by U.S. religious organizations is $3.4 billion for 2000. American universities have markedly increased their scholarship aid to foreign students in the past couple of decades. But the really dramatic private assistance now flowing from the United States to developing countries consists of remittances sent to their homelands by immigrants. In 2000 those payments totaled $18 billion; the leading recipient areas, in descending order, were Latin America, India, the Middle East, and Eastern Europe.

All told, U.S. private giving to the developing world amounts to some $35 billion annually, or more than three times its ODA. When you combine private aid flows with ODA and with various forms of U.S. government assistance that do not qualify as ODA, the grand total comes to around $56 billion of U.S. international assistance in 2000. That is undeniably a large figure, and it will grow larger in coming years as the Millennium Challenge and AIDS initiatives reach full funding levels. Whether the recalculated total should erase the U.S. reputation for aid stinginess is another question. Ms. Adelman seems to think it should. Yet if the private financial flows from other developed countries are estimated, and revised total aid numbers are then converted to percentages of GNP, the United States continues to be a laggard among the wealthy countries (USAID 2003, 134).

Immigration

Most Americans believe that their country has some kind of moral obligation to assist the less well off in the world. There are some standard ways to go about this. We have already considered foreign aid. Whether it flows through public or private channels, aid can make a positive difference. Another way for rich countries to help poorer ones is by opening their markets to the products of the developing world. A number of Asian countries have made decisive economic gains on the strength of their expanding export sales. We also saw, in chapter 2, that it would be enormously helpful to some developing countries if the United States and the EU countries would cut the subsidies they pay to their farmers, thus taking some surplus agricultural output off the world market and lifting the prices paid to producers in less developed countries. Standard policy options like these revolve around the movement of goods and funds. But what about a more radical idea for reducing world poverty, one based on the movement of *people?* Specifically, should the United States start viewing immigration as a policy option for achieving the worthy goal of reducing world poverty? (What more appropriate way of honoring the commitment inscribed on the Statue of Liberty to the "tired," "poor," and "huddled masses" abroad?) Taking this to its logical conclusion, what about an open-border policy as the ultimate gesture of solidarity with the world's poor?

The first thing to note is that the United States has been receiving large numbers of mostly poor immigrants from its earliest years of nationhood. Some of the immigrants arrived unwillingly—slaves from Africa—and some came seeking political asylum, but the rest made the journey in search of "opportunity." They came, and still come, in hopes of enjoying a better future, including a higher standard of living. Motivations for moving can be explained in terms of a "push-pull" theory of migration. People make the decision to migrate because the negative circumstances under which they have been living—ethnic persecution, political turmoil, poverty, and so forth—push them, or because the positive circumstances of the country to which they are headed—job possibilities, personal security, freedom—pull them. Historically, migrants to the United States have responded to both types of forces. Sometimes it is easy to identify a push force, like the Irish potato famine of the 1840s or the end of the Vietnam War in the 1970s. Much of the time, however, it is impossible to say whether push or pull was the stronger force. A simpler way to theorize migration would be to say that people migrate when there is a gap between the income they presently receive and the one they expect they could earn in the new country. The wider the gap, the stronger the motivation to migrate.

Current Sources of U.S. Immigration

To estimate what the effects would be of opening U.S. borders to all comers, we need to know what the current pattern of immigration is. In recent decades immigrants have become much more diverse in terms of geographic origins. Broadly speaking, it's fair to say that most immigrants to the United States during the nineteenth century came from northern and western Europe; from 1890 to 1920 the main "donor area" shifted to southern and eastern Europe; and from 1920 to 1960 northwest Europe resumed its dominance as a supplier of immigrants. Following the Immigration Act of 1965, northwest Europe fell behind Latin America, and after 1970, *far* behind both Latin America and Asia as a source of migrants to the United States. Legal immigrants in 2002 numbered just over 1 million, of which Europe provided only one-sixth. One country alone, Mexico, supplied more legal immigrants to the United States in 2002 than all of Europe combined. Indeed Mexico dwarfed all other countries, with 219,000 migrants; if illegal immigration were counted, that number might be doubled. The other leading "donor" countries were India (71,000), China (61,000), the Philippines (51,000), Vietnam (34,000), and El Salvador (31,000).

Theory and common sense both tell us that migrants to the United States hope, and can reasonably expect, to raise their long-run incomes significantly by making the move. Insofar as they are right, world poverty is thereby reduced. It's a simple proposition of arithmetic that lowering the number of people living in poor countries, and raising the number in rich ones, helps the world make progress against poverty. Consider the data in table 3.2.

The incomes in table 3.2 represent between 6 and 24 percent of U.S. per capita gross national income. Thus the income gaps

Table 3.2
Per Capita Incomes* of Countries Supplying the Most Immigrants to the United States, 2002

Mexico	$8,240
India	$2,820
China	$3,950
Philippines	$4,070
Vietnam	$2,070
El Salvador	$5,160

*Income data are in Purchasing Power Parity terms.

Source: World Bank. 2003. *World Development Indicators 2003.* Washington, DC: World Bank.

are large, and the motivation to migrate strong. (How many Americans could resist moving to another state if it would allow them to multiply their incomes between four and sixteen times?) It's a safe bet that the countries from which the United States receives the most immigrants today would send many more if there were no legal impediments.

Obviously, there *are* legal restrictions on immigration to the United States. Their rationale and impact are not our focus, however. Our question is whether a more liberal immigration system ought to be considered as a policy option for reducing global poverty. The ultimate liberalization would be open borders—no restrictions at all on immigration. For all intents and purposes, this actually was the U.S. policy until the late nineteenth century. In recent times support for open borders, with certain qualifications, has come from the political right (Ben Wattenberg, Julian Simon, Milton Friedman, many libertarians, the *Wall Street Journal*) as well as the egalitarian left (John Rawls, Joseph Carens, Peter Singer). The arguments of the latter tend to be more pertinent to questions of world poverty, as we see in the next section.

Open Border Ethics, in Brief

Proponents of unrestricted immigration ground their case on the principle that all individuals are of equal moral worth, whatever their social or economic status. The right to live where one chooses, and not to have one's movements limited, is equally fundamental. Americans would not dream of accepting any restrictions on where they are allowed to live within their own country.

Why, then, should such restrictions be accepted at the global level? People migrate across borders for many good reasons, the most important of which is to improve their economic prospects. Is there any morally defensible reason that they should be disallowed from doing so? The fact that their entry in large numbers into an affluent country might adversely affect the native-born citizens' standard of living can hardly be a justification for keeping them out. Protecting and perpetuating privilege is not defensible in most moral systems. When the wealthy, or their border guards, turn back poor immigrants trying to find a better livelihood, they do so out of political or economic expediency, not out of any consideration of justice. Or so it is argued by egalitarian philosophers.

Open Border Impacts

Although no one can say what exactly would happen if the United States were to declare its borders open to all comers, it is possible to speculate. With the exception of Canada and the UK, nearly all immigrants today hail from countries much poorer than the United States. There is every reason to think that the same regions that supply the most immigrants today—Latin America and Asia—would continue to dominate the migration flow. Given a policy objective of reducing world poverty, that would be a good thing, much better than receiving immigrants from, say, western Europe. In a best-case scenario, all the immigrants would find employment, earn the going wage, build up assets, and perhaps relieve some pressure on overcrowded labor markets in their home countries. Immigrant remittances, already about $20 billion, would swell to much greater amounts and be a further means of cutting poverty abroad.

It all sounds too good to be true, and perhaps it is. One concern would be how the influx of workers would affect U.S. labor markets. The majority of the arriving workers would be less skilled and less educated than native-born Americans. In the 1990s, more than half the legal immigrants to the United States came from Latin America, and their educational levels were below the native-born levels, on average. The Census Bureau reports that in 2002 only 49 percent of U.S. residents born in Latin America were high school graduates, a far lower figure than for those born in Asia, Europe, or the United States itself. This means that workers flocking through the open borders would be heading for labor markets already under pressure from previous migrant flows. The theory of supply and demand predicts what the outcome would be: lower wage rates for *all* low-skill workers, whether foreign- or native-born, and probably a rise in unemployment. To date, statistical studies have found that wage effects from immigration tend to be significant at local levels but not at the national level. However, those studies were based on limited, not unlimited, immigration.

Experts tell us that the economic impact of immigration on the U.S. economy has been mainly distributional. Immigration does not have much of a short-run impact on GNP, but it shifts some income away from labor, especially low-income workers, toward the owners of capital. (See the Borjas work in *Further Reading*.) How those findings would change with a doubling, tripling, or quadrupling of immigration is anyone's guess. The absorptive capacity of U.S. labor markets is great but not infinite. At the other end of the spectrum, there would be some concerns with regard to immigrants with *above*-average educational and job credentials—the computer scientists, the physicists, the engineers, and the trained medical doctors. Their departure from their native lands represents a kind of "brain drain" that, to some degree, worsens prospects for social and economic progress abroad. If open U.S. borders meant a larger "drain" of such skilled individuals, it would undercut the goal of lowering world poverty.

These speculations have been based on the initial assumption that reducing world poverty would be the sole objective of a liberalized U.S. immigration policy. On that basis we could afford to ignore the many political and cultural complications that would follow such a policy change. In the real world, policymaking can never proceed in such a vacuum. Placing the interests of the world's poor above every other consideration is a morally bracing idea but also a utopian one, and U.S. immigration policy is not likely to be shaped by such an approach in the years ahead. Just as U.S. aid and trade policies are formulated mainly with an eye to domestic interests, U.S. immigration policy is responsive to the concerns and interests of various groups within society. When all is said and done, using the tools of aid, trade, and investment looks like a much simpler way to achieve global poverty reductions than moving large numbers of people across borders.

Drug Pricing for Poor Nations

There is nothing fair about the fact that the world's poorest people are also, by and large, the world's unhealthiest people. They do not have the same access to preventive health care, reproductive health care, high-tech diagnostic equipment, expensive medical treatments, and high-priced drugs as people in the developed world, and as a result they spend more of their lives ill and die earlier. This ought to present a moral challenge to those who enjoy all that modern medicine has to offer. (This is not to say that everyone living in the developed world has access to high-quality health services; health coverage can be very unequal in rich countries, especially in the United States.) In the last few years, an issue that has brought these concerns into sharp focus is the price of key drugs needed by patients suffering from malaria, TB, and HIV/AIDS.

This is an issue that has received attention at the highest levels of international policy-making. At the Millennium Summit, held in September 2000, eight development goals were adopted (see chapter 6), the last of which was to "develop a global partnership for development." One of the targets under that overall goal was formulated in this way: "In cooperation with pharmaceutical companies, provide access to affordable, essential drugs in developing countries." The appropriate indicator of success was judged to be the "proportion of population with access to essential drugs on a sustainable basis." Such access is remarkably unequal at present. AIDS is a good example. The World Health Organization reported in November 2003 that in the Americas, 84 percent of those needing antiretroviral treatment were receiving it. In Eastern Europe and Central Asia, however, the proportion was only 19 percent, in Southeast Asia, only 7 percent, and in Africa, only 2 percent.

The access-to-drugs issue concerns Americans because some of the most effective drugs developed so far to fight AIDS have come out of the laboratories of U.S. pharmaceutical companies. The companies took out patents on the drugs and priced them at levels that they claimed were needed to recoup their research expenses and to finance new research. Initially the cost of the drugs ran as high as $10,000 per year for each AIDS patient, but over time the cost came down sharply. Even so, the price of antiretroviral drugs has remained beyond the reach of the vast majority of Africans and Asians.

Obstacles to Making Drugs Available

It is sometimes said that while the rich, industrialized countries have a moral obligation to provide AIDS drugs at affordable cost to those afflicted with the disease in poor countries, doing so might pose a serious risk of *worsening* the epidemic. How would that possibly be true? The concern is based on a belief that patients in developing countries might not be able to comply with the strict pill-taking schedules demanded for success of the therapy. Epidemiologists fear that if AIDS patients fail to take their pills at the right times and in the right doses, they will become, in effect, incubators of drug-resistant strains of the virus. Resistant strains of TB, malaria, and staphylococcus have already emerged in just that way, so the worry has a factual basis. In 2001 the director of USAID claimed that Africans "don't use clocks" and thus could not adhere to the required schedule for taking AIDS drugs. But this whole issue has since taken an unexpected turn. A study released in September 2003 found that AIDS patients in Africa were *more*, not less, compliant with their pill-taking regimens than Americans. While Americans complied about 70 percent of the time, Africans complied about 90 percent of the time!

A more concrete obstacle to the distribution of cheap drugs is the lack of an effective delivery system in many developing countries. Roads, if present, are often impassable, clinics are scarce, and there are inadequate numbers of trained personnel to explain medication details to patients and answer their questions. Thus even if lifesaving drugs were priced cheaper, the lack of medical infrastructure would make it very hard to deliver them to the individuals needing them the most.

Possibly the biggest obstacle in the way of distributing essential drugs to poor nations is the pharmaceutical industry's fear that its profits will be eroded. The industry does not actually expect to make profits on sales to poor countries. It understands that there is no prospect of AIDS patients in the developing world being able to pay the price that is charged in the richer countries. What worries drug companies in the United States (and Europe) is the possibility that drug makers now operating in countries like Brazil and India may produce generic versions of AIDS and other drugs, and those cheaper drugs may find their way into the markets of the rich countries. If that happens, prices—and profits—in the rich markets will tumble.

A WTO Breakthrough

It all comes down to WTO rules on intellectual property. Medicines developed by the big pharmaceutical companies are all patent-protected for many years. It seemed a great victory for poor countries when, at the WTO meeting in Doha (2001), they gained the right to override drug patents and produce "copycat" versions of their own if they faced a public health emergency. Many of these countries, however, lacked the technical capacity to produce such drugs. So at a subsequent WTO meeting, in late 2002, a proposal was put forward to allow poor countries to import cheap copies of patented drugs from *other* developing countries. This was vetoed by the United States. Why? Because the U.S. pharmaceutical industry feared that some of the copycat drugs produced under the terms of the agreement would be diverted into rich-nation markets. The industry also wanted the agreement to be limited to AIDS, malaria, and TB drugs, while the poorer nations wanted a broader range of drugs to be included— for example, drugs to treat diabetes and asthma. Whatever the merits of the U.S. position, the upshot was that the United States was seen as opposing cheap, lifesaving drugs for the poorest people in the world.

In late summer of 2003, the United States finally dropped its opposition to a WTO generic-drug agreement. It stopped insisting on a limit to the number of countries that could import cheap generic drugs and even accepted the wider range of drugs to be covered. In exchange the United States got assurances that patents would be overridden only "in good faith" and that special measures would be taken to prevent smuggling of cheap drugs into rich-country markets. Possible deterrents to such smuggling might include special packaging of pills and the use of differently colored pills.

It is sobering to realize that from the time this issue deadlocked in December 2002 to the announcement of a breakthrough in September 2003, almost 2.2 million Africans lost their lives to AIDS and other treatable diseases.

Poverty and Terrorism

The terrible events of September 11, 2001, fundamentally changed the way in which many Americans view their country's relationship to the rest of the world. Before that day, Americans usually associated acts of terrorism with faraway places like Israel, Chechnya, and Northern Ireland. But the comfortable illusion of security in the "homeland" crumbled as swiftly as the twin towers of the World Trade Center in lower Manhattan, leaving in its place a new and unwelcome sense of vulnerability. In the weeks and months following the attacks, questions were raised about the identities of the nineteen hijackers, and more generally about the origins of terrorism itself. Is it rooted in political ideology? In religious conflict and zealotry? In festering resentments over past injustices? Or is terrorism perhaps best explained as an outgrowth of *poverty?*

Some of the earliest commentaries on the attacks emphasized the link between terrorism and poverty. For example, Laura D'Andrea Tyson, head of the Council of Economic Advisers under President Clinton, observed in a *Business Week* column that in a world of sharp contrasts between "unprecedented opulence" and "remarkable deprivation," the United States was vulnerable to terrorists based in "remote regions" languishing in "poverty and despair." "In such a world," she stated, "our prosperity and freedom at home increasingly depend on the successful development of countries like Afghanistan." The president of the World Bank, James Wolfensohn, was careful not to assert an explicit causal link between poverty and terrorism when he said, just weeks after 9/11: "Poverty in itself does not immediately and directly lead to conflict, let alone to terrorism" (See his statement in chapter 6). Still, the title of his commentary, "Fight Terrorism and Poverty," juxtaposed the two issues in a way that implied some degree of connection between them. And President Bush, in an op-ed piece for the *New York Times* on the first anniversary of 9/11, observed: "Poverty, corruption and repression are a toxic combination . . . leading to weak governments that are . . . vulnerable to terrorist networks." On another occasion he said, more simply: "We fight against poverty because hope is an answer to terror."

If poverty offers fertile ground for the growth of terrorism, it presents one more good reason for the United States to pursue all the policies believed to be effective in reducing global poverty, whether in aid, trade, investment, or even migration. But how well established is the poverty-terror linkage?

Weak Evidence

There have been a number of studies, some dating from long before the 9/11 attacks, aimed at determining whether terrorists emerge from the ranks of the impoverished and uneducated. Surprisingly, most of the evidence runs the other way. In 1983, Charles Russell and Bowman Miller found that two-thirds of the 350 terrorists around the world about whom they could learn basic biographical information from newspaper articles had attended college. Many of the 9/11 hijackers had also attended college and were from middle-class families. Princeton economist Alan Krueger and Jitka Maleckova, a scholar at Prague's Charles University, recently did a statistical study of hate crimes against ethnic and religious groups in the Middle East—crimes that they saw as borderline terrorism. Among 129 Hezbollah fighters killed in action in the 1980s and early 1990s, the rate of poverty was *below* that of the general Lebanese population from whom they were recruited, and the educational level was higher. Claude Berrebi, a Princeton graduate student, has looked at the backgrounds of Palestinian suicide bombers in Israel and discovered that they were less than half as likely to be from poor families as the general population. They also were more than three times as likely as others of their age to have continued their education beyond high school.

Krueger and Maleckova also cite evidence concerning Israeli Jewish extremists who committed violent acts against Palestinians in the late 1970s and early 1980s, including attempts on the lives of three Palestinian mayors in the West Bank and an effort to blow up the Dome of the Rock, one of Islam's holiest shrines. They found the perpetrators to be "overwhelmingly well educated and in high-paying occupations." Michael Radu, a terrorism expert at the Foreign Policy Research Institute in Philadelphia, is particularly skeptical about a poverty "root cause" for revolutionary violence and terrorism, whether in the Middle East or elsewhere: "Terrorists have been middle class, often upper class, and always educated, but never poor. The South American Tupamaros and Montoneros of the 1970s were all middle class . . . as were their followers among the German Baader-Meinhof Gang, the Italian Red Brigades, France's Action Directe, the Sandinista leadership in Nicaragua and, before it, Fidel Castro's Cuban revolutionaries" (Radu 2002).

Fight Poverty Anyway

The evidence, then, does not appear to support an "explanation" of terrorism in terms of the impoverished backgrounds of those involved. Terrorists are by and large as well off as—or better off than—the populations from which they are drawn, and better educated as well. Does that completely invalidate the notion of a poverty-terrorism link? Maybe not. One could argue that, whatever their personal backgrounds, extremists and terrorists are driven to violence by the poverty they see in their own societies, or by outrage over the gulf they see between living standards in the affluent West and in their own nations. That is the kind of hypothesis that needs to be refined, examined, and tested against competing hypotheses as we try to improve our understanding of the nature of terrorism. In the meantime, Americans have plenty of compelling reasons to dedicate their personal efforts, and the programs of their government, to the relief and eradication of world poverty. In the first place, it is the moral thing to do. In the second place, the United States can reap long-term economic benefits from the lifting of other countries out of abject poverty, as the historical record of the past fifty years amply demonstrates. And finally, even if battling poverty in distant places will not reduce the risks of future terrorist assaults on the United States and its interests, neither is it likely to increase those risks.

References and Further Reading

Adelman, Carole C. 2003. "The Privatization of Foreign Aid: Reassessing National Largesse." *Foreign Affairs* 82, 6 (November/December), 9–14.

Borjas, George. 1999. *Heaven's Door: Immigration Policy and the American Economy.* Princeton, NJ: Princeton University Press.

Carens, Joseph. 1999. "A Reply to Meilander: Reconsidering Open Borders." *International Migration Review* 33, 4: 1081–1097.

Goozner, Merrill. 2002. "Medicine as a Luxury." *American Prospect* 13, 1 (January 1–14), A7.

Isbister, John. 1996. *The Immigration Debate: Remaking America.* West Hartford, CT: Kumarian.

Krueger, Alan. 2003. "Poverty Doesn't Create Terrorists." *New York Times,* May 29.

Krueger, Alan B., and Jitka Maleckova. 2003. "Seeking the Roots of Terrorism." *Chronicle of Higher Education* 49, 39 (June 6), B10.

McNeil, Donald G., Jr. 2003. "Africans Outdo Americans in Following AIDS Therapy." *New York Times,* September 3.

Perlez, Jane. 2002. "Educated Filipinos, Disillusioned at Home, Look Abroad for a Better Life." *New York Times,* April 8.

Program on International Policy Attitudes. 2001. "Americans on Foreign Aid and World Hunger: A Study of U.S. Public Attitudes." School of Public Affairs, University of Maryland. Accessed at http://www.pipa.org/OnlineReports/BFW/finding1.html.

Radelet, Steven. 2003. "Bush and Foreign Aid." *Foreign Affairs* 82, 5 (September/October), 104–117.

Radu, Michael. 2002. "Guest Comment: 'Root Cause' Futility: Terrorism Cannot Be Explained." *National Review Online,* April 29.

Russell, Charles, and Bowman Miller. 1983. "Profile of a Terrorist." Reprinted in L. Z. Freedman and Y. Alexander, eds., *Perspectives on Terrorism.* Wilmington, DE: Scholarly Resources.

Tyson, Laura D'Andrea. 2001. "It's Time to Step up the Global War on Poverty." *Business Week* (December 3), 26.

U.S. Agency for International Development. 2003. "Foreign Aid in the National Interest: Promoting Freedom, Security, and Opportunity." Accessed at http://www.usaid.gov/fani.

World Bank. 2003. *World Development Indicators 2003.* Washington, DC: World Bank.

World Health Organization. 2003. The 3 by 5 Initiative: Coverage and Need for Antiretroviral Treatment." Accessed at http://www.who.int/3by5/coverage.

4

Chronology

This chapter provides a time line of important conferences, commissions, declarations, awards, books, and founding dates of some organizations that have been involved with world poverty. It is of course a selective list, reflecting one person's sense of what is noteworthy. The emphasis on international declarations regarding poverty may be seen as an attempt to raise reader awareness of the commitments we as a global community have made, through our representatives, to deal with this issue.

ca. 745   The great Chinese poet Du Fu (712–770) reflects on the poverty and inequality he sees in his society: *Behind the brightly painted gates of the rich and powerful | the stench of spilled wine and rotting meat. | On the streets outside, the bones of the poor | who have frozen to death.*

1348   A flea-borne virus reaches Europe from the East, and within a few years approximately one-third of Europe's population has died of the plague, also known as the Black Death. It is one of history's clearest examples of the deadliness of infectious disease in a social environment of squalor and poverty.

1601   The Elizabethan Poor Law establishes the principle in Britain that the poor, in extreme circumstances, are entitled to assistance from their local parish. The funding comes from local property taxes. Much controversy surrounds the administration of the Poor Law in

1601 subsequent years, but the right to subsistence is main-
(cont.) tained without interruption from 1601 to the present
day.

1776 Scottish political economist Adam Smith publishes his
*Inquiry into the Nature and Causes of the Wealth of Na-
tions.* Smith describes in detail the workings of the
capitalist economy, including international trade, and
asserts the advantages to be reaped from letting the
system proceed without interference from the government. Workers, in particular, can expect a rising standard of living if the accumulation of private capital
and the specialization of labor are permitted to proceed and if commerce at all levels is kept free.

1798 The Reverend Thomas Robert Malthus, in his *Essay on
the Principle of Population*, presents a theory suggesting
that overly rapid population growth and even some
kinds of economic growth can result in increased
poverty. He further argues that government-provided
assistance to the poor is likely to create more, not less,
poverty.

1846 Ireland, long ruled (or misruled) by Britain, is hit by a
potato blight that causes a near-total failure of the potato crop upon which most inhabitants depend for
daily sustenance. Mass starvation and mass emigra-
tion quickly follow.

1848 Karl Marx and Friedrich Engels publish *The Communist Manifesto*, a blistering attack on English industrial
capitalism and the wretched poverty that, they argue,
is an integral part of the capitalist system. They call
upon workers of the world to unite, having nothing to
lose but "their chains."

1852–1853 English novelist Charles Dickens publishes *Bleak
House*, a classic depiction of the appalling poverty experienced by London's lower classes during the Victorian era.

1876–1879 Terrible droughts in India and China take a famine toll estimated as high as 23 million for the two nations.

1880 The U.S. social and economic critic Henry George publishes his *Poverty and Progress* and it soon becomes a huge international bestseller. George calls attention to the degrading poverty existing side by side with great wealth in the United States, and to the way in which the wealthy manage to avoid paying their fair share of taxes. He proposes a new system of taxation that would place the tax burden entirely on owners of property (rather than on labor).

1896–1902 The return of drought and famine to China and India brings a death toll that could exceed that of 1876–1879. (See Davis 2001, 7.)

1916 A theoretical explanation of Third World poverty is offered in V. I. Lenin's *Imperialism: The Highest Stage of Capitalism*. Lenin extends Marxian theory by arguing that capitalists in the most advanced industrial economies invest their surplus capital overseas and end up exploiting colonial workers in the same way as they exploit their own. The impoverishment of the colonies is normal under this theory. The most radical critics of globalization today see continued relevance in Lenin's vision of the exploitation of the Third World.

1919 Save the Children is founded in England by Eglantyne Jebb. Its assistance initially goes to young survivors of World War I in Vienna, but later this NGO extends its help to children around the world.

1942 The Oxford Committee for Famine Relief, later to become Oxfam, is established. Early activities focus on war-torn Europe, but in 1949 Oxfam broadens its mandate to cover human suffering anywhere in the world, caused by war or other events. It will eventually be a twelve-nation consortium, Oxfam International, which includes the United States, the United Kingdom, Ireland, Canada, Australia, and New Zealand.

1944   The Bretton Woods Conference, held at a resort hotel in New Hampshire, creates both the International Monetary Fund (IMF) and the International Bank for Reconstruction and Development (IBRD, or "World Bank"). The IMF is to function as a short-term lender of last resort to governments facing foreign-exchange crises, while the World Bank's role will be to raise and lend long-term development funds. Washington is chosen as the headquarters city for both institutions. The World Bank's first loans, in the late 1940s, are made to European countries ravaged by World War II.

1945   The Food and Agriculture Organization is established as a specialized UN agency. Its mandate is to improve agricultural productivity, rural standards of living, and nutrition worldwide. One of its central concerns is *food security*, meaning consistent access for all people to the food they require to live a healthy, active life. FAO headquarters are in Rome beginning in 1951.

1948   The UN's Universal Declaration of Human Rights, article 25(1), states: "Everyone has the right to a standard of living adequate for the health and well-being of himself and of his family, including food, clothing, housing and medical care and necessary social services, and the right to security in the event of unemployment, sickness, disability, widowhood, old age or other lack of livelihood in circumstances beyond his control."

1956   Argentina, heavily indebted to foreign lenders, agrees to meet in Paris with its official creditors to seek a rescheduling of its debt payments. This is the beginning of the *Paris Club*, an informal arrangement under which countries that are deeply in debt can negotiate with their creditors, as a group, for debt relief. The relief can take the form of reduced, deferred, or stretched-out payments. From 1983 to 2003, nearly 80 debtor countries will have participated in Paris Club negotiations involving more than $400 billion of debt.

1957   Father Joseph Wresinski, a French priest, founds ATD, Aide á Toute Detresse (Aid in Total Distress), to help the very poorest families through volunteer educational efforts, grassroots political organizing, and campaigns to combat social exclusion. The name is later changed to ATD Fourth World.

1958–1960 Mao Zedong's "Great Leap Forward," aimed at leapfrogging the normal obstacles to economic development, proves to be a monumental fiasco. The resulting famine claims the lives of 30 to 40 million Chinese, the worst famine in history.

1959   The first of the regional development banks, the Inter-American Development Bank (IADB), is chartered. Its overall aim is to advance the economic and social development of Latin America and the Caribbean region. With headquarters in Washington, D.C., the IADB eventually has forty-six member nations, both in the region and beyond. They own the bank, which is a nonprofit institution. Member nations in the region are borrowers; member nations outside, including the United States and Japan, are lenders.

            The first death of a person known to be infected with the HIV virus occurs in the Congo. In coming decades, this disease will take its heaviest toll on the world's poorest countries.

1960   With funding from the Ford and Rockefeller Foundations, the International Rice Research Institute (IRRI) opens in the Philippines. Its aim is to help develop better strains of rice to feed the hundreds of millions, mainly in Asia, for whom rice is the staple food. Actual research work begins in 1962.

1961   President Kennedy, in his inaugural address, states: "To those peoples in the huts and villages of half the globe struggling to break the bonds of mass misery, we pledge our best efforts to help them help themselves."

1961
(cont.)

The initiatives of Kennedy's presidency relating to world poverty include the Alliance for Progress, the Peace Corps, the Food for Peace program, and a major overhaul of the U.S. foreign aid program.

George McGovern, director of the U.S. Food for Peace program, proposes the creation of a multilateral food aid program to combat world hunger; the UN approves the idea (later it is named the World Food Programme) on an experimental basis.

The United Nations declares the 1960s to be the first UN Development Decade. The 1970s are later called the second UN Development Decade, and so on. This procedure continues through the 1990s (fourth Development Decade) but is then put aside in favor of declaring 1996–2007 the first United Nations Decade for the Eradication of Poverty.

1962

The World Food Programme assists earthquake victims in Iran and hurricane victims in Thailand.

1963

The first World Food Congress is convened in Washington, D.C. President Kennedy, in his keynote address, states: "We have the means, we have the capacity to eliminate hunger from the face of the earth in our lifetime. We need only the will."

1964

The African Development Bank (AfDB) is established to mobilize domestic and external financial resources for investment projects in Africa, to provide technical assistance, and to encourage economic reforms. Infrastructure investment is a primary interest of the AfDB. The majority of member countries are African, but two dozen non-African countries also have membership in the AfDB; the two biggest stakeholders are the United States and Japan.

1965

The UN authorizes the continuation of the World Food Programme for as long as multilateral food donations to the hungry are felt to be desirable.

The United Nations Children's Fund (UNICEF), established in 1946, is awarded the Nobel Peace Prize. A member of the Nobel committee makes the mordant observation that in working with 118 countries with a total of 750 million poor children, UNICEF has at its disposal an annual budget equal to what the world spends every two hours on armaments.

1966   The UN adopts an International Covenant on Economic, Social and Cultural Rights, which, in Article 11, recognizes "the right of everyone to an adequate standard of living for himself and his family, including adequate food, clothing and housing, and to the continuous improvement of living conditions." It singles out the "fundamental right of everyone to be free from hunger." In time, most countries ratify the covenant; the United States does not.

The Asian Development Bank (ADB) is established as a multilateral development-financing institution dedicated to combating poverty in Asia and the Pacific region. With headquarters in Manila and offices in many Asian countries, as well as in Frankfurt and Washington, D.C., the ADB gives loans and technical assistance to countries throughout Asia, mainly for infrastructure.

The Rockefeller Foundation formally establishes an agricultural research center in Mexico, to be called CIMMYT, a Spanish acronym for International Maize and Wheat Improvement Center. Under the leadership of Norman Borlaug, later to win the Nobel Peace Prize (1970), CIMMYT becomes an epicenter of the Green Revolution, a sharp shift in farming practices that permits greatly increased production and helps meet the rising food requirements of the developing world.

1967   The World Health Organization begins a global campaign to eradicate smallpox.

1967–1969 Famine in Biafra, ultimately claiming about 1.5 million lives, sets the pattern for several African famines of the late twentieth century. It occurs in circumstances of civil strife, when the national government of Nigeria refuses to permit food aid to flow into the province of Biafra because it is the site of a secession effort. The unfolding tragedy is widely covered in the Western news media.

1968 An International Conference on Human Rights is held in Teheran, under UN sponsorship. It has been twenty years since the Universal Declaration of Human Rights was issued. The "Proclamation of Teheran" includes item 12: "The widening gap between the economically developed and developing countries impedes the realization of human rights in the international community. The failure of the Development Decade to reach its modest objectives makes it all the more imperative for every nation, according to its capacities, to make the maximum possible effort to close this gap."

1969 A review of the first UN Development Decade chaired by former Canadian prime minister Lester Pearson (the Pearson Commission) finds unsatisfactory progress toward UN goals. It argues for a boost in aid by the developed countries to the less developed—to a target level of 0.7 percent of GNP. The target is supposed to be reached by 1975.

The International Labor Organization, on the fiftieth anniversary of its founding in 1919, is awarded the Nobel Peace Prize. The Nobel committee notes that in the years ahead the ILO's work will have to extend much more than previously to the developing countries, where "unemployment and underemployment are today social evils which hold millions of people in the grip of hopeless poverty."

1971 Doctors without Borders, or Medecins sans Frontieres (MSF), is founded in Paris. It becomes one of the most conspicuous NGOs in the world, consistently offering emergency medical aid wherever manmade or natural disasters occur, and bearing witness to the plight of the affected populations. For its work it is awarded the Nobel Peace Prize in 1999.

1972   At the UN Conference on the Human Environment (Stockholm), a forerunner to the 1992 Earth Summit in Rio, the Stockholm Declaration is adopted. It notes: "In the developing countries most of the environmental problems are caused by underdevelopment. Millions continue to live far below the minimum levels required for a decent human existence, deprived of adequate food and clothing, shelter and education, health and sanitation." For poor countries, economic development is seen as the main priority, though they are urged not to lose sight of environmental concerns.

1974   At the World Food Conference in Rome, Henry Kissinger, U.S. secretary of state, declares: "Within a decade, no child will go to bed hungry."

Muhammad Yunus, a Bangladeshi economist, discovers that poor village women need just a small amount of capital to start their own businesses and make other big changes in their lives. Yunus builds this insight into the idea of the Grameen (village) Bank, a revolving fund designed to help the poor, especially poor women, overcome their lack of access to loan funds. The Grameen Bank is chartered by the government in 1983 and eventually numbers 1,200 branches throughout Bangladesh, serving 40,000 villages and 2.5 million borrowers. The *microcredit* idea comes to be universally recognized as a key to achieving economic and social progress in the developing countries.

Gunnar Myrdal is honored with the Nobel Prize in Economics (cowinning with F. A. Hayek). In his acceptance speech, Myrdal speaks of the "new awareness of . . . poverty in underdeveloped countries" and how it is "bound to be morally disturbing in the Western world." He also calls attention to how the "political character of aid" from the United States to

1974
(cont.)

developing countries is becoming "more pro-nounced," even as aid is losing public support. Myrdal's books include *Asian Drama: An Inquiry into the Poverty of Nations* (1968) and *The Challenge of World Poverty* (1972).

1978

The People's Republic of China inaugurates the market-oriented economic reforms that will eventually reduce the number of Chinese poor by tens of millions. The pragmatic Deng Xiaoping, successor to Mao Zedong as China's paramount leader, authorizes the reforms and gives them consistent backing until his death in 1997. Collective farming is abandoned in favor of a system of individual responsibility that rewards farmers for their individual efforts—a daring departure from Maoist ideology. In industry, the state sector is allowed to gradually shrink as township and village enterprises are formed. Foreign capital and technology are permitted, even encouraged, to flow into China. (The nation will join the World Trade Organization in 2001.) China's growth rate from 1978 to the mid-1990s runs at about 9.5 percent annually. Observers take note, however, of the divergence between China's economic liberalization and the continuation of a political system featuring Communist one-party rule.

Former German chancellor Willy Brandt chairs a UN commission to consider ways to lessen world poverty and promote economic development. The commission's 1980 report, *North-South: A Program for Survival,* calls for improved cooperation between the rich and poor nations in the areas of trade, investment, and industrial policy. It also urges rich nations to meet the Pearson Commission's aid target of 0.7 percent of GNP, with the level rising to 1 percent by the year 2000.

1979

Mother Teresa is awarded the Nobel Peace Prize for her work and that of the Missionaries of Charity, which she founded in 1950 in Calcutta. This order of Catholic nuns carries out its mission in fifty cities in

India and in thirty other countries, ministering to orphans, lepers, the neediest, and the dying. In 2003, Mother Teresa is canonized by Pope John Paul II.

The eradication of smallpox worldwide, the result of a WHO initiative begun in 1967, is confirmed by extensive country-by-country verification activities.

1981   The UN High Commissioner for Refugees is awarded the Nobel Peace Prize for the second time, having received it also in 1955.

The first UN conference on the Least Developed Countries is held in Paris. (A second is held in 1990, again in Paris; a third in Brussels, in 2001.) By 2003 the list of LDCs runs to forty-nine, from Afghanistan to Zambia. Qualification for LDC status depends on a nation's per capita income, a human resource index number measuring health, nutrition, education, and literacy, and the nation's "economic vulnerability," which is a function of agricultural instability, merchandise export concentration, and export fluctuations. The majority of LDCs are in sub-Saharan Africa.

1989   The Convention on the Rights of the Child is agreed to by the UN General Assembly and eventually ratified by all nations in the world except Somalia and the United States, making it the most widely approved human rights document in history. (The United States has signed the convention but has not yet formally ratified it.) The convention defines "children" as persons under the age of eighteen and declares them entitled to "special care and assistance." Article 27 affirms "the right of every child to a standard of living adequate for the child's physical, mental, spiritual, moral and social development." Article 28 recognizes "the right of the child to education." Article 32 affirms "the right of the child to be protected from economic exploitation and from performing any work that is likely to be hazardous or to interfere with the child's education."

1990   World Summit for Children is held at the United Na-
            tions. It adopts a World Declaration on the Survival,
            Protection and Development of Children, one clause
            of which states: "Each day, millions of children suffer
            from the scourges of poverty and economic crisis—
            from hunger and homelessness, from epidemics and
            illiteracy, from degradation of the environment." Re-
            flecting the sudden end of the Cold War and wide-
            spread hopes for a peace dividend, the declaration
            also notes that "current moves towards disarma-
            ment . . . mean that significant resources could be re-
            leased for purposes other than military ones. Improv-
            ing the well-being of children must be a very high
            priority when these resources are reallocated."

            A World Conference on Education for All is held in
            Jomtien, Thailand. Attended by representatives from
            155 countries, it sets the goal that basic education
            should be made available to all children, youths, and
            adults, though with no target date specified. The
            goal is endorsed five years later by both the Copen-
            hagen social summit and the Beijing summit on
            women. In 2000 it becomes part of the UN Millen-
            nium Declaration.

            Octavio Paz, the Mexican poet and winner of the
            Nobel Prize for Literature, uses a striking phrase in his
            Oslo acceptance speech to describe the global division
            between rich and poor: "The advanced democratic so-
            cieties have reached an enviable level of prosperity; at
            the same time they are islands of abundance in the
            ocean of universal misery."

            The first *Human Development Report* is issued by the
            UN Development Programme, under the leadership
            of Mahbub ul Haq. Strongly reflecting ideas pioneered
            by economist Amartya K. Sen, the *HDR* presents for
            the first time an alternative measure of national well-
            being, called the "human development index." This
            index takes into account a range of socioeconomic
            variables, not just money income. Countries are

ranked according to their index number. Those with the highest numbers are thought to offer their citizens, if not the highest incomes, at least the best opportunities for living full and satisfying lives. The *HDR* continues to be issued annually.

1991　　Faced with dwindling reserves of foreign exchange and high rates of inflation, the government of India adopts a sweeping program of economic reforms. Many industries are deregulated, as is the financial sector. Foreign ownership of Indian companies, previously limited to 40 percent, can now rise to 51 percent. Tariffs on imports are reduced. The wide-ranging market-oriented reforms set the stage for a decade of strong economic growth that lifts millions of Indians out of poverty.

1992　　The United Nations declares October 17 an International Day for the Eradication of Poverty, to be observed each year starting in 1993.

At the Earth Summit in Rio de Janeiro, delegates adopt *Agenda 21: The Rio Declaration on Environment and Development*. It declares: "[A] development policy that focuses mainly on increasing the production of goods without addressing the sustainability of the resources on which production is based will sooner or later run into declining productivity, which could also have an adverse impact on poverty."

1993　　Delegates to the World Conference on Human Rights (Vienna) adopt, and the UN General Assembly later endorses, the "Vienna Declaration." It includes this statement: "The existence of widespread extreme poverty inhibits the full and effective enjoyment of human rights; its immediate alleviation and eventual elimination must remain a high priority for the international community." The document also calls on the world community to "make all efforts to help alleviate the external debt burden of developing countries."

1994   In Cairo, a third international conference on population is convened by the United Nations, following earlier conferences in Mexico City (1984) and Bucharest (1974). Formally titled the International Conference on Population and Development (ICPD), this meeting endorses an approach to population that stresses the value of, and need for, improvements in health and education programs and, particularly, the empowerment of women. High rates of maternal and infant mortality in the developing world are blamed on the poor state of women's health care. The ICPD Program of Action sets a goal of universal access to family planning by 2015, an objective adopted in 2000 as one of the Millennium Development Goals.

1995   The UN-sponsored World Summit for Social Development—or Social Summit, as it comes to be known—is held in Copenhagen. Among the goals adopted is a reduction by half in the global proportion of the "absolutely poor" (those living on less than $1 a day) by 2015, using 1990 as the base for calculation. Other goals set for 2015 include universal primary education and universal access to reproductive health services for those of appropriate age.

The UN General Assembly declares 1997–2006 the first United Nations Decade for the Eradication of Poverty.

At the UN-sponsored Fourth World Conference on Women (Beijing), delegates approve the Beijing Declaration. In item 28 they declare their determination to "promote women's economic independence, including employment, and eradicate the persistent and increasing burden of poverty on women by addressing the structural causes of poverty through changes in economic structures, ensuring equal access for all women, including those in rural areas, as vital development agents, to productive resources, opportunities and public services."

North Korea begins suffering from famine caused by floods, drought, and inept management of the economy by the government. Mortality estimates range up to 2 million.

1996   The Development Assistance Committee of the OECD adopts a set of goals for 2015 that echo those agreed to in Copenhagen the previous year. In particular, there is a call for *halving* the proportion of people living in extreme poverty by 2015. This becomes one of the Millennium Development Goals in 2000.

The World Bank and IMF jointly announce a new program of debt relief called the Highly Indebted Poor Countries (HIPC) initiative. It establishes criteria and timetables for relief, first on debt service payments and later on debt principal. The majority of countries eligible to apply for relief are in sub-Saharan Africa.

1997   A microcredit "summit" is held in Washington, D.C., attracting 2,900 delegates from 137 countries. Participants set a goal of reaching 100 million of the world's poorest families by 2005.

1998   Amartya K. Sen is awarded the Nobel Prize in Economics in recognition of his many contributions to welfare economics, including his work on the factors leading to famines and the theory and methods of constructing poverty indices.

1999   The World Bank and IMF, after reviewing the progress of their 1996 HIPC initiative, decide to accelerate and broaden the operation of the program. The "enhanced" HIPC initiative envisions more countries qualifying for debt relief, and sooner, than under the 1996 plan. By September 2003, twenty-seven countries have received assistance under HIPC, twenty-three of them in Africa; the approved debt packages promise an eventual $51 billion of relief on debt service.

1999
(cont.)
The International Monetary Fund and World Bank establish a new planning tool for poor countries, called the Poverty Reduction Strategy Paper (PRSP), which involves getting all interested parties in the country into a dialogue with each other and with external donors about how best to reduce poverty. A key goal of the PRSP is "country ownership," meaning that each country requesting aid should have a major say in, and accept responsibility for the outcome of, its own long-term economic and poverty planning. Filing an acceptable PRSP is a necessary step toward gaining HIPC aid.

Pope John Paul II, in a statement on September 23, lends his support to the Jubilee 2000 campaign for debt relief to the poorest nations. Debt relief, he argues, is "a precondition for the poorest countries to make progress in their fight against poverty."

2000
A World Education Forum, held in Dakar, Senegal, and attended by delegates from 164 nations, sets forth the "Dakar Framework for Action," which envisions universal education by 2015. It thus restates the goal set forth ten years earlier in Jomtien, Thailand, and sets the stage for its inclusion among the development goals of the UN Millennium Summit in the fall.

The Millennium Summit of the United Nations is held in New York. The central Millennium Development Goal is a halving of the proportion of people in extreme poverty by the year 2015. Other goals to be met by 2015 include universal primary education, a two-thirds reduction in infant and child mortality rates, a three-fourths reduction in maternal mortality rates, and a reversal of negative environmental trends. These are all goals previously enunciated at other gatherings (see above).

The African Growth and Opportunity Act (AGOA) is passed by the U.S. Congress as Title I of the Trade and Development Act of 2000. President Clinton's signature makes it law. AGOA eases previous tariffs and quotas on a variety of imports, mainly textiles and apparel, from thirty-five sub-Saharan nations. The overall aim is to help African economies integrate into the world economy through trade expansion.

On International Day for the Eradication of Poverty (October 17), the World March of Women concludes at the United Nations plaza with a presentation of petitions demanding "concrete measures" to end poverty, end violence against women, and establish equality between women and men. About 5,000 NGOs from 159 countries participate in this global campaign.

The UN Security Council discusses AIDS for the first time. By the following year, the number of infected persons worldwide will be 40 million, and the death toll will have reached 22 million.

2001   The Fourth WTO Ministerial Conference, in Doha, Qatar, sets out an ambitious schedule of negotiations among member states, to be completed by January, 2005, on issues ranging from subsidies and tariff rates to trade-related aspects of intellectual property. The overall goal of the "Doha development agenda" is a continuation of the trend toward reduced trade barriers among countries. Skeptics doubt that the developing countries will benefit as much as the developed ones from further trade liberalization.

A New Partnership for Africa's Development (NEPAD) is formally created in July at the 37th summit of the Organization of African Unity. The goals of NEPAD are to eradicate poverty, put African countries on a path of sustainable development, facilitate their integration into the global economy, and speed the empowerment of women. NEPAD calls for a new, more equal relationship between Africa and the industrialized nations (several of which are former colonial powers). It seeks, among other things, debt cancellation and higher rates of assistance from the developed countries to help Africa overcome its underdevelopment.

2001
(cont.)

The UN holds a special session of the General Assembly devoted to HIV/AIDS and adopts a declaration called "Global Crisis—Global Action." The declaration recognizes that "poverty, underdevelopment and illiteracy are among the principal contributing factors to the spread of HIV/AIDS" and notes "with grave concern that HIV/AIDS is compounding poverty and is now reversing or impeding development in many countries."

The Global Fund to Fight AIDS, Tuberculosis and Malaria is established. It is to be a financing mechanism to use funds donated by governments, foundations, corporations, and individuals to battle diseases that claim more than 6 million lives each year. Its funding will help increase six-fold the antiretroviral treatments to AIDS patients in Africa within five years. Global Fund grants go to prevention programs as well as treatment programs.

2002

At the World Summit on Sustainable Development held in Johannesburg as a ten-year follow-up to the 1992 Earth Summit at Rio, a Declaration is adopted which affirms: "We recognize that poverty eradication, changing consumption and production patterns, and protecting and managing the natural resource base for economic and social development are overarching objectives of and essential requirements for sustainable development." Thus, safeguarding the global environment and eradicating poverty are seen as interconnected goals, as they had been at Rio in 1992.

In a March speech at the Inter-American Bank in Washington, D.C., President Bush announces a roughly 50 percent increase in U.S. foreign aid. The additional funding, rising in stages to $5 billion by 2006, will be channeled through a Millennium Challenge Account. Access to these funds will be conditioned on recipient countries meeting certain performance standards.

The UN International Conference on Financing for Development is convened in Monterrey, Mexico. It gives participating nations an opportunity to review the development goals established by the 2000 Millennium Summit (New York) and their financial implications. Developing countries agree to higher levels of accountability and good governance, and the developed countries agree in principle to a substantial increase in aid. President Bush, who announced the new U.S. Millennium Challenge Account in the previous week (see above), gives a speech in which he declares: "We fight against poverty because hope is an answer to terror." Activists and NGOs are unhappy that there is no serious discussion of debt relief at the conference.

2003   The Fifth WTO Ministerial Conference, held in Cancun, Mexico, with lofty goals for further reductions in trade barriers and expansion of international commerce, ends in bitter discord. The developing countries assert that rich countries are not responding to their demand for a sharp cutback in rich-country government subsidies to agriculture. Such subsidies result in overproduction by farmers in the developed countries, and their surpluses end up being dumped on world markets. World prices are lowered, and farmers in developing regions are harmed.

References and Further Reading

Birdsall, Nancy, and John Williamson. 2002. *Delivering on Debt Relief: From IMF Gold to a New Aid Architecture.* Washington, DC: Center for Global Development.

Davis, Mike. 2001. *Late Victorian Holocausts: El Nino Famines and the Making of the Third World.* New York: Verso.

"FAO: What It Is, What It Does." Website at http://www.fao.org/UNFAO/e/wmain-e.htm.

John Paul II. 1999. "Pope John Paul II Statement on Debt Relief." Accessed at http://www.catholicrelief.org/get_involved/advocacy/economic_justice/international_debt/pope_statement4_00.cfm.

Kutzner, Patricia L. 1991. *World Hunger: A Reference Handbook*. Santa Barbara, CA, and Oxford: ABC-CLIO.

Pan, Philip P. 2003. "China Accelerates Privatization, Continuing Shift from Doctrine." *Washington Post*, November 12.

United Nations. 1989. *Convention on the Rights of the Child*. Accessed at http://www.unicef.org/crc/crc.htm.

———. 1990. *World Declaration on the Survival, Protection and Development of Children*. Accessed at http://www.unicef.org/wsc/declare.htm#Thetask.

———. 1993. *World Conference on Human Rights: Vienna Declaration*. Accessed at http://habitat.igc.org/undocs/vienna.html.

———. 1995. *Fourth World Conference on Women: Beijing Declaration*. Accessed at http://www.un.org/womenwatch/daw/beijing/platform/declar.htm.

———. 1997. *Milestones in United Nations History* website, accessible at http://www.un.org/Overview/milesto4.htm.

———. 2001. *Global Crisis—Global Action [on AIDS]*. Accessed at http://www.un.org/ga/aids/coverage/FinalDeclarationHIVAIDS.html.

UN Development Program (UNDP). 1990. *Human Development Report 1990*. New York: Oxford University Press.

———. 2002. *Human Development Report 2002: Deepening Democracy in a Fragmented World*. New York: Oxford University Press.

5

Biographical Sketches

This chapter presents thumbnail sketches of twenty-seven men and women whose theories, ideals, and actions regarding world poverty have been notable. Most are still living, though a few have retired from active careers or "official" duties of office. Economists are perhaps overrepresented, but it is economists who have been developing theories of wealth and poverty for more than two centuries now. Unfortunately, they have not yet discovered the master equation for abolishing poverty. If only it were possible! They have, however, found many ways to gather and assess data about poverty, and they regularly use that data to test hypotheses about poverty. One economist, Amartya Sen, has been a leader in broadening the definition of poverty to include much more than per capita income, and he has helped the United Nations devise a "human development index" consistent with that broader approach. Two well-known figures from the entertainment world (Bono, Geldof) are included for the simple reason that their efforts to publicize global hunger and debt have brought those issues home not only to the public at large but also to powerful policy-makers. Several individuals associated with the World Bank are among those featured. Activists have scorned, jeered, and picketed this "Bretton Woods" institution for many years now, along with the IMF, and while it cannot be pretended that the Bank has radically reshaped itself in response to the criticism, there have been significant initiatives, under McNamara and Wolfensohn, to make the Bank a more effective force for poverty reduction in the developing world.

It would certainly be possible to extend the list from 27 to 100 individuals—indeed to thousands. Many agricultural scientists are working hard, in the laboratory and in the field, to develop better strains of cereal and other food staples. This is critical work, because the world will be gaining almost 3 billion additional people by the middle of the century, and unless we find ever more efficient ways to produce and distribute food, world hunger will increase. Other researchers are working on cures for diseases that afflict the world's poor: HIV/AIDS, malaria, and tuberculosis, among others. The progress they make will help determine whether the life expectancy gap between the rich and poor nations widens or narrows in coming decades. (Africa already has far too many AIDS orphans.) Other dedicated individuals are working to make family planning a reality where up until now it has been only a hope or an empty promise. In many parts of the world, a reduction in poverty will be far more likely when girls are afforded the same educational opportunities as boys and thereby gain options beyond early marriage and frequent childbearing. Finally, an extended list would include many more people—well known or not—who are working to achieve economic justice. Many, like Dita Sari of Indonesia, do so at great personal cost.

Carol Bellamy (1942–)

If anyone has a special mandate to look out for the interests of the world's poor children, it is Carol Bellamy, executive director of the United Nations Children's Fund (UNICEF). Only the fourth UNICEF director since the agency's founding in 1946, Bellamy has a tough act to follow—her predecessor was the now-legendary James Grant. But no one has ever doubted her energy, dedication, political savvy, or sheer determination to achieve her goals.

Bellamy graduated from Gettysburg College, ran a school lunch program in Guatemala as a Peace Corps volunteer, and earned a law degree before starting a career that has alternated between the private sector and politics. She worked for several years at a top New York law firm, got elected to the New York State Senate, came back to New York City as the first woman president of the City Council, and then returned to Wall Street, where she eventually became a managing director at Bear Stearns & Co. In 1993, President Clinton appointed her director of the U.S. Peace Corps, the first "veteran" of that organization to be so named. The Peace Corps has about 7,000 volunteers in more than ninety countries; UNICEF has 9,000 employees in 160 countries. In both cases, the director's job requires communication skills, management skills, and a good set of luggage.

Following an early emphasis on restructuring UNICEF to make it more effective at meeting its objectives, Bellamy has pursued an agenda focused on universal child immunizations, universal primary schooling, reducing the spread of HIV/AIDS and its impact on children, and preventing the exploitation of children. She has UN mandates and declarations to back her up, and a term in office that extends to 2005.

Further Reading

Barbara Crossette. "From City Hall to the World's Stage: Carol Bellamy Uses Her UNICEF Perch to Fight for Children," *New York Times*, April 22, 2002, B1, B5.

Catherine Bertini (1950–)

Catherine Bertini's leadership of the UN World Food Programme from 1992 to 2002 was a case of the right person in the right job at the right time. A native of Syracuse, New York, and a 1971 graduate of the State University of New York (Albany), Bertini first worked as youth director for the Republican State Commission. In the mid-1970s she worked briefly for the Republican National Committee before entering the private sector. From 1977 to 1987 she held a variety of posts at the Container Corporation of America; at the same time, she was a member of the Illinois Human Rights Commission and the Illinois State Scholarship Commission. Bertini entered the federal government in 1987 as an acting assistant secretary in the Department of Health and Human Services. In 1989 she became assistant secretary for food and consumer services in the Department of Agriculture.

Bertini's appointment in 1992 as executive director of the World Food Programme put her into the record book on two scores: she was the first woman to head the WFP and the first American woman to head any UN agency. In her ten years with the WFP, Bertini oversaw programs of relief to Bangladesh, North Korea, Rwanda, Sudan, Sierra Leone, Angola, and scores of other countries. In late 2001, as her second term was nearing its end, she helped pull off a minor "miracle"—the prevention of mass starvation in Afghanistan when most experts believed such a tragedy to be inevitable. Timely WFP shipments made the difference. But in Afghanistan, as elsewhere, those who deliver vital food aid have faced deadly risks—indeed, many have been murdered—and Bertini has been vocal in bringing this fact to the world's attention.

Bertini's decade-long tenure at the WFP was marked by a significant increase in the percentage of women on the staff and a new emphasis on women's empowerment as a feature of food relief policy. It also saw growth in the size and role of the WFP as a front-line relief agency and a sharp increase in U.S. funding of the WFP budget. Bertini has been honored with numerous awards, including the prestigious World Food Prize (2003) for her contribution in "defeating large-scale famine in our time."

Further Reading

George McGovern, *The Third Freedom: Ending Hunger in Our Time* (New York: Simon and Schuster, 2001), chaps. 2, 4.

Nancy Birdsall (1946–)

People who speak and write on the subject of globalization often seem to belong to one of two camps. Either they are "cheerleaders" who celebrate the example of nations like India and China that in recent years have achieved poverty reduction through export growth, or they are "cynics" who see the whole globalization game as rigged in favor of the wealthy, industrialized countries. That is the take on globalization of Nancy Birdsall, president of the Center for Global Development in Washington, D.C. (Birdsall cofounded the CGD in 2001). The cheerleading group, according to Birdsall, includes most economists, heads of state, international financial institutions such as the World Bank and IMF, and the corporate community. In her camp of cynics are a few economists, most NGOs, various activists, and much of the popular press. But there is a third option. One can recognize some truth in what each camp asserts: Trade has indeed been an engine of growth and poverty reduction in some countries, yet it has not been a panacea. Nor has it been entirely free or fair on the side of the industrialized nations, with their quotas and subsidies on the very products in which the developing nations have a comparative advantage. Birdsall places herself in this camp of "doubters" and "worriers."

For some years now Birdsall has been one of the more

thoughtful observers of the development scene. She has consistently emphasized the importance of income inequality as a brake on economic growth, just as she has held poverty reduction to be one of the essential criteria of good development policy. Birdsall holds a master's degree from the Johns Hopkins School of Advanced International Studies (1969) and an economics Ph.D. from Yale (1979). Her career has included policy and managerial positions at the World Bank, the Inter-American Development Bank, and the Carnegie Endowment for International Peace.

Further Reading

Birdsall, N. "Is Globalization Good for Development?" *Global Agenda Magazine* (2003). Accessed at http://www.cgdev.org/other/birdsall_cheerleaders.pdf; N. Birdsall, A. C. Kelley, and S. W. Sinding, eds., *Population Matters: Demographic Change, Economic Growth, and Poverty in the Developing World* (Oxford University Press, 2003).

Bono (1960–)

One does not ordinarily encounter the phrases "rock star" and "African poverty" in the same news story, but Bono, of the rock band U2, is no ordinary rock star. For several years he has been advocating, publicly and vociferously, on behalf of the world's most impoverished continent. His interest in Africa dates from 1984, when he and his wife spent six weeks working in a refugee camp in Ethiopia. As the new millennium approached, Bono became active in the Jubilee 2000 movement, whose goal was forgiveness of foreign debt for the world's poorest countries. Over the years he has met with government officials, philanthropists, economists, and other interested parties, and made many visits to Africa. He welcomes the publicity that goes with these activities. Indeed, that is the point—to draw as much attention as possible to the poverty and health crisis affecting Africa. In May of 2002, Bono made an extensive tour of Africa in the company of U.S. treasury secretary Paul H. O'Neill, a former corporate executive and well-known aid skeptic. Press accounts likened the two to the Odd Couple. For the long run, Bono is establishing an organization called DATA, or Debt, Aid, Trade for Africa, which will push for something like a Marshall Plan for Africa. Its initial funding comes from the Bill and Melinda Gates Foundation.

Bono, whose real name is Paul David Hewson, was born in Dublin, Ireland, in 1960. His band, U2, was formed when its four members were still teenagers. U2 is sometimes called a "Christian band" because of the spiritual aspect of its lyrics (written mainly by Bono). To date it has won a total of fourteen Grammy awards.

Further Reading

Josh Tyrangiel, "Can Bono Save the World?" *Time,* March 4, 2002, 63–69.

Gro Harlem Brundtland (1939–)

In July 2003, Gro Brundtland completed her term as director-general of the World Health Organization (WHO). One of the messages Brundtland communicated often during her five-year term was that the world's poor are more vulnerable than the rich to a whole range of diseases, whether HIV, TB, or malaria, and yet "there are no health sanctuaries." One of her initiatives was the Roll Back Malaria campaign. In a speech in 2000 she estimated that if malaria had been tackled aggressively in 1990, Africa's GDP a decade later could have been $100 billion higher. Another priority for Brundtland was the need to curtail tobacco consumption. Globally, tobacco-related deaths could reach 10 million per year, or more than all infectious diseases combined, by 2030. Hence the WHO has launched a worldwide Tobacco Free Initiative. Improving women's health was another concern of Brundtland. She pointed out that maternal deaths are a "multiple tragedy," since the infant left behind faces a high risk of death, and any other children in the family are likely to suffer from impaired nutrition and health. Brundtland believes that the rich nations must offer more assistance, including debt relief, to poor nations if world health is to improve.

Born in Oslo, Norway, Gro Brundtland is the daughter of a physician who also served as defense minister in the Norwegian cabinet. Her father's example set her on the road to becoming a doctor herself; she earned her M.D. from the University of Oslo in 1963. Both father and daughter were highly political—Gro joined the Labor Party when she was seven. The high point of Brundtland's political career was reached when she served two terms as prime minister of Norway, in 1986–1989 and 1990–1996. She also chaired the commission that wrote the "Brundtland Report," a landmark of late-twentieth-century global environmentalism that set the stage for the Rio Earth Summit of 1992.

Further Reading

D. Brown, "Brundtland Leaves as Head of WHO," *Washington Post*, July 20, 2003; G. Brundtland, ed., *Our Common Future: The World Commission on Environment and Development* (Oxford: Oxford University Press, 1987); N. Gibbs, "Norway's Radical Daughter," *Time* (September 25, 1989).

Pieter Dijkhuizen (1941–)

As a young child, Pieter Dijkhuizen almost died of starvation in occupied Holland. It was the final year of World War II, and many of the Dutch were trying to survive on a diet of beets, boiled oats, and tulip bulbs. Years later Dijkhuizen came to realize that his childhood experience had planted in him a lifelong interest in the problems of malnutrition.

Dijkhuizen was born at The Hague. His education proceeded as far as a master's degree before he took a research post on a ship plying the waters off the west coast of Africa. The task was to measure fish populations. During the five years he spent at this job, Dijkhuizen came face to face with African poverty and wanted, increasingly, to do something about it. He returned to the Netherlands to earn a Ph.D. in medical nutrition at the University of Groningen (1977). A few years later, during a stint as senior nutritionist at the Royal Tropical Institute in Amsterdam, Dijkhuizen developed "blended foods" that poor nations could produce for themselves using local ingredients. A typical blended food would be a porridge made from boiled water, a nutrient-fortified blend of maize and soybean meal, some cooking oil, and a pinch of salt. Dijkhuizen helped set up factories to produce blended foods in several African countries, including Burundi, Mali, and Sierra Leone.

After nearly a decade at the Royal Tropical Institute, Dijkhuizen went to work for the World Food Programme. While deputy country director for Ethiopia, he introduced the first fortified biscuits to that country's school feeding programs. (The biscuit factories had previously produced rations for the army of General Mengistu.) Dijkhuizen soon shifted assignments within the WFP to become its senior nutrition advisor in the Rome headquarters. In that role he oversaw the establishment of blended-food factories in many developing countries, where nutritious, low-cost foods with names like "Famix," "Indiamix," and "Koryomix" are now being produced. The blended foods have been especially valuable for feeding infants, pregnant and lactating women, refugees, and disaster victims, and have undoubtedly saved many thousands of lives. In 2000, Dijkhuizen became the WFP's country director for Bangladesh, a position he held for two years before retiring to his native Netherlands.

Further Reading

H. Hill, "A Perfect Blend: Life and Times of Food Aid Pioneer Pieter Dijkhuizen," *In Depth* (World Food Programme), 2003. Accessed at http://www.wfp.org/newsroom/in_depth/asia/dijkhuizen0207.htm.

Bill Gates (1955–)

One of the most famous men on the planet—mainly because of his status as the *richest* man on the planet—is Bill Gates. His fortune fluctuates with the value of his Microsoft stock, but it stays in the tens of billions of dollars year in and year out. Gates was born in 1955 and grew up in Seattle. He took an interest in computers while in high school. Although he enrolled at Harvard in 1973, he dropped out in his junior year to give his full attention to Microsoft, the computer software company that he and his friend Paul Allen started in 1975. The rest, as they say, is history—or at least business history. Gates married Melinda French in 1994, and the couple has three children.

For years Gates had to face thinly veiled accusations that he lacked a social conscience. He had been a ruthless competitor in building up his fortune, it was said, but unlike Andrew Carnegie and John D. Rockefeller, he was giving nothing back. That began to change in 1994, when the software magnate created the William H. Gates Foundation, endowing it generously with Microsoft stock. In 2000 it was merged into the Bill and Melinda Gates Foundation. (Mid-2003 assets are in the range of $24 billion, dwarfing the next-largest U.S. charitable foundation.) In recent years the foundation has been gaining momentum as a force in global health, supporting initiatives to eradicate polio, get the world's children immunized against all vaccine-preventable diseases, and find a cure for some of the most debilitating and lethal diseases afflicting those who live in the developing world. Of the $6 billion granted by Gates's foundation since 1994, more than half has gone to global health. Much more is in the pipeline, according to Gates. "I think, within a decade, we'll be able to say because of this work there are millions of children alive who wouldn't have been here otherwise. It's an incredible thing, really."

Further Reading

T. Paulson, "Bill Gates' War on Disease, Poverty Is an Uphill Battle," *Seattle Post-Intelligencer,* March 22, 2001; S. Strom, "Gates Aims Billions to Attack Illnesses of World's Neediest," *New York Times,* July 13, 2003; "World Bank Launches Effort with Bill Gates, Others to Vanquish Polio," *Agence France Presse,* April 29, 2003.

Bob Geldof (1951–)

The advent of television news and celebrity culture has altered the way the global community perceives, and responds to, famines in "remote" places, and Bob Geldof played a central role in that change. An Irish singer and songwriter with the rock group Boomtown Rats, Geldof organized the Live Aid concerts of 1985 that raised some $70 million to benefit famine victims in Africa, especially Ethiopia. The previous November he had seen BBC reports on a looming African food crisis and responded by cowriting, with Midge Ure, "Do They Know It's Christmas?" Geldof recruited a number of rock musicians to record the song—the group was dubbed "Band Aid"—and it was released just before Christmas. The record sold very well, and eventually about £8 million were raised for famine relief. American musicians followed suit with their own benefit recording, "We Are the World," cowritten by Michael Jackson, which also went to the top of the charts.

In the summer of 1985, Geldof organized simultaneous Live Aid concerts on July 13, in London, Philadelphia, and several smaller cities. Combined attendance topped 170,000, but the worldwide audience was closer to 1.9 billion! It was an unprecedented media event of its kind; Joan Baez called it the "Woodstock of the 80s." About half of the funds raised were earmarked for immediate famine relief, the other half for long-term African development efforts. Geldof was nominated for a Nobel Peace Prize, and in 1986 he received a knighthood from Queen Elizabeth.

As famine again threatened Ethiopia (not to mention much of southern Africa) in the spring of 2003, Geldof made a highly publicized trip to that country to call attention to the crisis. His visit was made at the invitation of the UN children's agency, UNICEF, and Save the Children UK. Wherever he went, the news media were there to record his words and actions. The main message he tried to communicate was that donor countries needed to increase immediately their deliveries of food and medicine to Ethiopia in order to avert another famine. He also echoed a key point often made by his fellow Irish rock star, Bono: Africa desperately needs debt relief.

Further Reading

Rory Carroll, "Geldof Back in Ethiopia," *Guardian Unlimited*, May 28, 2003.

James P. Grant (1922–1995)

For fifteen years, from 1980 until his death in 1995, James P. Grant led UNICEF as its third executive director. By every account, his performance was extraordinary. During the 1980s he identified what he called a "global silent emergency" of premature death and preventable disease among children worldwide. His response was to launch a "child survival and development revolution," a key component of which was the GOBI initiative. G stood for growth monitoring—keeping tabs on each child's physical development for signs of possible malnutrition. O stood for oral rehydration therapy—the use of boiled water, salt, and sugar to combat deadly diarrheal dehydration. (Grant routinely carried around with him sample packets to pull out when making a point about cost-effective ways of dealing with preventable disease.) B stood for breast-feeding and birth-spacing as means of improving children's health, and I stood for immunizations. By the end of the 1980s the GOBI program was believed to have saved many millions of children's lives in the developing world. In the 1990s, Grant called attention to a different problem: deficiencies of micronutrients, like iodine, vitamin A, and iron, in poor children's diets. New goals were set, new programs launched.

Grant saw a larger role for the head of UNICEF than simply leading public health campaigns, as vital as those were. He was highly effective in the halls of Congress when it came to urging continued U.S. financial support of UNICEF. (No other UN agency fared as well during the 1990s.) He was also a strong advocate of the Convention on the Rights of the Child, adopted by the UN General Assembly in 1989, and a major force behind the convening of the 1990 World Summit for Children. That meeting represented the largest gathering of heads of state and government ever held; one outcome was a global Plan of Action setting out twenty-seven specific targets for improving child welfare. Grant followed through on the summit by getting nations to design their own individual plans of action.

With an undergraduate degree from Berkeley and a law degree from Harvard, Grant made a career of international aid and development. He worked for the UN Relief and Rehabilitation Administration (in China), for various agencies of the U.S. State Department, and then as president of the Overseas Development Council, a Washington, D.C., think tank he helped establish in 1969.

Further Reading

Patricia L. Kutzner, *World Hunger: A Reference Handbook* (Santa Barbara, CA: ABC-CLIO, 1991), 129–130.

Fatima Jibrell (1948–)

Somalia is one of the world's poorest countries, qualifying for both the LDC (least developed country) and HIPC (heavily indebted poor country) designations used by the World Bank. Life expectancy at birth is forty-seven, and only about one in five Somali children attends elementary school. There has not been a functioning central government since 1991, when a devastating civil war began. And environmental destruction now threatens the future of an already impoverished land. Against all odds, one Somali woman is findings ways, through activism and education, to move her country in the right direction. Fatima Jibrell, the founder and director of Horn of Africa Relief and Development Organization, has led a successful effort to save old-growth forests of acacia trees in northeast Somalia. Older trees were being logged for use in producing charcoal, a product heavily demanded in Saudi Arabia and the Gulf states. Severe ecological damage was being done. Jibrell campaigned against the practice and persuaded the regional government to ban further exports of charcoal. She has also taught young Somalis—as young as eight years old—how to pile up small rocks to form dams, preventing water runoff after seasonal rains. This not only conserves water in an arid land but also helps keep the ground moist enough to permit the germination of seeds. For her work on the conservation of natural resources in Somalia, Jibrell was awarded the Goldman Environmental Prize in 2002.

Jibrell's high school and university education—she holds a master's degree in community organizing—were received in the United States, and in fact she is a naturalized U.S. citizen, as well as the mother of five daughters. She admits that the decision to return to Somalia in the early 1990s after so many years abroad was a difficult one, especially for her children. "But America didn't need us. Somalia did." She continues to be deeply involved in environmental and women's issues and in efforts to develop leadership skills in the next generation of Somalis.

Further Reading

"Interview: Female Intuition," *New Scientist* (July 6, 2002); T. Szymanski, "Fatima Jibrell: Nursing Nature," *World Press Review* 49, 7 (July 2002).

Bernard Kouchner (1939–)

Winning the Nobel Peace Prize for 1999 brought long-overdue public recognition to Doctors without Borders (Medecins Sans Frontieres), an organization that has been on the front lines of global emergency medical assistance since its founding in 1971. MSF was started by a group of French doctors, with Bernard Kouchner often cited as having taken a leading role. Born in Avignon, Kouchner trained to be a specialist in internal medicine. When he and several other French doctors volunteered with the Red Cross to assist victims of the Biafran conflict from 1968 to 1970, the group's frustration with the political constraints of remaining "neutral" at all times led them to form MSF, with its headquarters in Paris. Kouchner subsequently led missions to Cambodia, Somalia, Thailand, Peru, Guatemala, and many other troubled areas. Knowing the value of publicity in advancing humanitarian causes, he organized a number of high-profile relief projects, like "A Boat for Vietnam" in 1978. This involved sending a hospital ship to the waters off Indonesia and Malaysia to assist the "boat people" who had fled Vietnam.

Aside from leading and participating in MSF activities, Dr. Kouchner has also pursued active political and literary careers. He was a minister in the French government for more than ten years, including a stint as minister of health. In 1994 he was elected to a seat in the European Parliament. And in 1999 he was appointed by UN secretary-general Kofi Annan as his personal representative in Kosovo. Kouchner has published a new book, on average, every three years for decades. (He also writes television scripts.) In the role of public intellectual, he has espoused a principle that he calls "the duty to interfere"—a moral duty to intervene on behalf of victims and to bear witness to human rights abuses. At the height of the 2003 SARS epidemic, Kouchner gave a speech at Harvard in which he proposed a global health insurance plan, saying, "In our day, no one deserves to die of a curable disease because he is poor. We know almost everything except how to convince people in the wealthiest countries to give all the inhabitants on Earth an equal chance."

Further Reading

Alvin Powell, "Kouchner Calls for Global Health Care," *Harvard University Gazette,* March 13, 2003.

Frances Moore Lappé (1944–)

Frances Moore Lappé's name is synonymous with globally conscious vegetarianism. Her 1971 book, *Diet for a Small Planet,* opened U.S. readers' eyes to the ethical dimensions of their meat-heavy diet and moved vegetarianism from fringe status into the cultural mainstream. At the time that *Diet* was published, many were concerned that a global "population bomb" was set to go off, with millions in the Third World doomed to starvation. Lappé rejected this nightmare vision, arguing that food production was adequate and that no one needed to starve if—and it was a big *if*—people in the richer countries would switch from a meat-centered diet to one heavy in grains and legumes. Many heeded her call, and others were at least challenged to connect their daily food choices with larger hunger issues. In 1975, Lappé and a colleague, Joseph Collins, founded the Institute for Food and Development Policy, or Food First, as a research center for issues of hunger and nutrition.

Lappé was born in Oregon but raised in Fort Worth, Texas. She graduated from Earlham College in 1966 and then became involved in community organizing in Philadelphia, before moving to California. There she enrolled in the graduate program in social work at the University of California, Berkeley. An interest in world hunger soon grew to be so consuming that she dropped out of her graduate program to research and write *Diet for a Small Planet.* It has been through multiple editions and printings, been translated into six languages, and has sold over 3 million copies. Lappé's fourteenth book, *Hope's Edge: The New Diet for a Small*

Planet, coauthored with her daughter Anna Lappé, was published in 2002. Frances Moore Lappé was the winner of the 1987 Right Livelihood Award, also known as the alternative Nobel Prize. She currently resides in Cambridge, Massachusetts.

Further Reading

D. Arnold, "Author with Recipe for Fight against Hunger Is Optimistic," *Boston Globe,* July 23, 2002.

Santiago Levy (1956–)

Around the world, poverty tends to be most deep seated and hopeless in rural areas. Until recently that could have been said about Mexico, where in 1996 about one-third of the population lived in poverty (by that country's own standards) and where a majority of the 20 percent in extreme poverty were rural residents. In 1997, however, a new government program targeting rural poverty was launched. It was named Progresa, a Spanish acronym for program of education, health, and nutrition. Conceived by Santiago Levy, deputy finance minister, Progresa provided bimonthly cash grants to rural families on the basis of their household income, size, and compliance with certain requirements. Those requirements included sending children to school and for medical checkups, and attendance by mothers at talks on health and nutrition. A unique feature of the program is its gender focus. Larger payments are received by families for a daughter's school attendance (after sixth grade) than for a son's, since the dropout rate for girls is higher. Also, monetary payments under Progresa are made to the *mother*—a departure from what might be expected in a male-dominated society. And health expenditures under Progresa go primarily to women, whether for pregnancy care, postnatal care, or reproductive health services.

Instituted under the administration of President Zedillo, Progresa survived the major political power shift when Vicente Fox was elected president in 2000. Indeed, President Fox approved an expansion of the program into *urban* areas and doubled its budget. Renamed Oportunidades, the expanded program now benefits more than 20 million people, or one in five Mexican families. An early evaluation of the program found that its recipients enjoyed better health and stayed in school longer than those not in the program. A more recent evaluation finds that every peso spent today brings long-term benefits that are five times as large, mainly through higher earnings. Progresa/Oportunidades now serves as a model for other Latin American countries, such as Argentina, Nicaragua, and Honduras.

Santiago Levy is a native of Mexico City. His university training, including a Ph.D. in economics, was received at Boston University. He has taught at several universities, consulted with the Inter-American Development Bank, and served in a variety of high government positions in Mexico. Currently he serves as director-general of Mexico's social security program.

Further Reading

Alan B. Krueger, "Economic Scene: A Model for Evaluating the Use of Development Dollars, South of the Border," *New York Times,* May 2, 2002; *PROGRESA: Breaking the Cycle of Poverty* (Washington, DC: IFPRI, 2002); Q. Wodon, B. Briere, C. Siaens, and S. Yitzhaki, "Mexico's PROGRESA: Innovative Targeting, Gender Focus and Impact on Social Welfare," *En Breve* 17 (January 2003)

George McGovern (1922–)

George McGovern has a message for all who will listen: Hunger can be erased from the face of the earth, and because it can, it *must.* Born and raised in South Dakota, McGovern saw Depression-era poverty in his youth and far more severe deprivation while stationed in Italy as a bomber pilot during World War II. (He flew thirty-five combat missions in that conflict.) After the war, McGovern completed his education and began a career in college teaching at Dakota Wesleyan University. He left academe for politics in 1956 with a successful run for the U.S. House of Representatives. Following two terms in Congress, McGovern was appointed by President Kennedy to head the new Food for Peace Program, under which U.S. farm surpluses were donated to poor nations experiencing food shortages. In his 2001 book *The Third Freedom: Ending Hunger in Our Time,* he writes of one of that program's early success stories: establishing a school feeding program in the Puno region of Peru. Two years later McGovern was back to electoral politics, winning the first of his three terms in the U.S. Senate. In 1972 he ran as the Democratic, antiwar candidate for president against the incumbent, Richard Nixon.

In the Senate, McGovern earned a reputation as a strong advocate for federal funding of nutrition programs, both for school children and for pregnant and nursing mothers. His frequent ally in these efforts—and later a candidate for president himself—was Bob Dole, a Kansas Republican. Upon concluding his political career, McGovern served as visiting professor at several leading universities and then as president of the Middle East Policy Council. In 1998, President Clinton named him the U.S. representative to the UN Food and Agriculture Organization in Rome. At the end of his term he was appointed the first global ambassador on hunger. McGovern believes that world hunger can be ended by 2030 through an international effort led by the United States. One of the principal means of achieving this goal would be a universal school lunch program—a proposal that, again, enjoys the support of his old Senate colleague, Bob Dole. As McGovern tells audiences, ending world hunger has become his "passion."

Further Reading

George McGovern, *The Third Freedom: Ending Hunger in Our Time* (New York: Simon and Schuster, 2001); "George McGovern, Son of Wesleyan, Citizen of the World." Accessed at http://www.mcgovernlibrary.com/george.htm.

Robert S. McNamara (1916–)

In the view of many, Robert S. McNamara stands out as the most dynamic of the nine presidents who have led the World Bank since its founding in 1945. Born in San Francisco, McNamara studied economics and philosophy at the University of California (Berkeley), taking his degree in 1937. He earned an MBA from Harvard two years later. Wartime service in the air force was followed by a stellar career at Ford Motor Company, where in 1960 McNamara was named the first president of the company from outside the Ford family. Almost immediately, though, McNamara was asked by another new president, John F. Kennedy, to become his secretary of defense, a position he held through most of the Vietnam War.

Under an informal understanding, the World Bank is customarily headed by an American, the IMF by a European. When McNamara became the Bank's fifth president in 1968, its annual lending to less developed nations was under $1 billion a year. By 1981, the year in which he completed his final term, lending exceeded $12 billion annually. In a frequently cited 1973 speech in Nairobi, McNamara called attention to the wide and growing gap in wealth between rich and poor nations, and to a similar gap *within* developing nations. He found it morally repugnant that 40 percent of the population of the developing world lived in absolute poverty, a poverty that, in his words, "degrades the lives of individuals below the minimal norms of human decency." He called for a new emphasis on rural development, stressing that most of the world's poorest were located outside of cities. Whereas the World Bank had previously focused its lending on huge infrastructure projects, the priority now was shifted to assisting small farmers in hopes of raising their productivity by an ambitious 5 percent annually.

McNamara's legacy at the World Bank is not uncontroversial. Detractors point to massive World Bank loans to poor countries in the 1970s as a source of the debt crisis of the 1980s. (Many countries have staggered into the twenty-first century bearing debt burdens they may never be able to pay off.) Critics also cite a decades-long record of World Bank support for large, environmentally harmful projects in the developing world. On the other hand, few have argued as urgently as McNamara for the need to make development assistance work for the most impoverished. In his Nairobi speech, he called for an end to absolute poverty by the close of the twentieth century—a worthy challenge that, sadly, was not met.

Further Reading

Jochen Kraske et al., *Bankers with a Mission: The Presidents of the World Bank, 1946–91* (New York: Oxford University Press, 1997); Robert S. McNamara, *The McNamara Years at the World Bank: Major Policy Addresses of Robert S. McNamara, 1968–1981* (Baltimore: Johns Hopkins University Press, 1981).

James T. Morris (1943–)

When Catherine Bertini, executive director of the World Food Programme, neared the end of her second five-year term in the winter of 2002, it was rumored that an Australian official was in line to succeed her. The United States let it be known, however, that it strongly favored a U.S. successor to the American-born Bertini. When Secretary-General Kofi Annan announced the name of the newest head of the WFP, it was James T. Morris, a son of Indiana with broad experience across the private, public, and not-for-profit sectors in that state. With a political science degree from Indiana University, Morris went to work for the Indianapolis city government in 1967, quickly becoming chief-of-staff to the mayor, Richard Lugar. (Lugar now represents Indiana in the U.S. Senate.) In 1973, Morris took the first of a series of jobs at Lilly Endowment, Inc., a large, Indianapolis-based charitable foundation created in 1937 by members of the Lilly family. By 1984 he had risen to the presidency of the foundation. From 1989 until his appointment to head the WFP, Morris was president and chief executive officer of IWC Resources Corporation, the parent company of Indianapolis Water Company.

Morris has taken leadership roles in a variety of nonprofit organizations, serving on the boards of the Chicago Theological Seminary, the NCAA Foundation, Indiana University, the United Way of Central Indiana, and the American Red Cross, among others. His managerial and consultative skills will undoubtedly be tested in overseeing the far-flung operations of the World Food Programme. The WFP, based in Rome, assisted 73 million people in eighty-four countries during 2001, on a budget of about $2 billion.

Further Reading

"Ask the World Food Programme's Executive Director," BBC News, *Talking Point*, June 17, 2002.

Andrew S. Natsios (1949–)

In early 2001, at his confirmation hearing to become administrator for the U.S. Agency for International Development (USAID), Andrew Natsios spoke movingly of the famine that claimed the lives of 10 percent of Greece's population during World War II. His family had mentioned it often over the years; one of the famine's victims was his great-uncle. Famines and other kinds of humanitarian emergencies have figured centrally in Natsios's career. He held two different senior-level positions relating to disaster assistance at USAID from 1989 to 1993, and he served as vice president of World Vision US, a Christian humanitarian organization, from 1993 to 1998. The agency he now heads has been providing assistance to developing countries since 1961. Essentially, USAID administers the foreign aid budget of the United States—nearly $10 billion a year. (That is approximately 0.1 percent of U.S. gross domestic product. Critics argue it should be seven times as much.)

Natsios is a 1971 graduate of Georgetown University, where he majored in history. He earned a master's of public administration degree from Harvard's Kennedy School of Government in 1979, during a twelve-year period of service in the Massachusetts House of Representatives (1975–1987). Just before returning to USAID, Natsios spent a year as chairman and CEO of the Massachusetts Turnpike Authority; in that role he had responsibility for Boston's Big Dig, one of the most ambitious public works projects ever undertaken in the United States. Natsios is married, the father of three children, a veteran of the Gulf War, and the author of two books, one of which deals with the North Korean famine of the 1990s.

Further Reading

A. Natsios, *The Great North Korean Famine* (Washington, DC: Institute of Peace Press, 2001).

Winston Hugh Njongonkulu Ndungane (1941–)

In the closing years of the twentieth century, a campaign to forgive the debts of impoverished nations around the world gained considerable momentum. Leading the effort was a group called Jubilee 2000, but the individual voice most clearly heard on this issue was that of Njongonkulu Ndungane, archbishop of Cape Town. Like many South Africans, Ndungane had his political views shaped by the struggle against apartheid. While a student at the University of Cape Town in 1960, he participated in demonstrations against the pass laws that were a part of that system. Further political activities led to a three-year prison term on the notorious Robben Island, where one of his fellow prisoners was Nelson Mandela. Later Ndungane earned divinity degrees at King's College, London, and served as an assistant priest in a London parish. By 1980 he had returned to South Africa, where he ascended through the Anglican hierarchy and, in 1996, succeeded Archbishop Desmond Tutu.

Ndungane hoped the Jubilee movement would bring relief to countries staggering under their debt burdens. The IMF did introduce a Heavily Indebted Poor Countries initiative (HIPC) in 1996 and an enhanced HIPC program in 1999, but the ensuing debt reductions were partial, selective, and, in the view of Ndungane, inadequate. Perhaps as a result, he sharpened his rhetoric. "As a follower of Jesus, committed to the health and salvation of every person, regardless of color or creed, I cannot keep silent on this issue [of debt]. It is a matter of life and death." Ndungane came out in favor of the controversial legal doctrine of "odious debt." This term refers to debts contracted by an unelected, oppressive government to advance its own interests rather than those of the nation as a whole. In theory such debts are not binding on, and may be repudiated by, a later government that is democratic. That is exactly what South Africa and other countries similarly placed should do, the archbishop says.

Further Reading

"Archbishop Njongonkulu Ndungane," *Focus* 10 (April 1998). Accessed at Helen Suzman Foundation, http://www.hsf.org.za/focus_10/F10_Anglican.htm; N. Birdsall and J. Williamson, *Delivering on Debt Relief: From IMF Gold to a New Aid Architecture* (Washington, DC: Institute for International Economics, 2002).

Kavita N. Ramdas (1963–)

World poverty is disproportionately the poverty of women. Well over half, perhaps as many as 70 percent, of the world's absolute poor are female. In many countries, education is not as available to girls as to boys, women have fewer legal rights, and property ownership is mainly in the hands of men. Women are subjected to domestic violence at epidemic rates. Childbirth can be a fatal experience in the developing world. What all of this shows—and the list of gender differences could easily be multiplied—is that the task of improving women's lives has a long way to go. The world's largest foundation devoted solely to supporting women's initiatives at the international level is the Global Fund for Women, based in Palo Alto, California, and headed by Kavita Ramdas. Since its founding in 1987, the GFW has disbursed more than $27 million to well over 2,000 women's groups in 160 countries. The funding goes to grass roots efforts to end poverty, violence, and illiteracy. In 2003, for example, a GFW grant was awarded to a rural organization, Rxiin Tnamet, that operates local clinics for Mayan women, giving them health information and education about their reproductive rights.

Kavita Ramdas was born in India and remains an Indian citizen, but she came to the United States in 1981 to attend Mount

Holyoke College and has stayed ever since. She earned a master's degree in international development from Princeton University (1988) before going to work at the John D. and Catherine T. MacArthur Foundation as a program officer. She joined GFW as president and chief executive officer in 1996. In 1999 she received the Changing the Face of Philanthropy Award from the Women's Funding Network. She has served on the Committee on Women and Development, a board that advises the UN Economic Commission for Africa, and she is fluent in English, German, Hindi, and Urdu.

Further Reading

V. Kashyap, "Enabling Women to Have a Say, Their Way," *India Currents* (December 3, 1999); GFW website at http://www.globalfundforwomen. org.

Jeffrey Sachs (1954–)

One of the world's best known economists now applies himself to the task of understanding and combating global poverty. Jeffrey Sachs, director of the Earth Institute at Columbia University, is a prolific scholar—his curriculum vitae runs to twenty-seven pages—and a globetrotting consultant to governments on a wide range of economic issues. Sachs came to prominence during the 1980s and early 1990s as a highly visible adviser to governments in Eastern Europe and the former Soviet Union on how to make the transition from central planning to a market economy. Before joining the faculty at Columbia, Sachs had obtained three degrees from Harvard University, joined its faculty in 1980, and raced to full professor status in just three years. Around the time he was hired to lead the Earth Institute in 2002, Sachs was also named a special adviser to Secretary-General Kofi Annan on the UN's Millennium Development Goals. These goals are an ambitious set of targets all nations are pledged to meet in the areas of poverty reduction, health, education, gender equality, and environmental protection by the year 2015. There is concern that many nations are behind schedule in meeting their goals.

Sachs believes that sustainable development faces significant obstacles in many parts of the world. His research has shown that landlocked countries, for example, suffer a serious economic handicap compared with those that have access to the sea. A poor, or tropical, climate can also hinder economic progress, for both agricultural and epidemiological reasons. (Sachs considers it a scandal that research to find a cure for malaria is so underfunded.) Besides physical constraints, many countries are also impeded by political mismanagement and outright corruption. Hence he shares the view of many that "good governance" is a requirement for making effective use of outside aid. But it is the overall *level* of such aid that concerns Sachs the most. The United States, he notes, currently falls short of the aid commitment it gave at an important international summit in 2002 by a whopping $60 billion. That sum, he further notes, equals the increase in U.S. military spending since President Bush took office.

Further Reading

D. Appell, "Science to Save the World," *Scientific American* 288, 1 (January 2003): 36–37; J. Sachs, "Weapons of Mass Salvation," *Economist* (October 26, 2002), 101–102.

Dita Sari (1972–)

A defining feature of globalization has been the transfer of manufacturing jobs from high-wage countries to low-wage ones. Although that clearly brings economic pain to the communities losing jobs, there can be gains at the receiving end in the form of expanded employment, higher incomes, and reduced poverty. But getting from potential to *actual* gains requires, in the view of many, a level of worker organization not often found in the poorer countries. In recent years, one of Indonesia's leading labor activists has been Dita Sari, the head of the National Front for Indonesian Workers' Struggle (FNPBI). Sari, a daughter of the middle class who attended the University of Indonesia in Jakarta intending to become a lawyer, came to public attention in 1995 when she led a strike against Indoshoes Inti Industry, a supplier of athletic shoes to Reebok and Adidas. She was only twenty-three at the time. The next year Sari was caught up in an escalating crisis of labor and political unrest that ended in her being arrested and charged with subversion. At the 1997 trial, she was convicted and sentenced to five years in prison. She served two years. In that time her country was hit by economic calamity and a radical change of government (the fall of Suharto). At the urging of the International Labor Organization and Amnesty International, among others, Sari was released in 1999. The young woman's mother had died during her imprisonment.

In what might seem an ironic twist, Reebok, in January 2002, named Sari a recipient of its Human Rights Award, worth $50,000. She declined it, however, issuing a statement that read, in part: "We cannot tolerate the way multinational companies treat the workers of the third world countries." An honor that she did accept, however, was the 2001 Ramon Magsaysay Award, in the "emergent leadership" category. Sometimes called "Asia's Nobel prize," the award recognized Sari's "resolute activism on behalf of working people and their place in Indonesia's evolving democracy."

Further Reading

"Noted Award Means Struggle Goes On: Dita," *Jakarta Post,* August 21, 2001; N. Walter, "Political Activist Rejects Award from Shoe Firm," *Independent* (London), February 8, 2002.

Amartya K. Sen (1933–)

In 1981 the Indian economist Amartya K. Sen published a book that became, almost immediately, the standard work on its subject: *Poverty and Famines.* Already widely recognized for his contributions to several distinct fields within economics, Sen solidified his reputation with a penetrating analysis of the true cause of famines. In simplest terms, famines resulted not from a shortage of food relative to the population of consumers—a "Malthusian" explanation—but from a scarcity of "entitlements," that is, too little purchasing power in the hands of the people. Sen's interest in extreme poverty began with a searing experience when he was eight years old. One day at the school he was attending, an emaciated man appeared on the school grounds, acting deranged. There followed another, and ten more, and then what seemed like thousands more. These were the road-weary victims of what would later be known as the Bengali famine of 1943–1944, straggling toward Calcutta. As Sen would later show in *Poverty and Famines,* the supply of food produced in East Bengal in 1943 was no lower than it had been in 1941, yet in the earlier year famine had *not* struck. Likewise, he argued, in Ethiopia in 1972–1974 and Bangladesh in 1974, famine occurred not because of disastrous crop failures but because of inflation or unemployment, which shrank real incomes and left the poor unable to purchase the needed quantities of food.

Sen was born in Santiniketan, a city near Calcutta in West

Bengal. His father was a chemistry professor, his grandfather a famous scholar of Sanskrit (*amartya* means "immortal" in Sanskrit). With an undergraduate degree from Presidency College, Calcutta, Sen went on to Cambridge University for his Ph.D. in economics (1957). Over a long career, he has taught at some of the most prestigious universities in the world, including Harvard, Cambridge, and the London School of Economics. In 1998, to no one's surprise, he was awarded the Nobel Prize in Economics. In the fall of 2002, Sen resigned as master of Trinity College, Cambridge, after six years as the first Asian head of an Oxbridge college, to return to Harvard. He has been awarded dozens of honorary degrees and was the first non-American elected as president of the American Economic Association.

Further Reading

A. K. Sen, *Poverty and Famines: An Essay on Entitlement and Deprivation* (Oxford: Clarendon, 1981); Sen, *Development as Freedom* (New York: Knopf, 2000); Jonathan Steele, "Guardian Profile: Food for Thought," *Guardian* (London), March 31, 2001.

Alfred Sommer (1942–)

One of the diseases doctors rarely see in the industrialized world is nutritional blindness, or xerophthalmia. Diets in the richer countries effectively prevent this disease. But in the developing countries, millions of children have lost their sight, and millions more their lives, for lack of a basic micronutrient in their diet: vitamin A. The man most responsible for discovering this simple, and easily remedied, problem is Dr. Alfred Sommer. A graduate of Union College with an M.D. from Harvard Medical School (1967), Sommer began his career at the Centers for Disease Control, working in the Epidemic Intelligence Service. From there he was recruited to join a team studying cholera in East Pakistan (now Bangladesh), in the wake of a devastating cyclone. He and his research partner, Henry Mosely, later published a landmark paper in the journal *Lancet* on assessing natural disasters using an epidemiological approach.

Back in the United States, Sommer completed his residency at the Wilmer Ophthalmologic Institute at Johns Hopkins before embarking on another international research project. This time he studied the effects of vitamin A deficiency in El Salvador and Haiti. In the late 1970s, Sommer, along with his family, moved to

Indonesia, where he supervised an in-depth investigation of the effects of vitamin A deficiency in children. He discovered that the deficiency was very common and, because it lowered resistance to measles and diarrhea, deadly. Sommer then found the same pattern in Nepal and Africa. He also found that *oral* doses of vitamin A, not just injections, could effectively treat or prevent deficiency diseases. By one UN estimate, between 1 million and 3 million children's lives could be saved every year by the taking of two or three vitamin A pills each. The cost: 4 to 6 cents per child annually. It would be difficult to find anything remotely as cost effective in medicine.

Sommer currently serves as dean of the Bloomberg School of Public Health at Johns Hopkins, where he is also a professor in the epidemiology and international health departments. He has published five books and hundreds of scientific articles. For his work in saving the lives and eyesight of millions of children around the world, Sommer has received numerous international awards. He was elected in 2001 to the National Academy of Sciences.

Further Reading

Richard Cohen interview with Sommer, "Lasker Luminaries." Accessed at http://www.laskerfoundation.org/awards/library/lumin_as_int.html.

Joseph E. Stiglitz (1943–)

Of all the critics of globalization in recent years, Joseph Stiglitz has been one of the hardest to ignore. From 1997 to 2000, Stiglitz served as a senior vice president and chief economist at the World Bank, but that did not prevent him, in early 2000, from publishing a stinging critique of the Bank's sister institution, the International Monetary Fund, in the pages of the *New Republic* magazine. Shortly thereafter he left the World Bank for a chair in the economics department of Columbia University, and in 2002 he published *Globalization and Its Discontents*. At book length he expanded on his earlier analysis of what the global financial institutions are doing wrong and how they might reform their policies. His main target remains the IMF, which, in his view, lacks a coherent understanding of what causes a country to fall into a financial crisis or what the proper remedy should be.

Stiglitz holds that "market fundamentalism"—an unquestioning faith in the operations of the unfettered market—guides IMF policy as it relates to the developing countries. Hence the

IMF has not hesitated to demand that these nations decontrol prices, abolish subsidies, boost interest rates, and open up their markets to short-term capital flows, regardless of the potential havoc that may follow. Worse, it now acts as if it has a mandate to protect the interests of the financial community—that is, international banks like Citibank—above the interests of the borrower nations. Short-sighted, rigid IMF policies were behind the Asian crisis of 1997 and the Russian crisis of 1998, in Stiglitz's view. Indeed, under the current rules enforced by the IMF, World Bank, and World Trade Organization, globalization is not helping very many of the world's poor achieve economic or social progress. But it is the rules, not globalization as such, that are to blame.

Coming from Stiglitz, the indictment cannot easily be dismissed. He is one of the economics profession's brightest lights, a former chairman of the Council of Economic Advisers under President Clinton, and a Nobel laureate in 2001. Born in Gary, Indiana, he went to Amherst College on scholarship, then to MIT for his Ph.D. (1967). He has held teaching appointments at Yale, Oxford, Princeton, and Stanford prior to his current position at Columbia, and has been awarded numerous honorary degrees in the United States and abroad.

Further Reading

J. Stiglitz, *Globalization and Its Discontents* (New York: W. W. Norton, 2002); Stiglitz, "The Insider," *New Republic* 222, 16/17 (April 17/April 24, 2000) 56–60.

Paul E. Tierney, Jr. (1943–)

In the era of globalization, many would-be entrepreneurs in the developing world are handicapped by a resource scarcity they have little power to overcome on their own—the scarcity of practical business savvy in starting and sustaining a small enterprise. Even the best business ideas will not get off the ground unless the individual knows how to develop a product, locate a market, and obtain financing. In 1968 a Connecticut businessman, Edward Bullard, started a nonprofit organization called TechnoServe to meet this need. Since 1992, Paul Tierney has led TechnoServe as its chairman and chief fundraiser. TechnoServe employs 400 people and has an annual budget of $15 million, with projects in ten countries of Africa and Latin America. Its oldest country program, dating back to 1971, is in Ghana, where it maintains a staff of 80 in eight cities. TechnoServe tries to help local entrepreneurs find a "niche market" for locally grown crops, whether coffee, shea nuts, pineapples, or cashews. This can mean organizing small growers into cooperatives, helping with the development of processing plants, identifying high-value specialty crops, putting growers in touch with supermarket chains, and locating sources of finance. When new businesses have been successfully mentored into being, the payoff takes the form of higher incomes, increased employment, and, ultimately, a stronger private sector. TechnoServe's record of success has earned it a place among "America's 100 Best Charities," according to *Worth* magazine.

Tierney has the ideal background to lead TechnoServe. A philosophy major at the University of Notre Dame (1964), he served as a Peace Corps volunteer in Chile, earned an MBA at the Harvard Business School (1968), and went on to a career in investment banking and venture capital in New York and London. In 2001 he was named executive-in-residence and adjunct professor at the Columbia Graduate School of Business.

Further Reading

Susan Young, "Straddling Two Worlds: Paul Tierney," Harvard Business School *Online Bulletin* (December, 2002).

James D. Wolfensohn (1933–)

There is an informal understanding—rarely discussed in public—that the person heading the World Bank is an American, while the IMF is led by a European. James Wolfensohn, the Bank's current president, is Australian by birth but a U.S. citizen by naturalization. Wolfensohn was educated at the University of Sydney, competed on the Australian fencing team at the 1956 Olympics, served in his country's air force, and practiced law for an Australian firm before moving to London to start a career in finance. Along the way, he earned an MBA degree from Harvard and then spent many years on Wall Street, where, in 1981, he founded his own firm, James D. Wolfensohn, Inc., to give advice to major US and multinational corporations. He assumed the World Bank presidency in 1995, and is the first Bank president since Robert S. McNamara to be appointed to a second five-year term.

The so-called Bretton Woods institutions (World Bank and IMF) have been subjected to strong criticism from various quarters. On the left, they are seen, along with the WTO, as part of the institutional machinery of a globalization that exploits the developing countries for the benefit of "capital"—that is, the wealthy. On the right, they are seen as wasteful, useless entities that would best be abolished. Even mainstream critics, including former employees, have questioned the effectiveness of the World Bank and IMF in reducing poverty. Wolfensohn, acutely aware of the criticism, has introduced major changes at the Bank. In 1996 he joined with his IMF counterpart to launch the HIPC (highly indebted poor countries) initiative, which has written off billions of dollars of debt owed by the poorest countries. He also introduced a new loan-approval process that requires governments to consult widely throughout civil society before submitting "poverty reduction strategy papers." The resulting PRSPs can be read off the Internet—an indication of the Bank's new commitment to transparency. In addition, Wolfensohn has attempted to lessen the distance between the Bank and its borrowing constituency by increasing from 500 to 2,500 the number of staff working "in the field." He has been quite vocal in asking the developed countries to increase their aid to the developing countries, and to open their markets to imports from those countries.

Further Reading

P. Blustein, "With Critics Quieter, Wolfensohn Is Looking Ahead," *Washington Post,* June 11, 2003; S. Schifferes, "James Wolfensohn: A New Broom at the World Bank," *BBC News Online,* September 14, 2000.

Muhammad Yunus (1940–)

When Muhammad Yunus, an economics professor at Chittagong University in Bangladesh, wanted to understand why poverty was so widespread in his country in the early 1970s, he went to a village near his university. He found a woman there making bamboo stools and asked her how much she earned. The answer: two cents a day. The reason: She was continually in debt to the trader who provided her with bamboo material and bought her finished product for next to nothing. He set the terms of trade for her, and two cents a day was all she was allowed. Yunus then asked her what she could do if she had the money to buy her own bamboo and then sell her finished stools freely. Her answer: She could double or triple her daily income. The picture was the same throughout the village—dirt-poor laborers unable to get control of their own livelihoods for lack of capital. Yunus then made a personal loan of only $27 to forty-two village women, and the entire sum was quickly repaid. That was the beginning of the Grameen Bank.

The Grameen principle is a kind of social experiment. Women in groups of five borrow sums of money from Grameen and agree to repay it within a relatively short period. If anyone is slow to make her payments, the other members of the group exert peer pressure on her. But the rate of repayment is very high. (It seems to have fallen off, however, since the massive Bangladesh floods of 1998.) The loans can be used to open a shop, buy a cow, or start a craft business. All who borrow must take a pledge to uphold "16 decisions"—a set of practices such as keeping family size small, not paying or accepting dowries, keeping houses in good repair, and planting vegetables every year. Grameen has lent nearly $4 billion to over 2.5 million women, and the microcredit idea has been replicated in Vietnam, the Philippines, China, and dozens of other countries.

Yunus was born in Bangladesh, came to the United States to study economics, and holds a Ph.D. from Vanderbilt University (1969). For a simple idea now considered revolutionary, Yunus has won many prizes, including the King Baudoin International Development Prize (1992) and the World Food Prize (1994).

Further Reading

D. Bornstein, *The Price of a Dream: The Story of the Grameen Bank* (New York: Simon and Schuster, 1996); D. Pearl and M. W. Phillips, "Bank that Pioneered Loans for the Poor Hits Repayment Snag," *Wall Street Journal* (November 27, 2001); M. Yunus and A. Jolis, *Banker to the Poor: The Autobiography of Muhammad Yunus, Founder of the Grameen Bank* (New York: Oxford University Press, 2001).

6

Data and Documents

Statistics on Global Poverty

The amount of information available to those with an interest in global poverty is nothing short of oceanic. (Wade into it at your own risk!) While it might seem that this vast quantity of data must reflect in some way the urgency of the issue and the public's desire to be well informed about it, a more mundane explanation might be closer to the mark. There are a number of international agencies whose mandated tasks include, among other things, the collection and publication of data, much of which relates to poverty. By and large, these agencies came into being at the end of World War II, when the United Nations and the so-called Bretton Woods institutions—the International Monetary Fund and the World Bank—were established. The UN system now includes not only the familiar agencies whose names begin with UN—such as UNDP, UNICEF, UNCTAD, UNCED, and UNFPA—but also the World Health Organization (WHO), the Food and Agriculture Organization (FAO), the World Food Programme (WFP), and the International Labor Organization (ILO). Great volumes of information are churned out, almost continuously, by these organizations. Most issue an annual yearbook that develops a policy topic and includes annually updated tables of relevant statistics.

Two institutions stand above the rest when it comes to publishing "official" statistics that quantify global poverty: the World Bank and the UN Development Programme. Both employ highly

131

professional staffs who are expert at gathering, organizing, presenting, and interpreting data. Each year their work bears fruit in the form of "flagship publications"—the *World Development Indicators* (World Bank) and the *Human Development Report* (UNDP). It is no exaggeration to say that the release of these annual documents is anticipated by journalists, government officials, scholars, and policy-makers alike. They are an excellent place to begin any study of world poverty.

The roughly two hundred nations and territories of the world can be categorized according to their economic standing, whether measured by money income alone or by a composite index that takes both income and other factors into account. Table 6.1 is the World Bank's 2003 grouping of countries on the basis of their per capita income. In the world's sixty-six poorest ("low income") countries, per capita incomes are $745 or less. By contrast, the richest fifty-two countries have per capita incomes of at least $9,206. (The figure for the United States is over $30,000.)

An alternative to the World Bank's "low income" grouping of countries is displayed in table 6.2, which lists the forty-nine "least developed countries" in the world, as determined by the United Nations Conference on Trade and Development (UNCTAD). There are three requirements for inclusion in this list: low per capita GDP (under $900), low levels of human resources, and high economic vulnerability. UNCTAD's index of human-resource weakness is based on measures of nutrition, health, education, and adult literacy. Its index of economic vulnerability is based on various measures, such as instability of exports, concentration of exports, and instability of agricultural production. If a country meets all the criteria for inclusion in the list of least developed countries, a final consideration is population size. Countries with populations in excess of 75 million are excluded. Incidentally, the term "LDC" used to stand for *less* developed country, but in recent years it has become the accepted abbreviation for *least* developed country. Note that the majority of the LDCs are in sub-Saharan Africa, as are most of the "low income countries" in table 6.1.

By far the most widely cited international definition of poverty is the $1 a day standard (see chapter 1 for a full explanation). When people are living on the equivalent of less than $1 a day, they are said to be in extreme, severe, or absolute poverty. Table 6.3 presents international rates of poverty under both the $1-a-day and $2-a-day standards for most countries in the world. A blank space indicates data are not available. Of course, the lack of

Table 6.1
208 Countries Grouped by Per Capita Income, 2003

Low-income Economies: $745 or Less

Afghanistan	Ghana	Nicaragua
Angola	Guinea	Niger
Armenia	Guinea-Bissau	Nigeria
Azerbaijan	Haiti	Pakistan
Bangladesh	India	Papua New Guinea
Benin	Indonesia	Rwanda
Bhutan	Kenya	Sao Tome and Principe
Burkina Faso	Korea, Democratic	Senegal
Burundi	Republic	Sierra Leone
Cambodia	Kyrgyz Republic	Solomon Islands
Cameroon	Lao People's Democratic	Somalia
Central African Republic	Republic	Sudan
Chad	Lesotho	Tajikistan
Comoros	Liberia	Tanzania
Congo, Democratic	Madagascar	Timor-Leste
Republic	Malawi	Togo
Congo, Republic of the	Mali	Uganda
Cote d'Ivoire	Mauritania	Ukraine
Equatorial Guinea	Moldova	Uzbekistan
Eritrea	Mongolia	Vietnam
Ethiopia	Mozambique	Yemen, Republic of
Gambia, The	Myanmar	Zambia
Georgia	Nepal	Zimbabwe

Lower-middle-income Economies: $746–$2,975

Albania	Guatemala	Philippines
Algeria	Guyana	Romania
Belarus	Honduras	Russian Federation
Belize	Iran, Islamic Republic	Samoa
Bolivia	Iraq	South Africa
Bosnia/Herzegovina	Jamaica	Sri Lanka
Bulgaria	Jordan	St. Vincent/Grenadines
Cape Verde	Kazakhstan	Suriname
China	Kiribati	Swaziland
Colombia	Macedonia, Republic of	Syrian Arab Republic
Cuba	Maldives	Thailand
Djibouti	Marshall Islands	Tonga
Dominican Republic	Micronesia, Federal States	Tunisia
Ecuador	Morocco	Turkey
Egypt, Arab Republic	Namibia	Turkmenistan
El Salvador	Paraguay	Vanuatu
Fiji	Peru	West Bank and Gaza

(continues)

Table 6.1
208 Countries Grouped by Per Capita Income, 2003 (cont.)

Upper-middle-income Economies: $2,976–$9,205

American Samoa	Grenada	Palau
Antigua and Barbuda	Hungary	Panama
Argentina	Isle of Man	Poland
Barbados	Latvia	Puerto Rico
Botswana	Lebanon	Saudi Arabia
Brazil	Libya	Seychelles
Chile	Lithuania	Slovak Republic
Costa Rica	Malaysia	St. Kitts and Nevis
Croatia	Malta	St. Lucia
Czech Republic	Mauritius	Trinidad and Tobago
Dominica	Mayotte	Uruguay
Estonia	Mexico	Venezuela, Republica
Gabon	Oman	Bolivariana de

High-income Economies: $9,206 or More

Andorra	Germany	New Caledonia
Aruba	Greece	New Zealand
Australia	Greenland	North Mariana Islands
Austria	Guam	Norway
Bahamas, The	Hong Kong, China	Portugal
Bahrain	Iceland	Qatar
Belgium	Ireland	San Marino
Bermuda	Israel	Singapore
Brunei	Italy	Slovenia
Canada	Japan	Spain
Cayman Islands	Korea, Republic of	Sweden
Channel Islands	Kuwait	Switzerland
Cyprus	Liechtenstein	United Arab Emirates
Denmark	Luxembourg	United Kingdom
Faeroe Islands	Macao, China	United States
Finland	Monaco	Virgin Islands (U.S.)
France	Netherlands	
French Polynesia	Netherlands Antilles	

Source: World Bank. 2003. *World Development Indicators 2003.* Washington, DC: World Bank.

data probably implies something different in the case of, say, Denmark than it does in the case of Haiti. In Denmark it is unlikely that even 1 percent of the population experiences the kind of poverty that this table aims to measure, whereas in Haiti (and some other countries) poverty is so profound that the government may not have the means to conduct surveys to quantify it. Note that the years for data collection vary from country to country.

Table 6.2
The World's 49 Least Developed Countries

Afghanistan	Madagascar
Angola	Malawi
Bangladesh	Maldives
Benin	Mali
Bhutan	Mauritania
Burkina Faso	Mozambique
Burundi	Myanmar
Cambodia	Nepal
Cape Verde	Niger
Central African Republic	Rwanda
Chad	Samoa
Comoros	Sao Tome and Principe
Democratic Republic of Congo	Senegal
Djibouti	Sierra Leone
Equatorial Guinea	Solomon Islands
Eritrea	Somalia
Ethiopia	Sudan
Gambia	Togo
Guinea	Tuvalu
Guinea-Bissau	Uganda
Haiti	United Republic of Tanzania
Kiribati	Vanuatu
Lao People's Democratic Republic	Yemen
Lesotho	Zambia
Liberia	

Source: United Nations, Office of the High Representative for the Least Developed Countries, Landlocked Developing Countries, and Small Island Developing States. 2003. Accessed at http://www.un.org/special-rep/ohrlls/ldc/list.htm.

Table 6.4 takes the data on poverty under the $1/day and $2/day standards and organizes it by region, giving both the numbers of people and the percentages that are living below the two lines. It would be a tough call to say which region, South Asia or sub-Saharan Africa, has a more serious poverty problem, since sub-Saharan Africa has a higher rate of poverty under the $1/day standard, while South Asia has a higher rate under the $2/day standard. Clearly, both regions are much worse off than the rest of the world. This table, incidentally, provides the basis (see bottom line) for the estimates, often cited by the news media, that there are 2.8 billion people living in poverty and 1.2 billion in severe poverty.

In chapter 1 we took note of the way in which Amartya Sen and others have worked to broaden the concept of poverty. Sen has argued that poverty is about not only a lack of income but also a lack of "capabilities" to participate fully in society, and he

Table 6.3
National Poverty Rates by $1/day and $2/day Standards

Country	Survey Year*	Percentage of Population below $1 a Day	Percentage of Population below $2 a Day
Afghanistan			
Albania			
Algeria	1995	<2	15.1
Angola			
Argentina	1998		
Armenia	1998	12.8	49.0
Australia			
Austria			
Azerbaijan	2001	3.7	9.1
Bangladesh	2000	36.0	82.8
Belarus	2000	<2	<2
Belgium			
Benin			
Bolivia	1999	14.4	34.3
Bosnia and Herzegovina			
Botswana	1993	23.5	50.1
Brazil	1998	9.9	23.7
Bulgaria	2001	4.7	23.7
Burkina Faso	1994	61.2	85.8
Burundi	1998	58.4	89.2
Cambodia			
Cameroon	1996	33.4	64.4
Canada			
Central African Republic	1993	66.6	84.0
Chad			
Chile	1998	<2	8.7
China	2000	16.1	47.3
Hong Kong, China			
Colombia	1998	14.4	26.5
Congo, Democratic Republic			
Congo, Republic of the			
Costa Rica	1998	6.9	14.3
Côte d'Ivoire	1995	12.3	49.4
Croatia	2000	<2	<2
Cuba			
Czech Republic	1996	<2	<2
Denmark			
Djibouti			
Dominican Republic	1998	<2	<2

(continues)

Table 6.3
National Poverty Rates by $1/day and $2/day Standards (cont.)

Country	Survey Year*	Percentage of Population below $1 a Day	Percentage of Population below $2 a Day
Ecuador	1995	20.2	52.3
Egypt, Arab Republic of	2000	3.1	43.9
El Salvador	1997	21.4	45.0
Eritrea			
Estonia	1998	<2	5.2
Ethiopia	1999–2000	81.9	98.4
Finland			
France			
Gabon			
Gambia, The	1998	59.3	82.9
Georgia	1998	<2	12.4
Germany			
Ghana	1999	44.8	78.5
Greece			
Guatemala	2000	16.0	37.4
Guinea			
Guinea-Bissau			
Guyana	1998	<2	6.1
Haiti			
Honduras	1998	23.8	44.4
Hungary	1998	<2	7.3
India	1999–2000	34.7	79.9
Indonesia	2000	7.2	55.4
Iran, Islamic Republic of	1998	<2	7.3
Iraq			
Ireland			
Israel			
Italy			
Jamaica	2000	<2	13.3
Japan			
Jordan	1997	<2	7.4
Kazakhstan	1996	1.5	15.3
Kenya	1997	23.0	58.6
Korea, Democratic Republic of			
Korea, Republic of	1998	<2	<2
Kuwait			
Kyrgyz Republic	2000	2.0	34.1
Lao People's Democratic Republic	1997–1998	26.3	73.2

(continues)

Table 6.3
National Poverty Rates by $1/day and $2/day Standards (cont.)

Country	Survey Year*	Percentage of Population below $1 a Day	Percentage of Population below $2 a Day
Latvia	1998	<2	8.3
Lebanon			
Lesotho	1993	43.1	65.7
Liberia			
Libya			
Lithuania	2000	<2	13.7
Macedonia	1998	<2	4.0
Madagascar	1999	49.1	83.3
Malawi	1997–1998	41.7	76.1
Malaysia	1997	<2	9.3
Mali	1994	72.8	90.6
Mauritania	1995	28.6	68.7
Mauritius			
Mexico	1998	8.0	24.3
Moldova	2001	22.0	63.7
Mongolia	1995	13.9	50.0
Morocco	1999	<2	14.3
Mozambique	1996	37.9	78.4
Myanmar			
Namibia	1993	34.9	55.8
Nepal	1995	37.7	82.5
Netherlands			
New Zealand			
Nicaragua	1998	82.3	94.5
Niger	1995	61.4	85.3
Nigeria	1997	70.2	90.8
Norway			
Oman			
Pakistan	1998	13.4	65.6
Panama	1998	7.6	17.9
Papua New Guinea			
Paraguay	1998	19.5	49.3
Peru	1996	15.5	41.4
Philippines	2000	14.6	46.4
Poland	1998	<2	<2
Portugal	1994	<2	<0.5
Puerto Rico			
Romania	2000	2.1	20.5
Russian Federation	2000	6.1	23.8
Rwanda	1983–1985	35.7	84.6
Saudi Arabia			
Senegal	1995	26.3	67.8
Sierra Leone	1989	57.0	74.5
Singapore			

(continues)

Table 6.3
National Poverty Rates by $1/day and $2/day Standards (cont.)

Country	Survey Year*	Percentage of Population below $1 a Day	Percentage of Population below $2 a Day
Slovak Republic	1996	<2	2.4
Slovenia	1998	<2	<2
Somalia			
South Africa	1995	<2	14.5
Spain			
Sri Lanka	1995–1996	6.6	45.4
Sudan			
Swaziland			
Sweden			
Switzerland			
Syrian Arab Republic			
Tajikistan	1998	10.3	50.8
Tanzania	1993	19.9	59.7
Thailand	2000	<2	32.5
Togo			
Trinidad and Tobago	1992	12.4	39.0
Tunisia	1995	<2	10.0
Turkey	2000	<2	10.3
Turkmenistan	1998	12.1	44.0
Uganda	1996	82.2	96.4
Ukraine	1999	2.9	45.7
United Arab Emirates			
United Kingdom			
United States			
Uruguay	1998	<2	<2
Uzbekistan	1998	19.1	44.2
Venezuela, Republica Bolivariana de	1998	15.0	32.0
Vietnam	1998	17.7	63.7
West Bank and Gaza			
Yemen, Republic of	1998	15.7	45.2
Yugoslavia, Federal Republic of			
Zambia	1998	63.7	87.4
Zimbabwe	1990–1991	36.0	64.2

*Survey year is the year in which the underlying data were collected.

Note: Population below $1 a day and population below $2 a day are the percentages of the population living on less than $1.08 a day and $2.15 a day at 1993 international prices (equivalent to $1 and $2 in 1985 prices, adjusted for purchasing power parity).

Source: World Bank. 2003. *World Development Indicators 2003.* Washington, DC: World Bank, 58–60.

Table 6.4
World Poverty by Region, 1999

Region	Living on Less Than $1 a Day		Living on Less Than $2 a Day	
	Millions	Percent	Millions	Percent
East Asia and Pacific	279	15.6	897	50.1
Excluding China	57	10.6	269	50.2
Europe and Central Asia	24	5.1	97	20.3
Latin America and the Caribbean	57	11.1	132	26.0
Middle East and North Africa	6	2.2	68	23.3
South Asia	488	36.6	1,128	84.8
Sub-Saharan Africa	315	49.0	480	74.7
Total	1,169	23.2	2,802	55.6

Source: World Bank. 2003. *Global Economic Prospects 2003.* Washington, DC: World Bank, pp. 30–31.

has accepted the challenge to devise quantitative methods for measuring such capabilities. His efforts led to the creation of an index of national well-being called the Human Development Index, first computed and published in 1990. Table 6.5 presents the HDI and its components for most countries in the world and for some major groupings of countries in 2001 (as published in 2003). No one will deny that there is a certain arbitrariness in the choice of index components, the weighting of those components in the index, and the cutoffs that separate "high," "medium," and "low" human development. Togo's HDI, for example, is a mere .002 above Cameroon's, yet that tiny difference puts Togo in a higher category! Unfortunately, there is no way to avoid such problems when dealing with indices like the HDI, which suggests the need for caution in making use of this data.

The Human Poverty Index is a close cousin of the Human Development Index, as explained in chapter 1. The HDI comes at poverty *in*directly, through measures of life expectancy, literacy, and so on, while the HPI takes a more *direct* approach, incorporating such factors as the probability of not surviving to the age of forty, adult illiteracy rates, and percentage of children who are underweight. Table 6.6 ranks ninety-four developing countries according to their HPI in 2001 (as published in 2003). The ranking is in best-to-worst order. Note that twelve of the top fifteen nations are in the Western Hemisphere, and all of the lowest twenty are in sub-Saharan Africa.

Table 6.5
Human Development Index

HDI Rank[a]	Life Expectancy at Birth (Years) 2001	Adult Literacy Rate (% Age 15 and Above) 2000–2001	School Enrollment Ratio (%) 2001[b]	GDP Per Capita (PPP U.S.$) 2001	Human Development Index (HDI) Value 2001
High Human Development					
1 Norway	78.7	d	98 e	29,620	0.944
2 Iceland	79.6	d	91 e	29,990	0.942
3 Sweden	79.9	d	113 e,f	24,180	0.941
4 Australia	79.0	d	114 e,f	25,370	0.939
5 Netherlands	78.2	d	99 e	27,190	0.938
6 Belgium	78.5	d	107 e,f,g	25,520	0.937
7 United States	76.9	d	94 e	34,320	0.937
8 Canada	79.2	d	94 e,g	27,130	0.937
9 Japan	81.3	d	83 e	25,130	0.932
10 Switzerland	79.0	d	88 e	28,100	0.932
11 Denmark	76.4	d	98 e	29,000	0.930
12 Ireland	76.7	d	91 e,h	32,410	0.930
13 United Kingdom	77.9	d	112 e,f	24,160	0.930
14 Finland	77.8	d	103 e,f,h	24,430	0.930
15 Luxembourg	78.1	d	73 e,i	53,780 j	0.930
16 Austria	78.3	d	92 e	26,730	0.929
17 France	78.7	d	91 e	23,990	0.925
18 Germany	78.0	d	89 e,g	25,350	0.921
19 Spain	79.1	97.7 d	92 e	20,150	0.918
20 New Zealand	78.1	d	99 e	19,160	0.917
21 Italy	78.6	98.5 d	82 e	24,670	0.916
22 Israel	78.9	95.1	90	19,790	0.905
23 Portugal	75.9	92.5 d	93 e	18,150	0.896
24 Greece	78.1	97.3 d	81 e,h	17,440	0.892
25 Cyprus	78.1	97.2	74 g,k	21,190 l	0.891
26 Hong Kong, China (SAR)	79.7	93.5	63 h	24,850	0.889
27 Barbados	76.9	99.7 d	89	15,560	0.888
28 Singapore	77.8	92.5	75 h	22,680	0.884
29 Slovenia	75.9	99.6 d	83 h	17,130	0.881
30 Korea, Republic of	75.2	97.9 d	91 e	15,090	0.879
31 Brunei Darussalam	76.1	91.6	83	19,210 g	0.872
32 Czech Republic	75.1	d	76 e	14,720	0.861
33 Malta	78.1	92.3	76 g	13,160 l	0.856
34 Argentina	73.9	96.9	89 e,g	11,320	0.849
35 Poland	73.6	99.7 d	88 e	9,450	0.841
36 Seychelles	72.7 m	91.0 m	n	17,030 o	0.840
37 Bahrain	73.7	87.9	81 g	16,060	0.839
38 Hungary	71.5	99.3 d	82 e,g	12,340	0.837

(continues)

Table 6.5
Human Development Index *(cont.)*

HDI Rank[a]	Life Expectancy at Birth (Years) 2001	Adult Literacy Rate (% Age 15 and Above) 2000–2001	School Enrollment Ratio (%) 2001[b]	GDP Per Capita (PPP U.S.$) 2001	Human Development Index (HDI) Value 2001
39 Slovakia	73.3	100.0 d,p,q	73 e	11,960	0.836
40 Uruguay	75.0	97.6	84 e	8,400	0.834
41 Estonia	71.2	99.8 d	89	10,170	0.833
42 Costa Rica	77.9	95.7	66	9,460	0.832
43 Chile	75.8	95.9	76 e	9,190	0.831
44 Qatar	71.8	81.7	81	19,844 g,r	0.826
45 Lithuania	72.3	99.6 d	85	8,470	0.824
46 Kuwait	76.3	82.4	54 g	18,700 l	0.820
47 Croatia	74.0	98.4	68 h	9,170	0.818
48 United Arab Emirates	74.4	76.7	67 g	20,530 g,l	0.816
49 Bahamas	67.2	95.5	74 h	16,270 g	0.812
50 Latvia	70.5	99.8 d	86	7,730	0.811
51 Saint Kitts and Nevis	70.0 s	97.8 s	70 s	11,300	0.808
52 Cuba	76.5	96.8	76	5,259 g,r	0.806
53 Belarus	69.6	99.7 d	86	7,620	0.804
54 Trinidad and Tobago	71.5	98.4	67	9,100	0.802
55 Mexico	73.1	91.4	74 e	8,430 l	0.800
Medium Human Development					
56 Antigua and Barbuda	73.9 s	86.6 s	69 s	10,170	0.798
57 Bulgaria	70.9	98.5	77	6,890	0.795
58 Malaysia	72.8	87.9	72 e	8,750 l	0.790
59 Panama	74.4	92.1	75 g	5,750	0.788
60 Macedonia	73.3	94.0 q,t	70	6,110	0.784
61 Libyan Arab Jamahiriya	72.4	80.8	89 e	7,570 g,u	0.783
62 Mauritius	71.6	84.8	69	9,860	0.779
63 Russian Federation	66.6	99.6 d	82 e	7,100	0.779
64 Colombia	71.8	91.9	71	7,040	0.779
65 Brazil	67.8	87.3	95 e	7,360	0.777
66 Bosnia and Herzegovina	73.8	93.0 p,q	64 v	5,970	0.777
67 Belize	71.7	93.4	76 e	5,690	0.776
68 Dominica	72.9 s	96.4 s	65 s	5,520	0.776
69 Venezuela	73.5	92.8	68	5,670	0.775
70 Samoa (Western)	69.5	98.7	71	6,180	0.775

(continues)

Table 6.5
Human Development Index *(cont.)*

HDI Rank[a]	Life Expectancy at Birth (Years) 2001	Adult Literacy Rate (% Age 15 and Above) 2000–2001	School Enrollment Ratio (%) 2001[b]	GDP Per Capita (PPP U.S.$) 2001	Human Development Index (HDI) Value 2001
71 Saint Lucia	72.2	90.2 s	82 g	5,260	0.775
72 Romania	70.5	98.2	68	5,830	0.773
73 Saudi Arabia	71.9	77.1	58 g	13,330	0.769
74 Thailand	68.9	95.7	72 e	6,400	0.768
75 Ukraine	69.2	99.6 d	81 g	4,350	0.766
76 Kazakhstan	65.8	99.4 d	78	6,500	0.765
77 Suriname	70.8	94.0 p,q	77 e	4,599 l,o	0.762
78 Jamaica	75.5	87.3	74 e	3,720	0.757
79 Oman	72.2	73.0	58 g	12,040 g	0.755
80 St. Vincent/ Grenadines	73.8	88.9 s	58 s	5,330	0.755
81 Fiji	69.3	93.2	76 e,g	4,850	0.754
82 Peru	69.4	90.2	83 e,g	4,570	0.752
83 Lebanon	73.3	86.5	76	4,170	0.752
84 Paraguay	70.5	93.5	64 e,h	5,210	0.751
85 Philippines	69.5	95.1	80 e	3,840	0.751
86 Maldives	66.8	97.0	79	4,798 l,o	0.751
87 Turkmenistan	66.6	98.0 q,t	81 h	4,320	0.748
88 Georgia	73.4	100.0 d,p,q	69	2,560	0.746
89 Azerbaijan	71.8	97.0 p,q	69 g	3,090	0.744
90 Jordan	70.6	90.3	77 e,g	3,870	0.743
91 Tunisia	72.5	72.1	76 e	6,390	0.740
92 Guyana	63.3	98.6	84 e,g	4,690	0.740
93 Grenada	65.3 s	94.4 s	63	6,740	0.738
94 Dominican Republic	66.7	84.0	74 e	7,020	0.737
95 Albania	73.4	85.3	69	3,680	0.735
96 Turkey	70.1	85.5	60 e,g	5,890	0.734
97 Ecuador	70.5	91.8	72 e	3,280	0.731
98 Occupied Palestinian Territory	72.1	89.2 w	77 g	x	0.731
99 Sri Lanka	72.3	91.9	63 e,g	3,180	0.730
100 Armenia	72.1	98.5	60	2,650	0.729
101 Uzbekistan	69.3	99.2 d	76 h	2,460	0.729
102 Kyrgyzstan	68.1	97.0 p,q	79	2,750	0.727
103 Cape Verde	69.7	74.9	80 e	5,570 l	0.727
104 China	70.6	85.8	64 e,g	4,020	0.721
105 El Salvador	70.4	79.2	64	5,260	0.719

(continues)

Table 6.5
Human Development Index (cont.)

HDI Rank[a]	Life Expectancy at Birth (Years) 2001	Adult Literacy Rate (% Age 15 and Above) 2000–2001	School Enrollment Ratio (%) 2001[b]	GDP Per Capita (PPP U.S.$) 2001	Human Development Index (HDI) Value 2001
106 Iran, Islamic Republic of	69.8	77.1	64	6,000	0.719
107 Algeria	69.2	67.8	71 e	6,090 l	0.704
108 Moldova, Republic of	68.5	99.0	61	2,150	0.700
109 Viet Nam	68.6	92.7	64	2,070	0.688
110 Syrian Arab Republic	71.5	75.3	59 g	3,280	0.685
111 South Africa	50.9	85.6	78	11,290 l	0.684
112 Indonesia	66.2	87.3	64 e	2,940	0.682
113 Tajikistan	68.3	99.3 d	71	1,170	0.677
114 Bolivia	63.3	86.0	84 e	2,300	0.672
115 Honduras	68.8	75.6	62 e	2,830	0.667
116 Equatorial Guinea	49.0	84.2	58 g	15,073 g,y	0.664
117 Mongolia	63.3	98.5	64	1,740	0.661
118 Gabon	56.6	71.0 p,q	83 e	5,990	0.653
119 Guatemala	65.3	69.2	57 e	4,400	0.652
120 Egypt	68.3	56.1	76 e,h	3,520	0.648
121 Nicaragua	69.1	66.8	65 e,g	2,450 g,l	0.643
122 São Tomé and Principe	69.4	83.1 m	58 m	1,317 g,r	0.639
123 Solomon Islands	68.7	76.6 m	50 m	1,910 l	0.632
124 Namibia	47.4	82.7	74 g	7,120 l	0.627
125 Botswana	44.7	78.1	80	7,820	0.614
126 Morocco	68.1	49.8	51 g	3,600	0.606
127 India	63.3	58.0	56 e,g	2,840	0.590
128 Vanuatu	68.3	34.0 m	54 g	3,190 l	0.568
129 Ghana	57.7	72.7	46	2,250 l	0.567
130 Cambodia	57.4	68.7	55	1,860	0.556
131 Myanmar	57.0	85.0	47	1,027 g,u	0.549
132 Papua New Guinea	57.0	64.6	41 g	2,570 l	0.548
133 Swaziland	38.2	80.3	77 g	4,330	0.547
134 Comoros	60.2	56.0	40 g	1,870 l	0.528
135 Lao People's Democratic Republic	53.9	65.6	57	1,620 l	0.525
136 Bhutan	62.5	47.0 p,q	33 h	1,833 o	0.511
137 Lesotho	38.6	83.9	63	2,420 l	0.510
138 Sudan	55.4	58.8	34 g	1,970	0.503
139 Bangladesh	60.5	40.6	54	1,610	0.502

(continues)

Table 6.5
Human Development Index *(cont.)*

HDI Rank[a]	Life Expectancy at Birth (Years) 2001	Adult Literacy Rate (% Age 15 and Above) 2000–2001	School Enrollment Ratio (%) 2001[b]	GDP Per Capita (PPP U.S.$) 2001	Human Development Index (HDI) Value 2001
140 Congo	48.5	81.8	57 e	970	0.502
141 Togo	50.3	58.4	67 g	1,650	0.501
Low Human Development					
142 Cameroon	48.0	72.4	48 e,g	1,680	0.499
143 Nepal	59.1	42.9	64	1,310	0.499
144 Pakistan	60.4	44.0	36	1,890	0.499
145 Zimbabwe	35.4	89.3	59 e	2,280	0.496
146 Kenya	46.4	83.3	52	980	0.489
147 Uganda	44.7	68.0	71	1,490 l	0.489
148 Yemen	59.4	47.7	52 g	790	0.470
149 Madagascar	53.0	67.3	41 g	830	0.468
150 Haiti	49.1	50.8	52 h	1,860 l	0.467
151 Gambia	53.7	37.8	47 e	2,050 l	0.463
152 Nigeria	51.8	65.4	45 h	850	0.463
153 Djibouti	46.1	65.5	21 g	2,370	0.462
154 Mauritania	51.9	40.7	43	1,990 l	0.454
155 Eritrea	52.5	56.7	33	1,030	0.446
156 Senegal	52.3	38.3	38 e	1,500	0.430
157 Guinea	48.5	41.0 p,q	34 e	1,960	0.425
158 Rwanda	38.2	68.0	52 g	1,250	0.422
159 Benin	50.9	38.6	49 e	980	0.411
160 Tanzania, United Republic of	44.0	76.0	31	520	0.400
161 Côte d'Ivoire	41.7	49.7	39 g	1,490	0.396
162 Malawi	38.5	61.0	72 e	570	0.387
163 Zambia	33.4	79.0	45	780	0.386
164 Angola	40.2	42.0 q,t	29 g	2,040 l	0.377
165 Chad	44.6	44.2	33 g	1,070 l	0.376
166 Guinea-Bissau	45.0	39.6	43 g	970	0.373
167 Congo, Dem. Rep. of the	40.6	62.7	27 g	680 l	0.363
168 Central African Rep.	40.4	48.2	24 h	1,300 l	0.363
169 Ethiopia	45.7	40.3	34	810	0.359
170 Mozambique	39.2	45.2	37	1,140 l	0.356
171 Burundi	40.4	49.2	31	690 l	0.337
172 Mali	48.4	26.4	29 g	810	0.337
173 Burkina Faso	45.8	24.8	22 e	1,120 l	0.330
174 Niger	45.6	16.5	17	890 l	0.292
175 Sierra Leone	34.5	36.0	51 p,q	470	0.275

(continues)

Table 6.5
Human Development Index *(cont.)*

HDI Rank[a]	Life Expectancy at Birth (Years) 2001	Adult Literacy Rate (% Age 15 and Above) 2000–2001	School Enrollment Ratio (%) 2001[b]	GDP Per Capita (PPP U.S.$) 2001	Human Development Index (HDI) Value 2001
Developing countries	64.4	74.5	60	3,850	0.655
Least developed countries	50.4	53.3	43	1,274	0.448
Arab States	66.0	60.8	60	5,038	0.662
East Asia/Pacific	69.5	87.1	65	4,233	0.722
Latin America/ Caribbean	70.3	89.2	81	7,050	0.777
South Asia	62.8	56.3	54	2,730	0.582
Sub-Saharan Africa	46.5	62.4	44	1,831	0.468
Central/Eastern Europe & CIS	69.3	99.3	79	6,598	0.787
OECD	77.0		87	23,363	0.905
High-income OECD	78.1		93	27,169	0.929
High human development	77.1		89	23,135	0.908
Medium human development	67.0	78.1	64	4,053	0.684
Low human development	49.4	55.0	41	1,186	0.440
High income	78.1		92	26,989	0.927
Middle income	69.8	86.6	70	5,519	0.744
Low income	59.1	63.0	51	2,230	0.561
World	66.7		64	7,376	0.722

Source: United Nations Development Programme, *Human Development Report 2003,* pp. 237–240.

Note: As a result of revisions to data and methodology and varying country coverage, human development index values and ranks are not strictly comparable with those in earlier Human Development Reports. The index has been calculated for UN member countries with reliable data in each of its components as well as for Hong Kong, China (SAR), and the Occupied Palestinian Territories.

a. The HDI rank is determined using HDI values to the sixth decimal point.

b. Data refer to the 2000/2001 school year. Data for some countries may refer to national or UNESCO Institute for Statistics estimates. For details, see http://www.uis.unesco.org. Because data are from different sources, comparisons across countries should be made with caution.

c. A positive figure indicates that the HDI rank is higher than the GDP per capita (PPP U.S.$) rank, a negative the opposite.

d. For purposes of calculating the HDI, a value of 99.0% was applied.

e. Preliminary UNESCO Institute for Statistics estimate, subject to further revision.

f. For purposes of calculating the HDI, a value of 100% was applied.

g. Data refer to a year other than that specified.

h. Data refer to the 1999/2000 school year. They were provided by the UNESCO Institute for Statistics for Human Development Report 2001 (see UNESCO Institute for Statistics 2001).

i. The ratio is an underestimate, as many secondary and tertiary students pursue their studies in nearby countries.

j. For purposes of calculating the HDI, a value of $40,000 (PPP US$) was applied.

k. Excludes Turkish students and population.

l. Estimate based on regression.

m. Data are from national sources.

n. Because the combined gross enrollment ratio was unavailable, the Human Development Report Office estimate of 78% was used.

o. Preliminary World Bank estimate, subject to further revision.

p. UNICEF 2003b.

q. Data refer to a year or period other than that specified, differ from the standard definition or refer to only part of the country.

r. Aten, Heston and Summers 2002.

s. Data are from the Secretariat of the Organization of Eastern Caribbean States, based on national sources.

t. UNICEF 2000.

u. Aten, Heston and Summers 2001.

v. UNDP 2002.

w. Birzeit University 2002.

x. In the absence of an estimate of GDP per capita (PPP US$), the Human Development Report Office estimate of $2,788, derived using the value of GDP in US dollars and the weighted average ratio of PPP US dollars to US dollars in the Arab States, was used.

y. World Bank 2002.

A commonly cited, though far from perfect, measure of the commitment of rich countries to the development of poorer countries is the amount of foreign aid the donor countries provide each year. The technical term for foreign aid is "official development assistance" (ODA), and table 6.7 gives the figures on ODA for 1996 and 2001 in millions of dollars, as a percentage of gross

Table 6.6
Human Poverty (HPI-1) Ranking for Ninety-Four Developing Countries, 2001

1 Barbados	33 Indonesia	65 Pakistan
2 Uruguay	34 Sri Lanka	66 Lao People's
3 Chile	35 Syrian Arab	Democratic Republic
4 Costa Rica	Republic	67 Yemen
5 Cuba	36 Mongolia	68 Haiti
6 Singapore	37 Tunisia	69 Eritrea
7 Jordan	38 Honduras	70 Nepal
8 Trinidad and	39 Viet Nam	71 Iraq
Tobago	40 Cape Verde	72 Bangladesh
9 Panama	41 Fiji	73 Cambodia
10 Colombia	42 Algeria	74 Congo, Democratic
11 Venezuela	43 Guatemala	Republic of the
12 Belize	44 Nicaragua	75 Botswana
13 Mexico	45 Myanmar	76 Senegal
14 Jamaica	46 Ghana	77 Rwanda
15 Lebanon	47 Egypt	78 Cote d'Ivoire
16 Paraguay	48 Comoros	79 Gambia
17 Mauritius	49 South Africa	80 Burundi
18 Brazil	50 Oman	81 Benin
19 Peru	51 Congo	82 Malawi
20 Maldive	52 Sudan	83 Lesotho
21 Ecuador	53 India	84 Guinea-Bissau
22 Turkey	54 Nigeria	85 Central African
23 Guyana	55 Djibouti	Republic
24 Thailand	56 Morocco	86 Mauritania
25 Dominican Republic	57 Madagascar	87 Mozambique
26 China	58 Cameroon	88 Chad
27 Bolivia	59 Tanzania, United	89 Zambia
28 Philippines	Republic of	90 Zimbabwe
29 Libyan Arab	60 Uganda	91 Mali
Jamahiriya	61 Papua New Guinea	92 Ethiopia
30 Saudi Arabia	62 Namibia	93 Burkina Faso
31 Iran, Islamic Rep.	63 Kenya	94 Niger
32 El Salvador	64 Togo	

Source: United Nations Development Programme. 2003. *Human Development Report 2003.* New York: United Nations Development Programme, p. 247.

Table 6.7
Net Official Development Assistance

	1996 ($ Millions)	2001 ($ Millions)	1996 (Percent of GNI)	2001 (Percent of GNI)	Average Annual % Change in vol. 1995–1996 to 2000–2001	Per Capita of Donor Country, 1996	Per Capita of Donor Country, 2001
Australia	1,074	873	0.27	0.25	0.6	46	49
Austria	557	533	0.24	0.29	0.2	51	66
Belgium	913	867	0.34	0.37	3.5	67	85
Canada	1,795	1,533	0.32	0.22	-2.6	59	51
Denmark	1,772	1,634	1.04	1.03	4.4	265	306
Finland	408	389	0.33	0.32	5.0	61	75
France	7,451	4,198	0.48	0.32	-6.6	95	72
Germany	7,601	4,990	0.32	0.27	-1.2	67	62
Greece	184	202	0.15	0.17	24.3	14	19
Ireland	179	287	0.31	0.33	11.9	43	74
Italy	2,416	1,627	0.20	0.15	-2.3	34	28
Japan	9,439	9,847	0.20	0.23	3.0	73	89
Luxembourg	82	141	0.44	0.82	18.1	156	325
Netherlands	3,246	3,172	0.81	0.82	5.0	161	195
New Zealand	122	112	0.21	0.25	5.6	22	30
Norway	1,311	1,346	0.84	0.83	1.7	278	299
Portugal	218	268	0.21	0.25	6.7	18	26
Spain	1,251	1,737	0.22	0.30	7.3	25	43
Sweden	1,999	1,666	0.84	0.81	4.4	173	207
Switzerland	1,026	908	0.34	0.34	3.0	108	123
United Kingdom	3,199	4,579	0.27	0.32	5.8	58	80
United States	9,377	11,429	0.12	0.11	3.2	38	39
Total or average	55,622	52,336	0.26	0.22	1.8	59	63

*2000 exchange rates and prices
Source: World Bank. 2003. *World Development Indicators 2003*. Washington, DC: World Bank.

national income, and on a per capita basis. One has to be impressed by the amount of per capita assistance offered by Denmark, Norway, Luxembourg, and The Netherlands, all of which exceed the benchmark commitment of 0.7 percent of GNI.

The modern plague, AIDS, has become both a cause and effect of poverty across the globe. Regional variations in the incidence of the disease are reported for late 2003 in table 6.8. One change from previous reporting is the specification of ranges of values, rather than single values; for example, the total number of adults and children living with HIV/AIDS is estimated to be 34

Table 6.8
Estimated Regional Impact of HIV/AIDS, End of 2003

Region	Adults and Children Living with HIV/AIDS	Adults and Children Newly Infected with HIV	Adult Prevalence (%)**	Adult and Child Deaths Due to AIDS
Sub-Saharan Africa	25.0–28.2 M*	3.0–3.4 M	7.5–8.5	2.2–2.4 M
North Africa and Middle East	470,000–730,000	43,000–67,000	0.2–0.4	35,000–50,000
South and Southeast Asia	4.6–8.2 M	610,000–1.1 M	0.4–0.8	330,000–590,000
East Asia and Pacific	700,000–1.3 M	150,000–270,000	0.1–0.1	32,000–58,000
Latin America	1.3–1.9 M	120,000–180,000	0.5–0.7	49,000–70,000
Caribbean	350,000–590,000	45,000–80,000	1.9–3.1	30,000–50,000
Eastern Europe and Central Asia	1.2–1.8 M	180,000–280,000	0.5–0.9	23,000–37,000
Western Europe	520,000–680,000	30,000–40,000	0.3–0.3	2,600–3,400
North America	790,000–1.2 M	36,000–54,000	0.5–0.7	12,000–18,000
Australia and New Zealand	12,000–18,000	700–1,000	0.1–0.1	<100
Total	40 (34–46) M	5 (4.2–5.8) M	1.1% (0.9–1.3%)	3 (2.5–3.5) M

* M = million
** The proportion of adults (15 to 49 years of age) living with HIV/AIDS in 2003
Source: UNAIDS and World Health Organization, AIDS Epidemic Update: December 2003.

Figure 6.1 Extreme Poverty:
Percent Living on Less Than $1 a Day, 1999

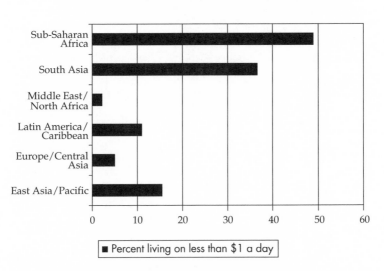

Source: Millennium Development Goals page of the World Bank Website, accessed at http://www.developmentgoals.org/Poverty.htm.

Figure 6.2 Infant Mortality Rate per 1,000 Live Births, 2001

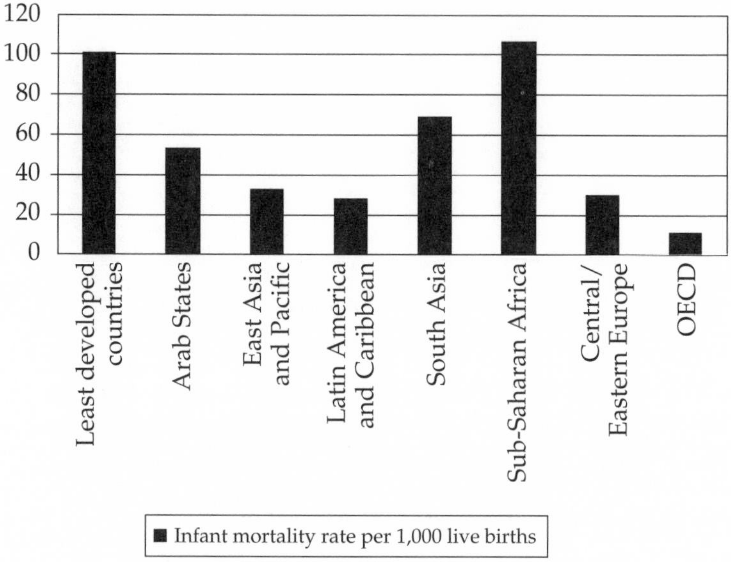

Source: United Nations Development Program. 2003. *Human Development Report 2003.* New York: United Nations Development Program, p. 265.

to 46 million, with a midrange estimate of 40 million. By far the heaviest burden of the disease is seen in sub-Saharan Africa.

Some dimensions of world poverty become clearer when presented in a graphical format. Figure 6.1 depicts extreme poverty rates by region of the world. What stands out immediately is the extraordinarily high rate of extreme poverty in sub-Saharan Africa and in south Asia.

Figure 6.2 graphs the infant mortality rates for key world regions or country groupings. The highest death rate is seen in sub-Saharan Africa, at a level many times that seen in the OECD countries. As previously noted, the "least developed countries" are forty-nine nations sharing certain characteristics of income, human resources, and economic vulnerability. The OECD consists of thirty countries, mainly in Europe but including the United States, Canada, Mexico, Japan, Korea, and Australia. Incidentally, one can separate out a "wealthy" subset of the OECD for

**Figure 6.3 Tuberculosis Cases
per 100,000 People, 2001**

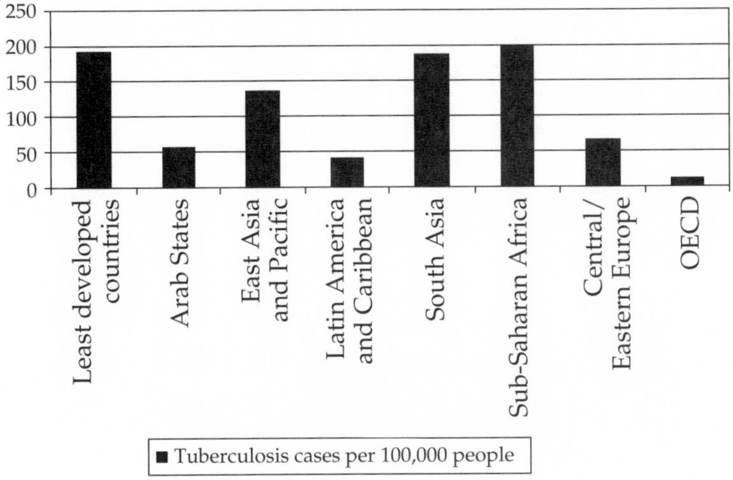

Tuberculosis cases per 100,000 people

Source: United Nations Development Program. 2003. *Human Development Report
2003.* New York: United Nations Development Program, p. 261.

which the infant mortality rate and other social indicators are
even more favorable than is seen in the graph.

Among the age-old diseases that are making comebacks in
the contemporary world and hitting poor countries especially
hard is tuberculosis. As we see in Figure 6.3, the rates in South
Asia and sub-Saharan Africa are the highest in the world, although East Asia and the Pacific are not far behind. In all these
areas, the TB rate is at least twelve times what it is in the OECD.
(In some African nations the rate is 100 times what it is in the
United States.)

The contrasting disease rates of poor and rich countries is
starkly evident when it comes to HIV/AIDS, as seen in Figure 6.4.
No region of the world comes close to sub-Saharan Africa in the
toll taken by the AIDS pandemic, as noted earlier (table 6.8).
Roughly 70 percent of the global incidence of the disease is in
Africa, and 95 percent of all cases are in developing countries.
There are concerns, moreover, that if forceful steps are not taken
soon in India and China, the disease could spread rapidly in those

**Figure 6.4 HIV/AIDS Adult Prevalence
Rates by Region, 2002**

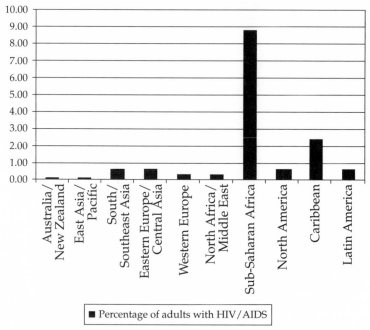

Source: UNAIDS and World Health Organization. *AIDS Epidemic Update:*
December 2002.

heavily populated countries. (Such concerns help explain the October 13, 2003, announcement of a $200 million grant by the Bill
and Melinda Gates Foundation to combat AIDS in India.) For a
more detailed accounting of AIDS and its linkages to poverty, see
the UN Population Fund (UNFPA) document in the document
section.

Documents

*A number of declarations, briefs, and policy analyses are presented in the
balance of this chapter for the purpose of illustrating some of the ways*

in which global poverty issues are understood at the present time. This selection of eleven documents has been guided in part by a desire to cover a wide range of issues, whether they be the environment, gender, or global nutrition. Many other possible readings are suggested in chapter 8. We begin with an overview of the Millennium Development Goals that were approved by the UN General Assembly in September 2000 and adopted by the world community at the Millennium Summit in the fall of 2000. There are just eight goals—all simple to state and difficult to dispute. But as diplomats are always reminding us, "The devil is in the details." This document specifies those details in the form of targets that must be met if the goals are to be achieved and indicators that will make it possible to gauge whether the targets are being met.

Millennium Development Goals (2000)

Goals and Targets

Goal 1—Eradicate extreme poverty and hunger.
Target 1: Halve, between 1990 and 2015, the proportion of people whose income is less than $1 a day
Indicators:

1a. Proportion of population below $1 a day[a]

1b. National poverty headcount ratio*

2. Poverty gap ratio at $1 a day (incidence x depth of poverty)

3. Share of poorest quintile in national consumption

Target 2: Halve, between 1990 and 2015, the proportion of people who suffer from hunger
Indicators:

4. Prevalence of underweight in children (under five years of age)

5. Proportion of population below minimum level of dietary energy consumption

Goal 2—Achieve universal primary education.

Target 3: Ensure that, by 2015, children everywhere, boys and girls alike, will be able to complete a full course of primary schooling
Indicators:

6. Net enrollment ratio in primary education

7a. Proportion of pupils starting grade 1 who reach grade 5

7b. Primary completion rate*

8. Literacy rate of 15- to 24-year-olds

Goal 3—Promote gender equality and empower women.

Target 4: Eliminate gender disparity in primary and secondary education, preferably by 2005 and in all levels of education no later than 2015
Indicators:

9. Ratio of girls to boys in primary, secondary, and tertiary education

10. Ratio of literate females to males among 15- to 24-year-olds

11. Share of women in wage employment in the nonagricultural sector

12. Proportion of seats held by women in national parliament

Goal 4—Reduce child mortality.

Target 5: Reduce by two-thirds, between 1990 and 2015, the under-five mortality rate
Indicators:

13. Under-five mortality rate

14. Infant mortality rate

15. Proportion of one-year-old children immunized against measles

Goal 5—Improve maternal health.

Target 6: Reduce by three-quarters, between 1990 and 2015, the maternal mortality ratio
   Indicators:

   16. Maternal mortality ratio

   17. Proportion of births attended by skilled health personnel

Goal 6—Combat HIV/AIDS, malaria, and other diseases.

Target 7: Have halted by 2015 and begun to reverse the spread of HIV/AIDS
   Indicators:

   18. HIV prevalence among 15- to 24-year-old pregnant women

   19. Condom use rate of the contraceptive prevalence rate[b*]

   19a. Condom use at last high-risk sex*

   19b. Percentage of population aged 15–24 with comprehensive correct knowledge of HIV/AIDS[c*]

   19c. Contraceptive prevalence rate[b]

   20. Ratio of school attendance of orphans to school attendance on non-orphans aged 10–14

Target 8: Have halted by 2015 and begun to reverse the incidence of malaria and other major diseases
   Indicators:

   21. Prevalence and death rates associated with malaria

   22. Proportion of population in malaria-risk areas using effective malaria prevention and treatment measures[d]

   23. Prevalence and death rates associated with tuberculosis

   24. Proportion of tuberculosis cases detected and cured under directly observed treatment short course (DOTS)

Goal 7—Ensure environmental sustainability.
Target 9: Integrate the principles of sustainable development into country policies and program and reverse the loss of environmental resources
Indicators:

25. Proportion of land area covered by forest

26. Ratio of area protected to maintain biological diversity to surface area

27. Energy use per unit of GDP

28. Carbon dioxide emissions (per capita) and consumption of ozone-depleting chlorofluorocarbons

29. Proportion of population using solid fuels*

Target 10: Halve, by 2015, the proportion of people without sustainable access to safe drinking water and basic sanitation
Indicators:

30. Proportion of population with sustainable access to an improved water source, urban and rural

31. Proportion of population with access to improved sanitation

Target 11: Have achieved, by 2020, a significant improvement in the lives of at least 100 million slum dwellers
Indicators:

32. Proportion of households with access to secure tenure

Goal 8—Develop a global partnership for development.
Target 12: Develop further an open, rule-based, predictable, nondiscriminatory trading and financial system (includes a commitment to good governance, development, and poverty reduction—both nationally and internationally)

Some of the indicators listed below will be monitored separately for the least developed countries, Africa, landlocked countries, and small island developing states.

Official Development Assistance

Indicators:

33. Net ODA total and to least developed countries, as a percentage of OECD/DAC donors' gross income

34. Proportion of bilateral, sector-allocable ODA of OECD/DAC donors for basic social services (basic education, primary health care, nutrition, safe water, and sanitation)

35. Proportion of bilateral ODA of OECD/DAC donors that is untied

36. ODA received in landlocked countries as proportion of their GNI

37. ODA received in small island developing states as proportion of their GNI

Target 13: Address the special needs of the least developed countries (includes tariff- and quota-free access for exports, enhanced program of debt relief for HIPC and cancellation of official bilateral debt, and more generous ODA for countries committed to poverty reduction)
Target 14: Address the special needs of landlocked countries and small island developing states (through the Program of Action for the Sustainable Development of Small Island Developing States and 22nd General Assembly provisions)

Market Access

Indicators:

38. Proportion of total developed country imports (excluding arms) from developing countries and least developed countries admitted free of duties

39. Average tariffs imposed by developed countries on agricultural products and clothing from developing countries

40. Agricultural support estimate for OECD countries as a percentage of their GDP

41. Proportion of ODA provided to help build trade capacity

Target 15: Deal comprehensively with the debt problems of developing countries through national and international measures in order to make debt sustainable in the long term

Debt Sustainability

Indicators:

42. Total number of countries that have reached their HIPC decision points and completion points (cumulative)

43. Debt relief committed under HIPC initiative, US$

44. Debt service as a percentage of exports of goods and services

Target 16: In cooperation with developing countries, develop and implement strategies for decent and productive work for youth
Target 17: In cooperation with pharmaceutical companies, provide access to affordable, essential drugs in developing countries
Target 18: In cooperation with the private sector, make available the benefits of new technologies, especially information and communications

Other Indicators

45. Unemployment rate of 15- to 24-year-olds, male and female and total[e]

46. Proportion of population with access to affordable, essential drugs on a sustainable basis[f]

47. Telephone lines and cellular subscribers per 100 population

48a. Personal computers in use per 100 population

48b.Internet users per 100 population

* These indicators are proposed as additional MDG indicators, but have not yet been adopted.

[a] For monitoring country poverty trends, indicators based on national poverty lines should be used, where available.

[b] Amongst contraceptive methods, only condoms are effective in preventing HIV transmission. The contraceptive prevalence rate is also useful in tracking progress in other health, gender and poverty goals. Because the condom use rate is only measured amongst women in union, it is supplemented by an indicator on condom use in high-risk situations (indicator 19a) and an indicator on HIV/AIDS knowledge (indicator 19b).

[c] This indicator is defined as the percentage of population aged 15–24 who correctly identify the two major ways of preventing the sexual transmission of HIV (using condoms and limiting sex to one faithful, uninfected partner), who reject the two most common local misconceptions about HIV transmission, and who know that a healthy-looking person can transmit HIV. However, since there are currently not a sufficient number of surveys to be able to calculate the indicator as defined above, UNICEF, in collaboration with UNAIDS and WHO, produced two proxy indicators that represent two components of the actual indicator. They are the following: (a) Percentage of women and men 15–24 who know that a person can protect herself from HIV infection by "consistent use of condom"; (b) Percentage of women and men 15–24 who know a healthy-looking person can transmit HIV. Data for this year's report are only available on women.

[d] Prevention to be measured by the percentage of children under 5 sleeping under insecticide-treated bednets; treatment to be measured by percentage of children under 5 who are appropriately treated.

[e] An improved measure of the target is under development by ILO for future years.

[f] Under development by WHO.

A few months after the Millennium Summit, the U.S. presidential election occurred, and President George W. Bush took office in early 2001. On March 14, 2002, the president made a surprise announcement that the U.S. government would increase its foreign aid substantially, to an annual rate that, by 2006, would be $5 billion higher than it had been previously. The new program took its title from the millennial summit of 2000: Millennium Challenge Account. Much of the increased funding pledged by the United States was earmarked for AIDS programs. The following frequently asked questions are from a White House document issued in 2003.

Millennium Challenge Account: Frequently Asked Questions

Q: Why do we need the MCA?

A: Today there are more than one billion people living on less than $1 a day and nearly three billion living on less than $2 a day. Not only is it a moral imperative to address these humanitarian concerns, our national interests require that we seriously address global development. Terrorism, disease, environmental degradation, and other transnational issues are exacerbated by poverty, spill across borders, and greatly impact the lives of every American. Too few countries are achieving sustained economic growth, which is a prerequisite for reducing poverty. The MCA will challenge countries to adopt the governance, health, education and economic policies that enable growth. In qualifying countries, it will target investments to overcome the greatest obstacles to growth. Greater prosperity in the developing world—by alleviating the poverty that breeds discontent and instability, by expanding export markets, and by reducing the spread of disease—promotes our own security and well-being.

Q: Why is the MCA different?

A: The MCA brings together the lessons we have learned about development over the past 50 years: (1) Aid is more likely to result in successful sustainable economic development in countries that are pursuing sound political, economic and social policies; (2) Development plans supported by a broad range of stakeholders, and for which countries have primary responsibility, engender country ownership and are more likely to succeed; (3) Integrating monitoring and evaluation into the design of activities ensures that aid is going where it's most effective. President Bush's vision of the MCA recognizes the importance of each of these lessons. First, it rewards pro-growth policies. President Bush categorizes these policies as ruling justly, investing in people and encouraging economic freedom. These policies benefit developing countries by increasing growth, creating an environment conducive to foreign and domestic investment, and making development assistance more effective. The MCA provides a strong incentive for countries to adopt these good policies. Second, the MCA establishes a true partnership in which the developing country, with the participation of its citizens, proposes its own priorities and plans. Finally, the MCA will place a clear focus on results. Funds will go only to those countries with well-implemented programs that have clear objectives and benchmarks.

Q: How much assistance will the MCA provide?

A: When he announced the Millennium Challenge Account in March 2002, President Bush proposed a new "global development compact" in which "greater contributions from developed nations must be linked to greater responsibility from developing nations." He pledged that the United States would lead by example and increase our current core development assistance by $5 billion per year within three years. The President's budget request of $1.3 billion for the MCA in FY 2004 (beginning in October 2003) marks the first step towards the President's commitment of providing $5 billion per year in MCA funding by FY 2006.

Q: Will the MCA come at the expense of other development assistance?

A: The MCA does not displace other assistance and, in fact, the President has made clear that the MCA is in addition to current assistance. The Administration is committed to global development. . . .

Q: How does the MCA fit into the USG's overall development goals?

A: The MCA reaffirms development as a strategic priority and its targeted mission is a part of an integrated strategy for achieving our development objectives. The MCC will focus on spurring growth in the subset of developing countries that have policies in place to use such assistance most effectively to achieve lasting results. USAID, State, and other agencies will continue to deliver assistance for many other purposes, including to address humanitarian crises, regional development, complex emergencies, and the problems of failed and failing states, all issues critical to U.S. national interests. USAID will also work with countries that are MCA "near misses" to encourage them to achieve the development-readiness essential for the MCA.

Q: How will the MCA relate to the U.N.'s Millennium Development Goals?

A: As the President said in announcing the MCA, we support the international development goals set forth in the Millennium Declaration as a shared responsibility of the developed and developing countries. The MCA is focused precisely on supporting the economic growth that poor countries taking sound steps will need to meet those goals.

Q: Which countries are eligible?

A: Only poor countries, which are not otherwise prohibited from receiving foreign assistance, will be eligible for MCA grants. For the first year, starting in FY 2004 beginning October 2003, only countries that can borrow from the International Development Association (IDA) with per capita incomes below $1,435 would be eligible. In FY 2005, all countries with incomes below $1,435 would be considered and from FY 2006, all countries with incomes up to $2,975—the World Bank cutoff for "lower middle income countries"—would be eligible.

Q: How will MCA countries be selected?

A: The MCA will only select countries that are, in President Bush's words, "ruling justly, investing in their people, and encouraging economic freedom." The MCA will use 16 independent indicators to measure country performance on these three criteria. To qualify, countries would be expected to score above the median on half of the indicators in each of the three criteria areas and score above the median on the corruption indicator. The Millennium Challenge Corporation Board would then review the results, by taking into account other factors such as data gaps or lags, and make a recommendation to the President. . . .

Q: How will the MCA be administered?

A: A new Millennium Challenge Corporation (MCC) will administer the MCA. The MCC will be a government corporation headed by a Chief Executive Officer and staffed leanly with talent drawn from the public and private sector. A cabinet-level board, including the Secretary of the Treasury and the Director of the Office of Management and Budget and chaired by the Secretary of State, will oversee the MCC. . . .

Q: Why do we need a new, independent corporation to administer the MCA?

A: The MCA represents the President's vision for redefining and revitalizing development assistance. It signals at home and to the world a new high-profile approach to kick start economic growth and poverty reduction. It gives the developing country primary responsibility for defining its own development priorities. It works with a limited group of partners committed to development and rewards them for the sound policies they have already adopted. It acts as an incentive to other countries to adopt growth-enabling policies. It provides substantial resources for integrated programs to spur development and then holds countries accountable for lasting results in a business-like MCA contract. A new institution is the best way to implement and highlight this innovative approach. The MCA will complement assistance provided by other agencies to address key U.S. priorities, such as humanitarian crises, failed states, infectious disease, and regional challenges. Unlike the MCA, such assistance cannot be given based solely on country performance or business-like partnerships. Because of its unique mandate, the MCA should not be constrained but will need flexible personnel and program authorities to carry out this targeted and innovative concept. If it is to respond to developing country priorities, for example, it cannot be earmarked to fund specific areas. The MCA should start with a clean slate—an innovative, flexible, narrowly targeted, and highly visible Millennium Challenge Corporation (MCC)—that can give it the best chance to succeed and show that this approach works.

Q: Why does the MCA have such complex qualifying criteria?

A: To qualify as a better performer a country would have to score above the median on half of the indicators in each of the three policy areas. This methodology assures that countries are committed and perform strongly in all three policy areas of "ruling justly, investing in people, and encouraging economic freedom." Sixteen indicators measure underlying policies that are critical to economic growth and poverty reduction. The use of transparent indicators also allows countries to precisely identify areas needing improvement. Neither the indicators nor the methodology are set in stone. The key is to find and use information that reliably identifies partners most ready for development. The MCA is already spurring improvements in data coverage and content. We will be assessing the system as we go along to ensure we are selecting countries that have policies that allow them to achieve development results. This process will be transparent, dynamic and rigorous.

Q: Why include countries with per-capita income of nearly $3,000 in the third year at the expense of qualified, poorer countries?

A: Countries with per capita incomes between $1,435 and $2,975 (the current World Bank cutoff for lower middle income countries) are still very poor and have a long way to go to lift themselves out of poverty. It is possible that these countries may be able to benefit most from MCA investments, enabling them to get to the next level of development where they no longer need foreign aid. Because scores can correlate with income, separate competitions will be run for countries with incomes below $1,435 and those with incomes between $1,435 and $2,975. This will limit bias against lower income countries.

Q: Is the role of women in society a part of the MCA eligibility process?

A: Consistent with the President's often articulated commitment to the cause of advancing political and economic equality for women, the U.S. government will be sensitive to the status of women as the MCA is implemented. Certainly countries that fail to advance women's human rights would not be expected to pass the criteria established for MCA. The Administration is confident that MCA's emphasis on good governance and human rights for all, sustainable economic growth and free enterprise, health and education for all, anti-corruption efforts and inclusive processes will be extremely beneficial for women.

Q: Is a commitment to the environment part of the MCA eligibility process?

A: Consistent with the Administration's support for sustainable development, including development that helps to maintain a healthy natural environment, we will be sensitive to the impact of our shared efforts on the environment. We believe that extreme poverty, poor governance, and a bad investment climate often contribute to environmental degradation. The MCA's emphasis on an inclusive process for developing sound MCA proposals, and its emphasis on governance, opportunity, and innovation will promote and support environmental stewardship. Finally, if it is a key priority to promoting economic growth and poverty reduction, countries will be free to propose specific activities with beneficial impacts on the environment.

Q: What types of activities will the MCA fund?

A: The goal of the MCA is to achieve poverty reduction through economic growth. The legislation identifies six areas that are directly tied to a country's productivity and economic growth, namely agriculture development, education, enterprise and private sector development, governance, health, and trade and investment capacity building. These areas are meant to be illustrative, not exclusive. Because flexibility and country ownership are key concepts of the MCA, decisions on specific MCA investments will be made on a country-by-country basis. The MCC and the country will identify investments that fit within each country's overall growth strategy. While environment and water projects, for example, may not be mentioned specifically, a country in consultation with the MCC may choose to invest in these areas in order to help it achieve its growth and development objectives.

Source: White House release, 2003. Accessed at http://www.mca.gov.

Fight Terrorism and Poverty

One of the concerns expressed in the Millennium Challenge Account document is that "poverty . . . breeds discontent and instability"; reducing such poverty is seen as something that "promotes our own security and well-being." The possible linkage between poverty and insecurity was on the minds of many people in the weeks and months after 9/11. The president of the World Bank, James D. Wolfensohn, offered his thoughts on the subject several times. The following piece was written by Wolfensohn just a few weeks after the events of 9/11.

The horrifying events of Sept. 11 have made this, for many, a time of reflection on how to make the world a better and safer place. The international community has already moved strongly to do so, by confronting terrorism directly and increasing security. We have also seen real collaboration aimed at averting global recession. These are signs of a rising cooperative spirit—seeking international responses to international problems.

But we must go one step further. The greatest long-term challenge for the world community in building a better world is that of fighting poverty and promoting inclusion worldwide. This is even more imperative now, when we know that because of the terrorist attacks, growth in developing countries will falter, pushing millions more into poverty and causing tens of thousands of children to die from malnutrition, disease and deprivation.

Poverty in itself does not immediately and directly lead to conflict, let alone to terrorism. Rather than responding to deprivation by lashing out at others, the vast majority of poor people worldwide devote their energy to the day-in, day-out struggle to secure income, food and opportunities for their children.

And yet we know that exclusion can breed violent conflict. Careful research tells us that civil wars have often resulted not so much from ethnic diversity—the usual scapegoat—as from a mix of factors, of which, it must be recognized, poverty is a central ingredient. And conflict-ridden countries in turn become safe havens for terrorists.

Our common goal must be to eradicate poverty, to promote inclusion and social justice, to bring the marginalized into the mainstream of the global economy and society.

We can do this through steps that help prevent conflicts. Take the example of the Nile Basin Initiative. It is no secret that water shortages pose a challenge to development and peace in North Africa and the Middle East. The initiative is a coming-together of the 10 countries of the Nile River Basin, providing a vehicle for cooperation on a program of sustainable water use and development. This is a good example of multilateral action to prevent conflict and to work directly for poverty reduction.

Equally important, we can help peace set down roots in societies just emerging from conflict. For example in Bosnia, where international support is helping communities come together at the local level on small-scale projects, creating jobs and bridging ethnic differences. Or in post-conflict societies, such as East Timor and Rwanda—where the international community is helping to rebuild infrastructure, reintegrate soldiers into the society and work force and restore the capacity of governments to manage their economies. Success may take years of hard work, but the alternative is a never-ending cycle of violence.

Central to conflict prevention and peace-building must be strategies for promoting social cohesion and inclusion. Inclusion means ensuring that all have opportunities for gainful employment, and that societies avoid wide income inequalities that can threaten social stability. But inclusion goes well beyond incomes. It also means seeing that poor people have access to education, health care and basic services, such as clean water, sanitation and power. It means enabling people to participate in key decisions that affect their lives. That is what we mean by empowerment.

But can we really make progress against poverty? Recent history tells us that we can. After increasing steadily for 200 years, the total number of people living in poverty worldwide started to fall 15 or 20 years ago. Over 20 years, the number of poor people has fallen by perhaps 200 million, even as the global population grew by 1.6 billion. This has been a direct result of the better policies that developing countries have been putting in place.

And progress extends well beyond income measures. Education and health have also improved. Since 1970, the proportion of those in the developing world who are illiterate has fallen sharply, from 47 percent to 25 percent; and since 1960, life expectancy has risen from 45 to 64 years.

Yet we must not underestimate the challenges that remain. Half the developing world—some 2 billion people—live in countries that have seen little growth in the last two decades. And even in those developing countries that have been doing relatively well, hundreds of millions of people are marginal to the progress of growth. As a result, well over 1 billion people, around 20 percent of the population of this planet, live on less than $1 a day.

And the scale of the challenge is not only immense but rising. In the next 30 years the population of the world will increase from 6 to 8 billion. Virtually all those 2 billion will be in the poor countries of the world.

In the wake of the tragedy of Sept. 11, facing these challenges, and taking multilateral action to meet them, are more important than ever. What should be our agenda?

First, scale up foreign aid. This may be much harder in an international economy that is slowing, but the needs and the stakes were never greater. Aid to Africa fell from $36 per person in 1990 to $20 today. And yet it is Africa, a continent now making great efforts to improve, that may feel most sharply the poverty fallout of the terrorist attacks. We cannot let Africa fall off the map as we turn our attention elsewhere.

Second, reduce trade barriers. The World Trade Organization summit must go ahead, and it must be a development round, one that is motivated primarily by a desire to use trade as a tool for poverty reduction and development. Substantial trade liberalization would be worth tens of billions of dollars to poor countries, and yet we know that at times of economic downturn there are increased pressures for protectionism. We must fight these pressures.

Third, focus development assistance to ensure good results. This means improving the climate for investment, productivity, growth and jobs as well as empowering and investing in poor people so that they can fully participate in growth.

And, fourth, act internationally on global issues. This includes not only confronting terrorism, internationalized crime and money laundering but also combating communicable diseases like AIDS and malaria, building an equitable global trading system, safeguarding financial stability to prevent deep and sudden crises, and protecting the natural resources and environment on which so many poor people depend for their livelihoods.

And all this we must do with developing countries in the driving seat—designing their own programs and making their own choices.

But we must also bring in the private sector, civil society, faith-based groups and international and national donors. Ours must be a global coalition—to fight terrorism, yes, but also to fight poverty.

Whether we take up that challenge is up to us. Some generations have had the courage. Others have turned away. Our parents and grandparents responded to the unspeakable horrors of World War II not by withdrawing but by coming together to build an international system. By contrast, the choices taken after World War I led to calamity. Which course we choose will determine not just our future but whether our children and grandchildren can live in peace.

Source: Wolfensohn, James. 2001. "Fight Terrorism and Poverty." *Development OUTREACH* (fall). Washington, DC: World Bank. Reprinted with permission of the World Bank.

HIV/AIDS and Poverty

When future historians try to capture the tenor of the era we are living in now, there will be no way to minimize the catastrophe that is AIDS. It is a modern plague that has already claimed 20 million lives, and it will claim millions more in coming decades. AIDS is now the main cause of death in Africa, the continent that has been hit hardest by the infection. Some of the key facts about HIV/AIDS as it relates to global poverty are presented in this excerpt from the 2002 State of World Population *report issued by the UNFPA.*

HIV/AIDS is the deadliest and fastest spreading of the diseases of sex and reproduction. It poses a greater threat to development prospects in poor countries than any other disease. The impact is hardest among the poor, who have no economic cushion and the weakest social support of any group.

Twenty years after the first clinical evidence of AIDS, it has become the most devastating disease yet faced by humanity, striking, on average, 14,000 men, women and children daily, the leading cause of death in sub-Saharan Africa and the world's fourth biggest killer.

The disease spreads through infected blood products and drug abuse, but overwhelmingly by sexual contact, predominantly between men and women. Women are more vulnerable to infection for physiological and social reasons, and sex workers are far more likely than the population at large to be infected. But the sexual behavior of men is largely responsible for spreading the disease.

More than 60 million people have been infected with HIV, and AIDS has already killed more than 20 million people, according to the Joint United Nations Programme on HIV/AIDS (UNAIDS) and WHO. In sub-Saharan Africa alone, 3.5 million were newly infected in 2001.

An estimated 40 million people are living with the virus, over 28 million in Africa and almost 95 per cent in developing countries. It is spreading most rapidly now in Eastern Europe and Central Asia, where most new infections are among injecting drug users. India may have more than 4 million infected. Its prevalence in China is unknown, but it may be far more than the official estimate of about a million. Some estimates are as high as 6 million, with a possible 10 million by the end of the decade.

HIV can also be passed in utero from infected mothers to their children. About a third of infected mothers pass the disease to their children in this way.

UNAIDS and WHO now estimate that more than 4 million children under the age of 15 have been infected with HIV. Over 90 per cent were infants born to HIV-positive mothers and acquired the virus before or during birth or through breastfeeding.

These infections have resulted in an unprecedented increase in infant mortality, because HIV infection progresses quickly to AIDS in children and many of these children have died. Of the 580,000 children under the age of 15 who died of AIDS in 2001, 500,000—nearly nine out of ten—were African.

Half of new HIV infections are among young people aged 15–24, many of whom have no information or prevention services and are still ignorant about the epidemic and how to protect themselves. In studies of sexually active 15–19 year-olds in seven African countries, at least 40 per cent did not believe that they were at risk. In one country the figure was 87 per cent. At least 30 per cent of young people in 22 countries surveyed recently by UNICEF had never heard of AIDS; in 17 countries surveyed, over half of adolescents could not name a single method of protecting themselves against HIV. In all surveys, young women know less than young men, though young women are more vulnerable to infection.

In developing countries HIV/AIDS is destroying lives and livelihoods alike, wiping out decades of progress. Even in the industrial countries most infections are among the poor. No developed country has an AIDS epidemic even approaching those of the poor world.

"Economic and social changes . . . have created an enabling environment that places tens of millions of people at risk of HIV infection."* Initiatives that only "seek to change behavior are insufficient to stem the epidemic. Determinants of the epidemic go far beyond individual volition." We will not stop the pandemic by treating it only as a disease. HIV/AIDS accompanies poverty, is spread by poverty and produces poverty in its turn.

The relationship between poverty and HIV transmission is not simple. If it were, South Africa might not have Africa's largest epidemic, for South Africa is rich by African standards. Botswana is also relatively rich, yet this country has the highest levels of infection in the world. While most people with HIV/AIDS are poor, many others are infected.

Poverty's companions encourage the infection: undernourishment; lack of clean water, sanitation and hygienic living conditions; generally low levels of health, compromised immune systems, high incidence of other infections, including genital infections, and exposure to diseases such as tuberculosis and malaria; inadequate public health services; illiteracy and ignorance; pressures encouraging high-risk behavior, from labor migration to alcohol abuse and gender violence; an inadequate leadership response to either HIV/AIDS or the problems of the poor; and finally, lack of confidence or hope for the future.

Individuals, households and communities living with HIV/AIDS find that lost earnings, lost crops and missing treatment make them weaker, make their poverty deeper and push the vulnerable into poverty. The cycle intensifies.

Inequality sharpens the impact of poverty, and a mixture of poverty and inequality may be driving the epidemic. A South African truck driver is not well paid compared to the executives who run his company, but he is rich in comparison to the people in the rural areas he drives through. For the woman at a truck stop, a man with 50 rand ($10) is wealthy; her desperate need for money to feed her family may buy him unprotected sex, although she knows the risks.

*B. Rau and J. Collins, "AIDS in the Context of Development," unpublished paper, UN Research Institute for Social Development, 2000.

Source: United Nations Population Fund. 2002. *State of World Population 2002: People, Poverty, and Possibilities.* Reprinted with permission of the United Nations.

Rome Declaration on World Food Security (1996)

In 1996, a "world food summit" was held in Rome, sponsored by the Food and Agriculture Organization of the UN and attended by delegates from 187 countries. The conference adopted two important documents, the "Rome Declaration on World Food Security" and the "World Food Summit Plan of Action." The first is presented below; the second may be accessed at http://www.fao.org/docrep/003/w3613e/w3613e00.htm. Note that in the second paragraph of the Rome Declaration, a goal is set of reducing the number of undernourished people in the world by one-half by the year 2015. This goal was later incorporated into the Millennium Development Goals and reaffirmed at a follow-up world food summit held in June 2002.

We, the Heads of State and Government*, or our representatives, gathered at the World Food Summit at the invitation of the Food and Agriculture Organization of the United Nations, reaffirm the right of everyone to have access to safe and nutritious food, consistent with the right to adequate food and the fundamental right of everyone to be free from hunger.

We pledge our political will and our common and national commitment to achieving food security for all and to an ongoing effort to eradicate hunger in all countries, with an immediate view to reducing the number of undernourished people to half their present level no later than 2015.

We consider it intolerable that more than 800 million people throughout the world, and particularly in developing countries, do not have enough food to meet their basic nutritional needs. This situation is unacceptable. Food supplies have increased substantially, but constraints on access to food and continuing inadequacy of household and national incomes to purchase food, instability of supply and demand, as well as natural and man-made disasters, prevent basic food needs from being fulfilled. The problems of hunger and food insecurity have global dimensions and are likely to persist, and even increase dramatically in some regions, unless urgent, determined and concerted action is taken, given the anticipated increase in the world's population and the stress on natural resources.

We reaffirm that a peaceful, stable and enabling political, social and economic environment is the essential foundation which will enable States to give adequate priority to food security and poverty eradication. Democracy, promotion and protection of all human rights and fundamental freedoms, including the right to development, and the full and equal participation of men and women are essential for achieving sustainable food security for all.

Poverty is a major cause of food insecurity and sustainable progress in poverty eradication is critical to improve access to food. Conflict, terrorism, corruption and environmental degradation also contribute significantly to food insecurity. Increased food production, including staple food, must be undertaken. This should happen within the framework of sustainable management of natural resources, elimination of unsustainable patterns of consumption and production, particularly in industrialized countries, and early stabilization of the world population. We acknowledge the fundamental contribution to food security by women, particularly in rural areas of developing countries, and the need to ensure equality between men and women. Revitalization of rural areas must also be a priority to enhance social stability and help redress the excessive rate of rural-urban migration confronting many countries.

We emphasize the urgency of taking action now to fulfill our responsibility to achieve food security for present and future generations. Attaining food security is a complex task for which the primary responsibility rests with individual governments. They have to develop an enabling environment and have policies that ensure peace, as well as social, political and economic stability and equity and gender equality. We express our deep concern over the persistence of hunger which, on such a scale, constitutes a threat both to national societies and, through a variety of ways, to the stability of the international community itself. Within the global framework, governments should also cooperate actively with one another and with United Nations organizations, financial institutions, intergovernmental and non-governmental organizations, and public and private sectors, on programs directed toward the achievement of food security for all.

Food should not be used as an instrument for political and economic pressure. We reaffirm the importance of international cooperation and solidarity as well as the necessity of refraining from unilateral measures not in accordance with the international law and the Charter of the United Nations and that endanger food security.

We recognize the need to adopt policies conducive to investment in human resource development, research and infrastructure for achieving food security. We must encourage generation of employment and incomes, and promote equitable access to productive and financial resources. We agree that trade is a key element in achieving food security. We agree to pursue food trade and overall trade policies that will encourage our producers and consumers to utilize available resources in an economically sound and sustainable manner. We recognize the importance for food security of sustainable agriculture, fisheries, forestry and rural development in low as well as high potential areas. We acknowledge the fundamental role of farmers, fishers, foresters, indigenous people and their communities, and all other people involved in the food sector, and of their organizations, supported by effective research and extension, in attaining food security. Our sustainable development policies will promote full participation and empowerment of people, especially women, an equitable distribution of income, access to health care and education, and opportunities for youth. Particular attention should be given to those who cannot produce or procure enough food for an adequate diet, including those affected by war, civil strife, natural disaster or climate related ecological changes. We are conscious of the need for urgent action to combat pests, drought, and natural resource degradation including desertification, overfishing and erosion of biological diversity.

We are determined to make efforts to mobilize, and optimize the allocation and utilization of, technical and financial resources from all sources, including external debt relief for developing countries, to reinforce national actions to implement sustainable food security policies.

Convinced that the multifaceted character of food security necessitates concerted national action, and effective international efforts to supplement and reinforce national action, we make the following commitments:

- we will ensure an enabling political, social, and economic environment designed to create the best conditions for the eradication of poverty and for durable peace, based on full and equal participation of women and men, which is most conducive to achieving sustainable food security for all;
- we will implement policies aimed at eradicating poverty and inequality and improving physical and economic access by all, at all times, to sufficient, nutritionally adequate and safe food and its effective utilization;
- we will pursue participatory and sustainable food, agriculture, fisheries, forestry and rural development policies and practices in high and low potential areas, which are essential to adequate and reliable food supplies at the household, national, regional and global levels, and combat pests, drought and desertification, considering the multifunctional character of agriculture;
- we will strive to ensure that food, agricultural trade and overall trade policies are conducive to fostering food security for all through a fair and market-oriented world trade system;
- we will endeavor to prevent and be prepared for natural disasters and man-made emergencies and to meet transitory and emergency food requirements in ways that encourage recovery, rehabilitation, development and a capacity to satisfy future needs;
- we will promote optimal allocation and use of public and private investments to foster human resources, sustainable food, agriculture, fisheries and forestry systems, and rural development, in high and low potential areas;

- we will implement, monitor, and follow-up this Plan of Action at all levels in cooperation with the international community.

We pledge our actions and support to implement the World Food Summit Plan of Action.

Rome, 13 November 1996

*When the term "Government" is used, it means as well the European Community within its areas of competence.

Source: United Nations Food and Agriculture Organization, World Food Summit. 1996. "Rome Declaration on World Food Security." Accessed at http://www.fao.org/docrep/003/w3613e/w3613e00.htm. Reprinted with permission of the United Nations.

Undernourishment around the World

While the previous document sets out the goals and values of the international community regarding food security, the next one details where we stand today. It references the World Food Summit objective of halving global malnutrition by 2015, noting that progress so far has been much too slow to achieve that aim. The publication from which this excerpt is taken, State of Food Insecurity, *is considered the authoritative sourcebook on its subject.*

Hunger and Mortality

Millions of people, including 6 million children under the age of five, die each year as a result of hunger. Of these millions, relatively few are the victims of famines that attract headlines, video crews and emergency aid. Far more die unnoticed, killed by the effects of chronic hunger and malnutrition, a "covert famine" that stunts their development, saps their strength and cripples their immune systems.

Where prevalence of hunger is high, mortality rates for infants and children under five are also high, and life expectancy is low (see map and graphs). In the worst affected countries, a newborn child can look forward to an average of barely 38 years of healthy life (compared to over 70 years of life in "full health" in 24 wealthy nations). One in seven children born in the countries where hunger is most common will die before reaching the age of five.

Not all of these shortened lives can be attributed to the effects of hunger, of course. Many other factors combine with hunger and malnutrition to sentence tens of millions of people to an early death. The HIV/AIDS pandemic, which is ravaging many of the same countries where hunger is most widespread, has reduced average life expectancy across all of sub-Saharan Africa by nearly five years for women and 2.5 years for men.

Even after compensating for the impact of HIV/AIDS and other factors, however, the correlation between chronic hunger and higher mortality rates remains striking. Numerous studies suggest that it is far from coincidental. Since the early 1990s, a series of analyses have confirmed that between 50 and 60 per cent of all childhood deaths in the developing world are caused either directly or indirectly by hunger and malnutrition.

Relatively few of those deaths are the result of starvation. Most are caused by a persistent lack of adequate food intake and essential nutrients that leaves children weak, underweight and vulnerable.

As might be expected, the vast majority of the 153 million underweight children under five in the developing world are concentrated in countries where the prevalence of undernourishment is high.

Even mild-to-moderate malnutrition greatly increases the risk of children dying from common childhood diseases. Overall, analysis shows that the risk of death is 2.5 times higher for children with only mild malnutrition than it is for children who are adequately nourished. And the risk increases sharply along with the severity of malnutrition (as measured by their weight-to-age ratio). The risk of death is 4.6 times higher for children suffering from moderate malnutrition and 8.4 times higher for the severely malnourished.

Counting the Hungry: Latest Estimates

FAO's latest estimates of the number of undernourished people confirm an alarming trend—progress in reducing hunger in the developing world has slowed to a crawl and in most regions the number of undernourished people is actually growing.

Worldwide, the latest estimates indicate that 840 million people were undernourished in 1998–2000. This figure includes 11 million in the industrialized countries, 30 million in countries in transition and 799 million in the developing world. The latest figure of 799 million for the developing countries represents a decrease of just 20 million since 1990–92, the benchmark period used at the World Food Summit (WFS). This means that the average annual decrease since the Summit has been only 2.5 million, far below the level required to reach the WFS goal of halving the number of undernourished people by 2015. It also means that progress would now have to be accelerated to 24 million per year, almost 10 times the current pace, in order to reach that goal.

Closer examination reveals that the situation in most of the developing world is even bleaker than it appears at first glance. The marginal global gains are the result of rapid progress in a few large countries. China alone has reduced the number of undernourished people by 74 million since 1990–92. Indonesia, Viet Nam, Thailand, Nigeria, Ghana and Peru have all achieved reductions of more than 3 million, helping to offset an increase of 96 million in 47 countries where progress has stalled. But if China and these six countries are set aside, the number of undernourished people in the rest of the developing world has increased by over 80 million since the WFS benchmark period.

When the number of undernourished is considered as a proportion of a country's total population, the picture is somewhat more encouraging. In the majority of developing countries, the proportion has actually decreased since the WFS. In 26 of the 61 developing countries that achieved a proportional decrease in undernourishment, however, the absolute number of undernourished people has continued to rise as a result of rapid population growth. One of those 26 countries is India, where the ranks of the undernourished have swollen by 18 million, despite the fact that the proportion fell from 25 to 24 percent.

Sub-Saharan Africa continues to have the highest prevalence of under nourishment and also has the largest increase in the number of undernourished people. But the situation in Africa is not uniformly grim. Most of the increase took place in Central Africa, driven by the collapse into chronic warfare of a single country, the Democratic Republic of the Congo, where the number of undernourished people has tripled.

West Africa, with Southeast Asia and South America, has reduced significantly both the prevalence and the number of undernourished people. But prospects are troubling for Central America, the Near East and East Asia (excluding China), where both of these elements have increased.

Poverty and Hunger—Mutual Causes, Devastating Effects

Measures of food deprivation, nutrition and poverty are strongly correlated. Countries with a high prevalence of undernourishment also have high prevalences of stunted and underweight children. In these countries, a high percentage of the population lives in conditions of extreme poverty. In countries where a high proportion of the population is undernourished, a comparably high proportion struggles to survive on less than US$1 per day.

While poverty is undoubtedly a cause of hunger, hunger can also be a cause of poverty. Hunger often deprives impoverished people of the one valuable resource they can call their own: the strength and skill to work productively. Numerous studies have confirmed that hunger seriously impairs the ability of the poor to develop their skills and reduces the productivity of their labor.

Hunger in childhood impairs mental and physical growth, crippling the capacity to learn and earn. Evidence from household food surveys in developing countries shows that adults with smaller and slighter body frames caused by undernourishment earn lower wages in jobs involving physical labor. Other studies have found that a 1 percent increase in the Body Mass Index (BMI, a measure of weight for a given height) is associated with an increase of more than 2 percent in wages for those toward the lower end of the BMI range.

Micronutrient deficiencies can also reduce work capacity. Surveys suggest that iron deficiency anaemia reduces productivity of manual laborers by up to 17 percent. As a result, hungry and malnourished adults earn lower wages. And they are frequently unable to work as many hours or years as well-nourished people, as they fall sick more often and have shorter life spans.

Hunger and the Poverty of Nations

Widespread hunger and malnutrition impair economic performance not only of individuals and families, but of nations. Anaemia alone has been found to reduce GDP by 0.5–1.8 percent in several countries. Studies in India, Pakistan, Bangladesh and Viet Nam estimated conservatively that the combined effect of stunting, iodine deficiency and iron deficiency reduced GDP by 2 to 4 percent. Recent calculations by FAO suggest that achieving the WFS goal of reducing the number of undernourished people by half by the year

2015 would yield a value of more than US$120 billion. That figure reflects the economic impact of longer, healthier, more productive lives for several hundred million people freed from hunger.

Nobel Prize-winning economist Robert Fogel has pointed out that hungry people cannot work their way out of poverty. He estimates that 20 percent of the population in England and France was effectively excluded from the labor force around 1790 because they were too weak and hungry to work. Improved nutrition, he calculates, accounted for about half of the economic growth in Britain and France between 1790 and 1880. Since many developing countries are as poor as Britain and France were in 1790, his analysis suggests reducing hunger could have a similar impact in developing countries today.

Source: United Nations Food and Agriculture Organization. *State of Food Insecurity 2002.* Rome: United Nations Food and Agriculture Organization. Reprinted with permission of the United Nations.

Links between Gender Equality and Poverty Reduction

Women experience a higher rate of poverty than men the world over. When we measure poverty by the standard of "capabilities," rather than simply income, the gender gap appears even wider, since females have less access to education, are often legally disadvantaged compared to males, and in many parts of the developing world do not yet have an equal voice in the political process. The following discussion, from an important new World Bank publication, makes the point that gender inequities hinder economic development in complex ways, deepening poverty.

Many variables are critical for poverty reduction, both on the investment climate side and on the empowerment side. However, one of the key conclusions of recent research is that, other things being equal, gender inequality retards both economic growth and poverty reduction.

Among the links between gender equality and growth rate are:

- *Investment in human capital, especially girls' and women's education and health, raises productivity.* Educated, healthy women are more able to engage in productive activities, find formal sector employment, earn higher incomes, and enjoy greater returns to schooling than are uneducated women, who suffer from poor nutrition and health, or are victims of domestic violence. Moreover, educated women give greater emphasis to schooling their own children, thereby improving the productivity of the next generation. *For example, children of literate mothers in India spend two more hours per day studying than do the children of illiterate mothers.*

- *Increased access to productive assets and resources also raises productivity.* Many societies have institutions and practices that limit women's access to productive assets and resources such as land, financial services and employment in the formal sector. Land titling is especially problematic. Women rarely have title to land, even when they are its primary users, and are thus often unable to use land as collateral for credit. Evidence from several African countries suggests that female farmers are as efficient as male farmers, but are less productive because they have less access to productive inputs and human capital. *In Sub-Saharan Africa, if women's access to agricultural inputs was on a par with men's, total agricultural outputs could increase by 6–20 percent.*

- *Time poverty created by poor infrastructure reduces productivity.* In many settings, including the middle income countries of Eastern, Central, and Southern Europe, women work significantly more hours collecting fuel and water. This time poverty limits their ability to engage in income-generating activities and to participate in community affairs. Because the gender-based division of labor extends to children, women's time poverty means that girls are often kept out of school to help with household work.

- *Information and Communications Technologies (ICTs) can enable greater participation of poor women and men in the world economy.* ICTs have an enormous potential to reach dispersed rural populations and provide them with education and training, job opportunities, access to markets, availability of information important for their economic activities, and greater participation in the political process. *For example, Tortas Peru is a women-owned enterprise that uses the Internet to reach and service a wider market, selling cakes and desserts through their website, mainly targeting the 2 million Peruvians living outside the country, who send orders by email. With just three hours of instruction, the housewife-members of the network, who bake and deliver the cakes, learn to use email, find the website, and interact with clients through public computer booths.*

Not only does gender inequality exacerbate poverty; poverty also exacerbates inequality between males and females. Inequalities between girls and boys in access to schooling or health care are more acute among the poor than among those with higher incomes. Whether measured in terms of command over productive resources, or in terms of power to influence the political process, poor men tend to have less influence in the community than non-poor men, and poor women generally have the least influence. These disparities disadvantage women and girls and limit their capacity to participate in and benefit from development.

Source: Gender and Development Group of the World Bank. 2004. *Gender Equality and the Millennium Development Goals.* Washington, DC: The World Bank, pp. 6–7.

China and India: Impressive Growth, Important Differences

China and India are the world's most populous nations by far, with over one billion people each. If demographic forecasts are to be believed, it is unlikely there will ever be a third member of the billionaire's club. But these are also two poor countries, even if one of them is able to send a "taikonaut" into earth orbit. What happens to their economies drives global poverty trends to a significant degree. Indeed, it is because they have done so well—China, especially—in the past decade or so that the global poverty numbers have been going in the right direction. (The darker side of this truth is that trends in the developing world outside China and India have been decidedly less positive, and in some ways powerfully negative.)

China and India, together containing a third of the world's population, have enjoyed tremendous economic growth over the past decade. Their successes in advancing average well-being imply major improvements for a large portion of humanity. But their experiences also point to the importance of looking beyond national averages to understanding differences within countries.

Though both countries have achieved rapid, sustained economic growth, their rates of progress have been quite different. China has enjoyed the fastest sustained economic advance in human history, averaging real per capita growth of 8% a year over the past decade. Its per capita income is now $3,976 in purchasing power parity (PPP) terms. Meanwhile, real per capita income in India grew at a robust though more modest average rate of 4.4%, reaching $2,358 in 2001. Reflecting their successful economic growth, both countries have seen significant reductions in poverty. According to World Bank estimates based on consumption surveys, the proportion of people living on less than $1 a day declined in China from 33% in 1990 to 16% in 2000, and in India from 43% in 1993/94 to 35% in 2001. While highly contested because of differences in methodology, survey design, and samples, these calculations nonetheless provide a rough indication of poverty trends in these countries.

Market Reforms

China's exceptional growth is partly explained by its market-based reforms that started in 1978, well before India's similar reforms began in 1991. These reforms have enabled China to integrate with the global economy at a phenomenal pace. Today it is the largest recipient of foreign direct investment among developing countries, with annual investment rising from almost zero in 1978 to about $52 billion in 2002 (nearly 5% of GDP). Foreign direct investment in India has also increased significantly, though at much lower levels, growing from $129 million in 1991 to $4 billion in 2002 (less than 1% of GDP).

Robust export growth has contributed to the economic performance of both countries, with a growing dominance of manufactured exports—though again, China has had much more success in this realm. Its exports reached $320 billion in 2001, compared with $35 billion for India. Manufactured exports accounted for 53% of China's total exports in 1981 and for 90% in 2001; in India that share rose from 60% to 77%. China has had particular success in moving from labor-intensive to technology-intensive exports: telecommunications equipment and computers now account for a quarter of its exports.

Social Investments

Social investments are required for sustained economic growth. In China public spending on education is 2.3% of GDP while that on health is 2.1% of GDP. The outcomes for human development are clear. Literacy stands at 84%, infant mortality rates at 32 per 1,000 live births and under-five mortality rates at 40 per 1,000 live births.

India, in contrast, has traditionally had lower spending levels. Health spending stands at 1.3% of GDP (central and state governments combined). Spending on education has increased significantly, from 0.8% of GDP in 1950 to 3.2% today, though it still falls short of the government target of 6% of GDP. Human development indicators for India remain much lower than for China. Literacy stands at 65%, infant mortality at 68 per 1,000 live births, and under-five mortality rates at 96 per 1,000 live births.

Regional Variations and Other Challenges

It would be misleading to talk solely in terms of national averages for two countries so large in population and area. . . . [I]n China, the highest economic growth has occurred in the coastal provinces—while the geographically isolated north-western provinces have experienced much lower growth. India also harbors stark regional variations. In 1992–97 per capita economic growth ranged from –0.2% in Bihar to 7.8% in Gujarat. Similar variations appear in other human development indicators, such as those for education and health.

Both countries still face challenges, such as the spread of HIV/AIDS and other sexually transmitted diseases accompanying increased labor migration and international trade. And both face the challenge of fostering a knowledge-based economy to maintain consistently high economic growth as average skill levels increase. Both also need to focus on spreading the gains of growth to regions, communities, and ethnic groups that have seen so little benefit from the new prosperity. Inclusive public policies should focus on investments in health, education, and infrastructure for future development.

Source: United Nations Development Programme. 2003. *Human Development Report 2003*, p. 73. Reprinted with permission of the United Nations.

Rio Declaration on Environment and Development (1992)

Poverty and the environment are two issues that we have come to understand are inextricably linked to each other. A deteriorating natural environment can only exacerbate the poverty of those who depend on it for water, fuel, and food production. Likewise, deepening poverty forces people to exploit their local environment beyond what it can sustain. It's clear that the "health and integrity of the Earth's ecosystem," as noted in the next document, must be a global concern of both the developing and the developed nations. The document came out of the "Earth Summit" held in Rio de Janeiro, Brazil, in June 1992. Delegates from 178 countries gave their approval to this short statement of the principles of sustainable development.

The United Nations Conference on Environment and Development, having met at Rio de Janeiro from 3 to 14 June 1992 . . . proclaims that:

Principle 1

Human beings are at the centre of concerns for sustainable development. They are entitled to a healthy and productive life in harmony with nature.

Principle 2

States have, in accordance with the Charter of the United Nations and the principles of international law, the sovereign right to exploit their own resources pursuant to their own environmental and developmental policies, and the responsibility to ensure that activities within their jurisdiction or control do not cause damage to the environment of other States or of areas beyond the limits of national jurisdiction.

Principle 3

The right to development must be fulfilled so as to equitably meet developmental and environmental needs of present and future generations.

Principle 4

In order to achieve sustainable development, environmental protection shall constitute an integral part of the development process and cannot be considered in isolation from it.

Principle 5

All States and all people shall cooperate in the essential task of eradicating poverty as an indispensable requirement for sustainable development, in order to decrease the disparities in standards of living and better meet the needs of the majority of the people of the world.

Principle 6

The special situation and needs of developing countries, particularly the least developed and those most environmentally vulnerable, shall be given special priority. International actions in the field of environment and development should also address the interests and needs of all countries.

Principle 7

States shall cooperate in a spirit of global partnership to conserve, protect and restore the health and integrity of the Earth's ecosystem. In view of the different contributions to global environmental degradation, States have common but differentiated responsibilities. The developed countries acknowledge the responsibility that they bear in the international pursuit of sustainable development in view of the pressures their societies place on the global environment and of the technologies and financial resources they command.

Principle 8

To achieve sustainable development and a higher quality of life for all people, States should reduce and eliminate unsustainable patterns of production and consumption and promote appropriate demographic policies.

Principle 9

States should cooperate to strengthen endogenous capacity-building for sustainable development by improving scientific understanding through exchanges of scientific and technological knowledge, and by enhancing the development, adaptation, diffusion and transfer of technologies, including new and innovative technologies.

Principle 10

Environmental issues are best handled with the participation of all concerned citizens, at the relevant level. At the national level, each individual shall have appropriate access to information concerning the environment that is held by public authorities, including information on hazardous materials and activities in their communities, and the opportunity to participate in decision-making processes. States shall facilitate and encourage public awareness and participation by making information widely available. Effective access to judicial and administrative proceedings, including redress and remedy, shall be provided.

Principle 11

States shall enact effective environmental legislation. Environmental standards, management objectives and priorities should reflect the environmental and developmental context to which they apply. Standards applied by some countries may be inappropriate and of unwarranted economic and social cost to other countries, in particular developing countries.

Source: Report of the United Nations Conference on Environment and Development, Annex I, "Rio Declaration on Environment and Development," 1992. Accessed at http://www.un.org/documents.

Debt Relief under the Heavily Indebted Poor Countries (HIPC) Initiative: A Factsheet—September 2003

The world has rarely, if ever, seen a global movement like the Jubilee debt forgiveness initiative of the 1990s, which aimed to relieve the most impoverished nations, at the turn of the millennium, from the crushing burden of their accumulated foreign debt. The outcome of this important social movement was not "total victory" in the eyes of its supporters, but neither was it a total failure. The World Bank and the IMF developed a program in the late 1990s under which highly indebted countries could gain considerable debt relief by meeting certain conditions of financial reform and commitment to poverty reduction. An update on the HIPC program is offered in this IMF document.

The HIPC Initiative is a comprehensive approach to debt reduction for heavily indebted poor countries pursuing IMF- and World Bank-supported adjustment and reform programs. To date, debt reduction packages have been approved for 27 countries, 23 of them in Africa, providing $51 billion in debt service relief over time.

What Is the Heavily Indebted Poor Countries (HIPC) Initiative?

The HIPC Initiative was first launched in 1996 by the IMF and World Bank, with the aim of ensuring that no poor country faces a debt burden it cannot manage. The Initiative entails coordinated action by the international financial community, including multilateral organizations and governments, to reduce to sustainable levels the external debt burdens of the most heavily indebted poor countries. Following a comprehensive review in September 1999, a number of modifications were approved to provide faster, deeper and broader debt relief and to strengthen the links between debt relief, poverty reduction and social policies. Countries' continued efforts toward macroeconomic adjustment and structural and social policy reforms—including higher spending on social sector programs like basic health and education—are now central to the enhanced HIPC Initiative.

Yet the HIPC Initiative is not a panacea. Even if all of the external debts of these countries were forgiven, most would still depend on significant levels of concessional external assistance, since their receipts of such assistance have been much larger than their debt-service payments for many years.

How the HIPC Initiative Works

To be considered for HIPC Initiative assistance, a country must:

- face an unsustainable debt burden, beyond traditionally available debt-relief mechanisms;
- establish a track record of reform and sound policies through IMF- and World Bank–supported programs; and
- have developed a Poverty Reduction Strategy Paper (PRSP) through a broad-based participatory process (an interim strategy is sufficient to begin the process).

The first step is to carry out a debt sustainability analysis to determine the debt relief needs of the country. If a country's external debt ratio after traditional debt relief mechanisms is above a threshold for the value of debt to exports (or, in special cases, the value of debt to fiscal revenues), it qualifies for assistance under the Initiative. Once a country has made sufficient progress in meeting the criteria for debt relief, the Executive Boards of the IMF and World Bank formally decide on a country's eligibility, and the international community commits to reducing debt to the sustainability threshold. This is called the decision point.

Once a country reaches its decision point, it may immediately begin receiving interim relief on its debt service falling due. In order to receive the full and irrevocable reduction in debt available under the HIPC Initiative, however, the country must establish a further track record of good performance under IMF- and World Bank–supported programs. The length of this second period depends on (i) the satisfactory implementation of key policy reforms agreed at the decision point, (ii) the maintenance of macroeconomic stability, and (iii) the adoption and implementation for at least one year of the PRSP.

Once a country has met these criteria, it can reach its completion point, at which time lenders are expected to provide the full relief committed at the decision point.

How the HIPC Initiative Is Financed

The total cost of providing assistance to the 37 countries potentially qualified under the enhanced HIPC Initiative is estimated to be about $50 billion in net present value terms. A little over half of this will be provided by bilateral creditors, and the rest will come from multilateral lenders. The IMF's share of the cost is financed primarily by the investment income on the net proceeds from off-market gold sales in 1999 that were deposited to the IMF's PRGF-HIPC Trust. Additional contributions to this trust have been provided by member countries.

How Countries Have Benefited from the HIPC Initiative

For the 27 countries for whom packages have already been approved, debt service falling due between 1998 and 2004 will drop by more than half in relation to both exports and government revenue. Yet for debt reduction to have a tangible impact on poverty, the additional resources need to be targeted at the poor. Before the HIPC Initiative, eligible countries were, on average, spending slightly more on debt service than on health and education combined. This is no longer the case in the 27 countries receiving HIPC relief. Under their recent IMF- and World Bank–supported programs, these countries have increased markedly their expenditures on health, education and other social services and, on average, such spending is now almost four times the amount of debt service payments.

While country-by-country data demonstrate that these countries are seeing clear gains, it has taken time and effort to ensure that money is redirected to aid the poor in ways that most reduce poverty. And difficult problems remain. For example, in war-ravaged Rwanda and Ethiopia, pressing reconstruction needs may mean large new loans at the same time that old debt is being reduced.

Difficult problems also remain in HIPCs that have not yet been able to reach their decision points. Some of these countries are plagued by uneven policy records or poor governance, which in turn may be caused by the serious problems that their governments confront, including civil conflict. Some HIPCs have debts too large to write off given current funding for the Initiative. This is true, for example, in Liberia and Sudan, which are both afflicted by civil conflict.

None of these are easy problems. But the IMF and World Bank are looking for solutions, with poverty reduction as the central focus.

Source: International Monetary Fund. 2003. "Debt Relief under the Heavily Indebted Poor Countries (HIPC) Initiative: A Factsheet—September 2003." Accessed at the IMF website at http://www.imf.org. Reprinted with permission of the International Monetary Fund.

The Monterrey Consensus (2002): Selected Passages

In the spring of 2002, an international conference on financing development was hosted by the UN in Monterrey, Mexico. Attended by a number of world leaders, including President Bush of the United States, it provided an opportunity for dialogue among business people, civil society, government officials, and institutional "stakeholders" (IMF, World Bank, WTO) on how to support the development process, particularly with respect to funding, whether in the form of grants, credits, or loans. It was in the lead-up to this conference that President Bush announced the new U.S. funding commitment that became known as the Millennium Challenge Account. An edited selection from the Monterrey Consensus is given here. Note item 42, which calls attention once more to the 0.7%-of-GNP goal set long ago for developed countries to contribute in aid to the developing countries. As of now, only a small handful of European nations meet that goal.

I. Confronting the Challenges of Financing for Development: A Global Response

1. We the heads of State and Government, gathered in Monterrey, Mexico, on 21 and 22 March 2002, have resolved to address the challenges of financing for development around the world, particularly in developing countries. Our goal is to eradicate poverty, achieve sustained economic growth and promote sustainable development as we advance to a fully inclusive and equitable global economic system.

2. We note with concern current estimates of dramatic shortfalls in resources required to achieve the internationally agreed development goals, including those contained in the United Nations Millennium Declaration.

3. Mobilizing and increasing the effective use of financial resources and achieving the national and international economic conditions needed to fulfill internationally agreed development goals, including those contained in the Millennium Declaration, to eliminate poverty, improve social conditions and raise living standards, and protect our environment, will be our first step to ensuring that the twenty-first century becomes the century of development for all.

4. Achieving the internationally agreed development goals, including those contained in the Millennium Declaration, demands a new partnership between developed and developing countries. We commit ourselves to sound policies, good governance at all levels and the rule of law. We also commit ourselves to mobilizing domestic resources, attracting international flows, promoting international trade as an engine for development, increasing international financial and technical cooperation for development, sustainable debt financing and external debt relief, and enhancing the coherence and consistency of the international monetary, financial and trading systems. . . .

7. Globalization offers opportunities and challenges. The developing countries and countries with economies in transition face special difficulties in responding to those challenges and opportunities. Globalization should be fully inclusive and equitable, and there is a strong need for policies and measures at the national and international levels, formulated and implemented with the full and effective participation of developing countries and countries with economies in transition to help them respond effectively to those challenges and opportunities. . . .

II. Leading Actions: Mobilizing Domestic Financial Resources for Development

10. In our common pursuit of growth, poverty eradication and sustainable development, a critical challenge is to ensure the necessary internal conditions for mobilizing domestic savings, both public and private, sustaining adequate levels of productive investment and increasing human capacity. A crucial task is to enhance the efficacy, coherence and consistency of macroeconomic policies. An enabling domestic environment is vital for mobilizing domestic resources, increasing productivity, reducing capital flight, encouraging the private sector, and attracting and making effective use of international investment and assistance. Efforts to create such an environment should be supported by the international community.

11. Good governance is essential for sustainable development. Sound economic policies, solid democratic institutions responsive to the needs of the people, and improved infrastructure are the basis for sustained economic growth, poverty eradication, and employment creation. Freedom, peace and security, domestic stability, respect for human rights, including the right to development, and the rule of law, gender equality, market-oriented policies, and an overall commitment to just and democratic societies are also essential and mutually reinforcing.

12. We will pursue appropriate policy and regulatory frameworks at our respective national levels and in a manner consistent with national laws to encourage public and private initiatives, including at the local level, and foster a dynamic and well functioning business sector, while improving income growth and distribution, raising productivity, empowering women and protecting labor rights and the environment. We recognize that the appropriate role of government in market-oriented economies will vary from country to country.

13. Fighting corruption at all levels is a priority. Corruption is a serious barrier to effective resource mobilization and allocation, and diverts resources away from activities that

are vital for poverty eradication and economic and sustainable development.

14. We recognize the need to pursue sound macroeconomic policies aimed at sustaining high rates of economic growth, full employment, poverty eradication, price stability, and sustainable fiscal and external balances to ensure that the benefits of growth reach all people, especially the poor.

Governments should attach priority to avoiding inflationary distortions and abrupt economic fluctuations that negatively affect income distribution and resource allocation. Along with prudent fiscal and monetary policies, an appropriate exchange rate regime is required.

15. An effective, efficient, transparent and accountable system for mobilizing public resources and managing their use by Governments is essential. We recognize the need to secure fiscal sustainability, along with equitable and efficient tax systems and administration, as well as improvements in public spending that do not crowd out productive private investment. We also recognize the contribution that medium-term fiscal frameworks can make in that respect.

16. Investments in basic economic and social infrastructure, social services and social protection, including education, health, nutrition, shelter and social security programs, which take special care of children and older persons and are gender sensitive and fully inclusive of the rural sector and all disadvantaged communities, are vital for enabling people, especially people living in poverty, to better adapt to and benefit from changing economic conditions and opportunities. Active labor market policies, including worker training, can help to increase employment and improve working conditions. The coverage and scope of social protection needs to be further strengthened. Economic crises also underscore the importance of effective social safety nets. . . .

18. Microfinance and credit for micro-, small and medium-sized enterprises, including in rural areas, particularly for women, as well as national savings schemes, are important

for enhancing the social and economic impact of the financial sector. . . .

20. Private international capital flows, particularly foreign direct investment, along with international financial stability, are vital complements to national and international development efforts. Foreign direct investment contributes toward financing sustained economic growth over the long term. It is especially important for its potential to transfer knowledge and technology, create jobs, boost overall productivity, enhance competitiveness and entrepreneurship, and ultimately eradicate poverty through economic growth and development. . . .

21. To attract and enhance inflows of productive capital, countries need to continue their efforts to achieve a transparent, stable and predictable investment climate, with proper contract enforcement and respect for property rights, embedded in sound macroeconomic policies and institutions that allow businesses, both domestic and international, to operate efficiently and profitably and with maximum development impact. . . .

International Trade as an Engine for Development

26. A universal, rule-based, open, non-discriminatory and equitable multilateral trading system, as well as meaningful trade liberalization, can substantially stimulate development worldwide, benefiting countries at all stages of development. In that regard, we reaffirm our commitment to trade liberalization and to ensure that trade plays its full part in promoting economic growth, employment and development for all. We thus welcome the decisions of the World Trade Organization to place the needs and interests of developing countries at the heart of its work program, and commit ourselves to their implementation.

27. To benefit fully from trade, which in many cases is the single most important external source of development financing, the establishment or enhancement of appropriate institutions and policies in developing countries, as well as in countries with economies in transition, is needed. Meaningful trade liberalization is an important element in the sustainable development strategy of a country. Increased trade and foreign direct investment could boost economic growth and could be a significant source of employment.

28. We acknowledge the issues of particular concern to developing countries and countries with economies in transition in international trade to enhance their capacity to finance their development, including trade barriers, trade-distorting subsidies and other trade-distorting measures, particularly in sectors of special export interest to developing countries, including agriculture; the abuse of anti-dumping measures; technical barriers and sanitary and phytosanitary measures; trade liberalization in labor intensive manufactures; trade liberalization in agricultural products; trade in services; tariff peaks, high tariffs and tariff escalation, as well as non-tariff barriers; the movement of natural persons; the lack of recognition of intellectual property rights for the protection of traditional knowledge and folklore; the transfer of knowledge and technology; the implementation and interpretation of the Agreement on Trade-Related Aspects of Intellectual Property Rights in a manner supportive of public health; and the need for special and differential treatment provisions for developing countries in trade agreements to be made more precise, effective and operational. . . .

Increasing International Financial and Technical Cooperation for Development

39. Official development assistance (ODA) plays an essential role as a complement to other sources of financing for development, especially in those countries with the least capacity to attract private direct investment.

ODA can help a country to reach adequate levels of domestic resource mobilization over an appropriate time horizon, while human capital, productive and export capacities are enhanced. ODA can be critical for improving the environment for private sector activity and can thus pave the way for robust growth. ODA is also a crucial instrument for supporting education, health, public infrastructure development, agriculture and rural development, and to enhance food security. For many countries in Africa, least developed countries, small island developing States, and landlocked developing countries, ODA is still the largest source of external financing and is critical to the achievement of the development goals and targets of the Millennium Declaration and other internationally agreed development targets. . . .

41. We recognize that a substantial increase in ODA and other resources will be required if developing countries are to achieve the internationally agreed development goals and objectives, including those contained in the Millennium Declaration. To build support for ODA, we will cooperate to further improve policies and development strategies, both nationally and internationally, to enhance aid effectiveness.

42. In that context, we urge developed countries that have not done so to make concrete efforts towards the target of 0.7 per cent of gross national product (GNP) as ODA to developing countries and 0.15 to 0.20 percent of GNP of developed countries to least developed countries, as reconfirmed at the Third United Nations Conference on Least Developed Countries, and we encourage developing countries to build on progress achieved in ensuring that ODA is used effectively to help achieve development goals and targets. We acknowledge the efforts of all donors, commend those donors whose ODA contributions exceed, reach or are increasing towards the targets, and underline the importance of undertaking to examine the means and time frames for achieving the targets and goals. . . .

External Debt

47. Sustainable debt financing is an important element for mobilizing resources for public and private investment. National comprehensive strategies to monitor and manage external liabilities, embedded in the domestic preconditions for debt sustainability, including sound macroeconomic policies and public resource management, are a key element in reducing national vulnerabilities. Debtors and creditors must share the responsibility for preventing and resolving unsustainable debt situations. Technical assistance for external debt management and debt tracking can play an important role and should be strengthened.

48. External debt relief can play a key role in liberating resources that can then be directed towards activities consistent with attaining sustainable growth and development, and therefore, debt relief measures should, where appropriate, be pursued vigorously and expeditiously. . . . Noting the importance of re-establishing financial viability for those developing countries facing unsustainable debt burdens, we welcome initiatives that have been undertaken to reduce outstanding indebtedness and invite further national and international measures in that regard, including, as appropriate, debt cancellation and other arrangements.

49. The enhanced Heavily Indebted Poor Countries Initiative provides an opportunity to strengthen the economic prospects and poverty reduction efforts of its beneficiary countries. Speedy, effective and full implementation of the enhanced Initiative, which should be fully financed through additional resources, is critical. Heavily indebted poor countries should take the policy measures necessary to become eligible for the Initiative. Future reviews of debt sustainability should also bear in mind the impact of debt relief on progress towards the achievement of the development goals contained in the

Millennium Declaration. We stress the importance of continued flexibility with regard to the eligibility criteria. Continued efforts are needed to reduce the debt burden of heavily indebted poor countries to sustainable levels. . . .

50. We stress the need for the International Monetary Fund and the World Bank to consider any fundamental changes in countries' debt sustainability caused by natural catastrophes, severe terms of trade shocks or conflict, when making policy recommendations, including for debt relief, as appropriate. . . .

Source: United Nations, International Conference on Financing for Development, "Draft Outcome," adopted by acclamation on 22 March 2002, in Monterrey, Mexico. Accessed at http://www.un.org/documents.

7

Directory of Organizations

Thousands of organizations, agencies, foundations, trusts, and charities around the world are committed to the elimination of poverty. Their motivations and strategies vary widely, as do their resources. Some of the groups listed below have annual budgets in the mere millions of dollars, while others—the World Bank, for example—are financial giants. Money talks, but so do ideas. One of the most original and potent ideas of recent decades, for example, is *microcredit*, the lending of small amounts of money to poor individuals, usually women, so that they can make their labor more productive and thereby lift themselves and their children out of abject poverty. So important have microcredit institutions become that they are given a separate category of listings in this chapter. Other nongovernmental relief and development organizations are divided between those that are faith-based and those that are not. A fourth category is official agencies, such as the World Bank, the World Health Organization, and UNICEF; and a fifth category lists several organizations that are primarily involved in advocacy and/or research.

Any observer of the developing world understands that poverty is not a stand-alone issue, that it has connections to environmental issues and human rights. The connections are important, they are recognized in various international agreements and forums, and they receive some attention in other chapters of this book. But because of space limitations, the organizations whose primary missions relate to human rights or the environment are not listed here. (An exception is made for organizations that advocate for the right to *food*.)

This is a highly selective list—in some ways, not much more than a sampling. Because so many organizations are involved in the fight against global poverty, no other choice is feasible. Those who want a more extensive list, or want information about an organization that is not featured in this chapter, may consult http://poverty.worldbank.org/webguide/category/5#10425 for a "webguide" to NGOs as listed by the World Bank at its PovertyNet website, or http://www.charitywatch.org/toprated. html#intrelief for a list of international relief and development charities compiled by the American Institute of Philanthropy. Another good list, with names and links to more than 220 organizations, is BOND (British Overseas NGOs for Development); find it at http://www.bond.org.uk.

Official Agencies

African Development Bank
Rue Joseph Anoma
01 BP 1387
Abidjan 01
Cote d'Ivoire
afdb-webmaster@afdb.org
http://www.afdb.org

The African Development Bank is one of four regional development banks in the world, the others being the Asian Development Bank, the Inter-American Development Bank, and the recently established European Bank for Reconstruction and Development. The African Development Bank, or AfDB, lends to development projects and programs in Africa. When it began operations in 1964, only African nations could be "members" of the bank. That changed in 1982, when membership was opened to non-African nations, and today there are fifty-three African and twenty-four non-African member nations. (The non-African members include the United States, Canada, Japan, and the UK.) The AfDB gives loans and technical assistance in the areas of agriculture, transport, industry, public utilities, health, and education. Its priority is agricultural and rural development, so it makes large investments in roads, water projects, and other kinds of infrastructure. Most of its loans are made at market interest rates, but there is another option for borrowers who cannot afford those rates. They can borrow from one of the AfDB's two affiliates in the African

Development Bank *Group*—the African Development *Fund* or the smaller Nigerian Trust Fund—where the interest rate can be as low as zero.

Publications: The best way to get a sense of the full range of AfDB lending activities is to check, on its website, the current list of "Loan & Grant Approvals." Also valuable is the annual *African Development Report*, which reviews the state of the African economy as a whole, with the aid of many charts and tables.

Asian Development Bank
P.O. Box 789
0980 Manila, Philippines
(632) 632-4444
Fax: (632) 636-2444
information@adb.org
http://www.adb.org

Established in 1966, the Asian Development Bank has as its underlying mission the reduction of poverty in Asia and the Pacific region. Like the other three regional development banks (for Africa, Latin America, and Europe), it is owned by its members. The ADB has sixty-one member nations, of which forty-four are within the region and seventeen, including the United States and the United Kingdom, are not. Japan and the United States are the largest shareholders, with about 16 percent each. The real business of the bank is to make development loans and provide technical assistance to member countries that are in the "developing" category—a group of forty-one countries, from Afghanistan to Viet Nam. The largest borrower has been Indonesia, followed by the People's Republic of China, Pakistan, and India. Most of the $5 billion of fresh lending each year goes to projects in agriculture and rural development, although, as with the African Development Bank, an increasing volume of lending now goes toward "social infrastructure" projects related to health and education. All of the international financial institutions (World Bank, IMF, regional development banks) offer "soft loan" windows, through which very poor borrowers can obtain funds at below-market interest rates. At the ADB, such loans are financed from a special fund called the Asian Development Fund, mainly for programs aimed at reducing poverty.

Publications: The *Asian Development Outlook 2003*, a comprehensive look at development prospects for forty-one nations in the

Asia/Pacific region, can be ordered from the website or downloaded for free. The bimonthly *ADB Review,* with feature articles about the current Asian economy as well as ADB activities, may also be ordered (no charge) or read online. Finally, the ADB's *Annual Report* is a useful compendium of up-to-date statistics on the developing Asian economies.

Food and Agriculture Organization of the United Nations
Viale delle Terme di Caracalla, 00100
Rome, Italy
Fax: +39 06 5705 3152
FAO-HQ@fao.org
http://www.fao.org

The FAO is an intergovernmental organization with a mandate, from its founding in 1945, to raise the levels of nutrition worldwide, lift agricultural productivity, and improve the lives of rural populations. The largest autonomous UN agency, it has a membership of 183 nations and one organization, the European Community. In its title, "agriculture" is understood to include not only the ordinary raising of crops on soil but also aquaculture, fisheries, marine products, and forestry. In all these areas, the FAO engages in technical and policy advice, advocacy, and data-gathering. Its capacities for collecting, analyzing, and disseminating information are unparalleled (see *Publications*). That information is used by scientists, government planners, NGOs, traders, and, of course, farmers. The FAO hosts international conferences and technical gatherings of many kinds. Its director-general, Jacques Diouf, who served previously as Senegal's ambassador to the United Nations, was elected to a six-year term in 1993 and then re-elected for a second term in 1999.

Publications: The FAO is well known for its annual *State of . . .* reports, the most prominent perhaps being *The State of Food Insecurity in the World,* or *SOFI,* since this is the news media source for the number of people in the world who go to bed hungry (nearly 800 million). The others are *The State of the World's Forests, The State of Food and Agriculture,* and *The State of World Fisheries and Aquaculture.* Also worth noting is *Agriculture 21,* the highly readable bimonthly webzine published by the agriculture department of the FAO. Other FAO publications tend to be far more technical than a general reader would require.

Group of 77
Office of the Chairman of the Group of 77
United Nations Headquarters, Room S-3959
New York, NY 10017
(212) 963-0192
Fax: (212) 963-3515
G77off@unmail.org
http://www.g77.org

In 1964, seventy-seven developing nations joined together to establish the Group of 77, or G77, to speak and act collectively in the interests of the Third World (a term more in use then than now). The group holds meetings periodically, issues declarations and action programs, sponsors resolutions, and promotes economic and technical cooperation among the developing nations. At their website, go to "News Centre," then "News Links," for links to organizations and news sources little known to most people in the "First World." (Particularly informative is the Third World Network.)

Publication: The G77 publishes the *Journal of the Group of 77*, the current issue being available at their website. Its main function seems to be the documentation of official G77 positions on important pending issues.

Inter-American Development Bank
1300 New York Avenue, NW
Washington, DC 20577
(202) 623-1000
Fax: (202) 623-3096
webmaster@iadb.org
http://www.iadb.org

The Inter-American Development Bank is the oldest multilateral institution of its kind, having been chartered in 1959. Originally, nineteen Latin American and Caribbean countries, along with the United States, were members of the IADB. Over time, additional Western Hemisphere nations joined, followed by a large number of nonregional countries. Today, total membership is forty-six nations. At first the IADB made loans mainly to finance agriculture, industry, and infrastructure. As has been true of other regional banks and the World Bank, the emphasis has recently shifted toward more "social" lending—poverty reduction, the environment, and similar priorities. The IADB has also increased its lending to microentrepreneurs and the informal sector. Its total lending in 2002 amounted to about $4.5 billion.

Publications: Published every month or two, the online *IDBAmerica* is a forum for Latin American and Caribbean development issues that manages to be lively and topical; besides English, it can be read in Spanish, Portuguese, and French. For a good sense of the day-to-day lending activities of the bank, follow the "News" link to "Press Releases."

United Nations Children's Fund—UNICEF
UNICEF House
3 United Nations Plaza
New York, NY 10017
(212) 326-7000
Fax: (212) 888-7465
http://www.unicef.org

UNICEF was started in 1946 as a UN effort to assist children in war-torn Europe. It was made a permanent part of the United Nations in 1953. When the UN General Assembly adopted the Declaration of the Rights of the Child in 1959, and even more clearly when it adopted the Convention on the Rights of the Child in 1989, it gave the mission of UNICEF a solid basis in international law. In a critical phrase of its mission statement, UNICEF commits itself to "mobilize political will and material resources to help countries, particularly developing countries, ensure a 'first call for children' and to build their capacity to form appropriate policies and deliver services for children and their families." More recently, its mandate has been strengthened by the adoption of the Millennium Development Goals (2000), inasmuch as six of the eight goals involve children directly. "Most of the people living in poverty are children," UNICEF has noted in a recent statement. Most of what UNICEF does falls into the category of *advocacy*, whether it be advocating educational equality for girls, pushing governments to develop HIV/AIDS prevention programs for children and adolescents, campaigning for universal child immunizations, or giving its support to the Global Polio Eradication Initiative.

Publications: UNICEF's most important publication is *The State of the World's Children*, issued annually (2003 theme: child participation). A free summary may be ordered through the website, and both the report and summary may be downloaded as well. The *Annual Report* gives an overview of UNICEF's worldwide activities during the previous year. Many shorter works on topics related to UNICEF's work may be downloaded or ordered from the website. Highly recommended is a 50-page booklet, *Poverty Reduction Begins with Children*, published in 2000.

United Nations Conference on Trade and Development— UNCTAD

Palais des Nations
8–14, Av. De la Paix
1211 Geneva 10
Switzerland
info@unctad.org
http://www.unctad.org

UNCTAD was established in 1964 as an intergovernmental organization and the UN agency chiefly concerned with trade, investment, and development issues. It seeks the integration of the developing countries into the world economy on terms favorable (or, at any rate, not unfavorable) to those countries. UNCTAD provides a forum for discussions and consultations. Indeed it was at the conclusion of the first UNCTAD conference that the Group of 77, actually a coalition of well over a hundred developing countries, was formed. In the policy analysis/advocacy in which UNCTAD engages, it is understood that the interests and concerns of the "South" or developing nations will have priority. This is considered by many a reasonable, though perhaps only symbolic, counterbalance to the power held by the G8, or wealthy industrialized countries, at the World Bank and IMF. Of special concern to UNCTAD are the *least* developed, landlocked, and island developing countries.

Publications: Among the many studies, reports, and reviews published by UNCTAD, one has particular relevance for students of world poverty, the annual *Least Developed Countries Report*. It focuses on that set of countries at greatest risk of being left behind as globalization marches forward. The theme of the 2002 report is *Escaping the Poverty Trap*. It may be downloaded or purchased.

United Nations Development Programme—UNDP

One United Nations Plaza
New York, NY 10017

(212) 906-5558
Fax: (212) 906-5364
enquiries@undp.org
http://www.undp.org

The United Nations Development Programme was born in 1965 from the merger of two earlier UN programs, the Expanded Programme of Technical Assistance (EPTA) and the UN Special Fund. EPTA, created in 1949, had been designed as an agency through which the industrialized nations could provide technical assistance to the "underdeveloped nations," while the UN Special Fund, authorized in 1958, was meant to be a conduit for financial as well as technical assistance to the low-income countries. Today the UNDP is the UN's main development arm. It assists countries in devising poverty-reduction strategies, and works to ensure the success of any programs or projects that may emerge from that planning. The UNDP gives technical advice on projects related to health, nutrition, and education, as well as physical infrastructure. Part of the UNDP's mandate involves giving advice and support to other UN agencies in their interactions with the developing countries. The UNDP builds partnerships and coalitions within and among countries to achieve common development objectives, and advocates on behalf of developing countries in various global settings. It has been given the job of "connecting countries to the knowledge and resources needed to achieve" the Millennium Development Goals (MDGs) agreed to at the Millennium Summit in the fall of 2000, while at the same time monitoring the progress that countries are making toward those goals. The UNDP is currently active in 166 countries.

Publications: The UNDP issues what may well be called the UN's premier publication: the annual *Human Development Report*. Each year the *HDR* explores a particular development-related theme; for 2003 it was *Millennium Development Goals: A Compact among Nations to End Human Poverty*. A digest of the HDRs from 1990 to 1999 written specifically for younger readers, *Sustainable Human Development*, may be ordered from http://www.peacechild.org. The *Development Policy Journal*, which documents progress (or lack thereof) on the MDGs, may be read online at the UNDP website. And *Choices* is the UNDP's quarterly webzine, with feature stories on global development that are highly accessible to general readers.

United States Agency for International Development—USAID
Information Center
Ronald Reagan Building
1300 Pennsylvania Ave., NW
Washington, DC 20523-1000
(202) 712-0000
Fax: (202) 216-3524
pinquiries@usaid.gov
http://www.usaid.gov

From the days of the Marshall Plan in the late 1940s until early in the administration of President John F. Kennedy, the U.S. foreign aid effort was fragmented among several agencies, created at various times for various purposes. The Foreign Assistance Act of 1961 corrected this problem by creating USAID and centralizing all U.S. technical and economic assistance programs under one roof. Although USAID is the administrator of *nonmilitary* U.S. assistance, the agency is far from blind to matters of geopolitics. Since its inception, USAID has been guided by U.S. national security and foreign policy interests, as determined by the administration currently in office. Thus the earliest USAID programs were conceived as part of the Cold War effort to contain communism. That objective had largely disappeared by 1990, but other concerns—combating the narcotics trade and terrorism, for example—have replaced it. Today the range of USAID activities is immense, from financing family-planning programs, to developing oral rehydration therapies, to funding agricultural research overseas. The agency is a big supporter of UN and NGO programs in health, education, disease prevention, and disaster relief. The U.S. foreign aid budget is in the range of $8 billion per year—a much smaller percentage of the country's GDP than some other industrialized countries devote to aid. However, in early 2003, President Bush proposed and Congress approved a new initiative that will boost U.S. spending on HIV/AIDS efforts in Africa and the Caribbean to $15 billion over the next five years. USAID will have a key role in administering the initiative.

Publications: Brief factual accounts of USAID activities may be found in the *Press Releases, Fact Sheets,* and *Media Advisories* in the "Press" section of the website. In the "Development Experience Clearinghouse" there are, the website claims, more than 119,000 USAID reports, of which some 14,000 can be downloaded. These reports deal with technical aspects of aid programs. More readable are the pages of *Frontlines,* a monthly publication for USAID employees that can be read online.

World Bank
1818 H Street, N.W.
Washington, DC 20433
(202) 473-1000
Fax: (202) 477-6391
feedback@worldbank.org
http://www.worldbank.org

"Our dream," states the World Bank, "is a world free of poverty." Conceived at the legendary Bretton Woods conference in 1944, the World Bank—or International Bank for Reconstruction and Development—was intended to be the long-term finance partner to the IMF. (The IMF was to be a *short*-term lender to countries facing balance of payments difficulties.) Its first task was to help the European nations rebuild after World War II. Thereafter, it became increasingly involved in financing Third World projects to build up physical infrastructure, on the theory that such investments were essential to economic development. Dams, roads, port facilities, power plants—these were the typical World Bank investments. In recent years the World Bank has pulled back somewhat from the "hard" infrastructural investments in favor of "social" investments—for example, in health and education. Technically, the "World Bank" consists of the original IBRD *and* the International Development Agency (IDA). The IDA gives grants and interest-free credits to the world's poorest countries, using funds donated by the rich countries. The World Bank, on the other hand, sells bonds in the capital markets and then offers the funds at low interest rates, with long repayment schedules, to borrowing countries. The "World Bank *Group*" consists of these two core institutions and three other development-related agencies. Activities funded by the World Bank run the gamut from road construction to AIDS-awareness education, from microcredit lending to investments in health care delivery. The World Bank employs about 10,000 professionals at its headquarters in Washington, D.C., and "on the ground" in developing nations around the world.

Publications: The annual *World Development Indicators* compiled by the World Bank is one of the two essential sourcebooks for students of world poverty, the other being the *Human Development Report* issued by the United Nations. The *WDI* is available online, in paperback, and in a CD-ROM that contains more data series than the book itself. It should not be confused with the *World Development Report (WDR)*, also issued annually by the World Bank, which examines a different development theme each year (in 2003: *Sustainable Development in a Dynamic World*). The *WDR* has, as appendices, some of the key data tables from the *WDI*, which is very handy. There is probably no bookstore in the world better supplied with poverty and development publications than the InfoShop, run by the World Bank, at 701 18th Street, NW, Washington, DC.

World Food Programme
Via C.G. Viola 68
Parco dei Medici, 00148
Rome, Italy
Fax: +39-06-6513-2840
wfpinfo@wfp.org
http://www.wfp.org

Since the early 1960s, the World Food Programme has been the main food-assistance agency of the United Nations. Indeed it has become the world's largest international food relief organization, helping feed more than 72 million people in eighty-two countries in 2002. The WFP's formal mission statement, adopted in 1994, makes food security the ultimate goal of the organization. Food security is defined as "access of all people at all times to the food needed for an active and healthy life." In programmatic terms, this entails action by the WFP to (1) get food to people caught up in humanitarian crises; (2) support the most vulnerable people—children, pregnant women, the elderly—at the most critical times of their lives; and (3) help the hungry poor become more self-sufficient. The third task is accomplished through providing food in exchange for work on projects that enhance economic development, such as building schools, roads, and wells. The funds for WFP programs come not from the United Nations itself but from the contributions of national governments, corporations, and individuals. Government funding is by far the most important, and the contributions of the U.S. government, in cash and commodities, dwarf those of all other nations.

Publications: No printed periodicals or other general-readership materials are issued by the WFP, but its website is well organized and well stocked with information about hunger emergencies and WFP responses. Check the "Newsroom" and "Operations" links.

World Health Organization
Liaison Office in Washington
1775 K Street, NW
Suite 430
Washington, DC 20006
(202) 331-9081
Fax: (202) 331-9097
http://www.who.int

The World Health Organization was established in 1948 as the health agency of the United Nations. Its challenge—the "attainment by all peoples of the highest possible level of health"—has grown more daunting with the steady expansion of world population and the advent of HIV/AIDS, drug-resistant TB, SARS, and other diseases. Because the health of the world's poor lags so far behind that of the rich, it's a safe assumption that most WHO-supported and -directed activities contribute, on balance, to the reduction of global poverty. At the level of specific policy impact, a recently formed department of WHO deserves special notice: the Department of Health and Development (HDE). Created in 1999, HDE proceeds on the premise that "improved health can be a powerful exit route from poverty." It therefore works to integrate health concerns into the development strategies of poor countries. It offers advice to countries putting together Poverty Reduction Strategy Papers (PRSPs) on how to build improved health for the poor into their planning. And it does the same thing on an international level as it lobbies to keep health concerns near the center of global poverty reduction efforts.

Publications: Much of what is published by WHO is technical in nature, but the annual *World Health Report,* inaugurated in 1995, has become a widely cited global health "report card." Several publications at the HDE website (http://www.cct-freiburg. de/who/publications.htm) deal more specifically with questions of poverty and health policy.

World Trade Organization
Centre William Rappard,
Rue de Lausanne 154,

CH-1211 Geneva 21,
Switzerland
Fax: (41-22) 731 42 06
enquiries@wto.org
http://www.wto.org

The WTO came into existence on January 1, 1995, as the successor organization to GATT, or the General Agreement on Tariffs and Trade. After World War II, it was the hope of many nations to have a third institution, called the International Trade Organization, enforce the rules of international trade. The ITO was meant to stand alongside the two "Bretton Woods" institutions, the World Bank and IMF. An ITO charter was written and ratified by some governments, but it was doomed by opposition in the U.S. Congress. In its place, GATT, created in 1948, took on the role of rules-keeper for international commerce. Under the auspices of GATT, successive "rounds" of tariff-cutting were conducted over the next forty-five years, liberalizing trade to such an extent that the average tariff on manufactured goods fell from around 40 percent to just under 5 percent.

The WTO differs from GATT in several ways. While GATT was ad hoc and provisional—it was never ratified by the "contracting parties"—the WTO is permanent. GATT covered only merchandise (goods) trade, while the WTO covers trade in goods and services, and even the trade aspects of intellectual property. GATT was slow at resolving disputes, while the WTO has a relatively quick, efficient mechanism for conflict resolution. These differences have in no way insulated the WTO from criticism, however. In fact, the WTO has attracted fiercer criticism than GATT ever did, from activists concerned about environmental, human rights, and food safety issues to those who believe that the developing countries are still not receiving fair treatment in the world trading system. The round of trade negotiations recently begun under WTO auspices is being called the "Development Round," since it aims to establish a new aid-and-trade framework that works to the advantage of the poorest countries.

Publications: The WTO's online newsletter, *Focus,* appears irregularly (about six times annually) and gives a good overview of WTO activities. Many other publications relating to trade negotiations, trade disputes, and trade statistics are also available online or for purchase. The least technical and most readable of these are listed under the heading "Free publications."

Microcredit Organizations

ACCION International
56 Roland Street Suite 300
Boston, MA 02129
(617) 625-7080
Fax: (617)-625-7020
http://www.accion.org

The mission of ACCION International is to "give people the tools they need to work their way out of poverty." It began in 1961 when a group of American volunteers, or "ACCIONistas," went to Caracas, Venezuela, to engage in community development projects such as installing electricity and sewer lines and building schools and community centers. The program expanded to several other Latin American countries, but took a decisive turn in 1973, when ACCION started making small loans in Recife, Brazil, to "microenterprises." The idea was expanded to fourteen Latin American countries in the next decade, and in 1992, ACCION took another major step: it founded a "bank of the poor" in Bolivia, called BancoSol, the world's first commercial bank dedicated to microlending. ACCION began operating programs in the United States in 1991—its first loans were made in Brooklyn—and in sub-Saharan Africa in 2000. But its major commitments are still in Latin America. Outside the United States, two-thirds of ACCION's clients are female. In 2002 the organization had three-quarters of a million clients in the Caribbean and Latin America (and about 60,000 total in Africa and the United States). Its average loan is under $600.

Publications: Various speeches, articles, books, and manuals relating to microfinance are available from the ACCION website, in Spanish, English, and French. There is also a "media center" with news releases, a photo gallery, a "media kit," and story ideas.

FINCA
1101 14th Street, NW
Washington, DC 20005
(202) 682-1510
http://www.villagebanking.org

FINCA, the Foundation for International Community Assistance, was established by John Hatch, a consultant to USAID, in

1984 as a way to kick-start development in Bolivia. Its stated purpose is to provide "financial services to the world's poorest families so that they can create their own jobs, raise household incomes, and improve their standard of living." Funds are provided through Village Banking groups of ten to fifty peers, usually neighboring mothers, who use their loans (*not* gifts or grants) to start small businesses. The loans are minimal, in the range of $50 to $1,000, but sufficient for the purchase of a sewing machine, a used refrigerator, and other forms of working capital. Loan repayment rates are in excess of 96 percent. A fundamental goal of FINCA is to put more money in the hands of mothers so that they can better provide for their children's nutrition, health, and education. FINCA operates in twenty countries in Africa, Latin America, the former Soviet republics, and North America.

Freedom from Hunger
1644 DaVinci Court
Davis, CA 95616
(800) 708-2555
Fax: (530) 758-6241
info@freefromhunger.org
www.freefromhunger.org

Freedom from Hunger is a relatively small, private, nonsectarian organization that began in 1946 as Meals for Millions. Its mission is to reduce hunger in the developing world through the provision of information and resources that enable women to become more self-sufficient. Specifically, FFH operates a program called Credit with Education that combines a Grameen-type microcredit lending facility with informal weekly classes on subjects like managing a microbusiness, nutrition, health, HIV/AIDS, and family planning. Around 240,000 women in sixteen countries are currently participating in FFH programs. Thirty percent of FFH funding comes from USAID. The average loan is only $80.

Publications: At the FFH website there are useful links to other websites (and organizations) that deal with microfinance or public health, the twin aspects of Credit with Education. The quarterly *Freedom from Hunger* newsletter and occasional *Briefing Sheets,* available online, discuss FFH activities and concerns.

Grameen Bank Bhaban
Mirpur 2, Dhaka 1216
Bangladesh
http://www.grameen-info.org

In 1974, Bangladeshi economist Muhammad Yunus had the often-recounted experience of learning from some poor women in a Bangladesh village that all any of them needed was a small loan in order to move ahead economically. He lent forty-two women a total of $27 out of his own pocket, and the entire sum was repaid. The "experiment" was repeated several times, with similar success. In 1983 the Grameen Bank was officially chartered by the government, with ownership in the hands of the borrowers (mainly poor women) except for a small fraction of government ownership. In spring of 2003, there were roughly 1,200 GB branches, doing business in more than 40,000 Bangladesh villages, with 2.4 million borrowers. The microcredit concept has been much imitated around the world, and Professor Yunus has collected a slew of honors for it. Grameen loans now are made not only for business but also for nonbusiness purposes, such as for housing costs and education, and a Grameen Trust has been established to finance the costs of "replication" efforts and research on how to reduce poverty. (Replication projects have been supported in thirty-four countries.) There is a Grameen Foundation USA, founded in 1997, with an office in Washington, D.C. Its mission is to promote the microcredit idea globally. Professor Yunus sits on its board of directors. More information can be obtained at its website: http://www.gfusa.org.

Publications: A quarterly newsletter, *Grameen Dialogue,* can be read at the Grameen website. It has feature articles on various aspects of poverty and "country reports" on microcredit projects outside Bangladesh.

Faith-Based Relief and Development

ADRA International
12501 Old Columbia Pike
Silver Spring, MD 20904
(800) 424-2372
http://www.adra.org

The Adventist Development and Relief Agency, or ADRA International, has undergone several name changes since it was started by the Seventh Day Adventist Church in 1956. While it lacks the name recognition of some other faith-based NGOs, it has a presence in more than 120 countries. In 2002 it provided over $100 million of development and relief assistance. ADRA projects fall mainly into five categories: food security, economic development (oriented to small farmers and "microentrepreneurs"), primary health, disaster preparedness and response, and basic education. It receives funding from private contributions and the U.S. government. Like the other faith-based organizations in this list, ADRA helps people without regard to race, gender, creed, or political affiliation. Unlike some, though, it does not actively evangelize. (It sometimes calls itself "the gospel in work boots"). In 1997, ADRA was granted general consultative status by the Economic and Social Council of the United Nations.

Publications: The quarterly *ADRA Works,* with reports on ADRA activities around the world, is available on request and online. A weekly television program, "ADRA's World," deals with international development projects on which ADRA is engaged; it is broadcast weekly on 3ABN, the satellite network.

American Friends Service Committee
1501 Cherry Street
Philadelphia, PA 19102
(215) 241-7000
Fax: (215) 241-7275
http://www.afsc.org

The Quakers founded the American Friends Service Committee in 1917 to provide alternative service options for conscientious objectors. The relief they rendered to victims of World Wars I and II, and their work for peace and reconciliation, earned them the Nobel Peace Prize in 1947. AFSC has remained committed to helping victims of disaster and conflict. Relatively small in comparison to other faith-based groups listed below, the AFSC delivers relief assistance on a correspondingly smaller scale. It seeks to aid victims who may be overlooked by other agencies. Examples include blankets and food to Afghanistan; water purifiers to Iraqi hospitals; and tools, clothes, and toiletries to AIDS orphans in Africa. Where AFSC may have a larger poverty impact is in their peace-building programs. The Friends' commitment to justice and nonviolence goes back over three centuries, giving it a special moral authority in today's conflict-prone world. AFSC reaches out to youth, parties in conflict, diplomats, and others in its pursuit of peace and justice. It maintains offices in Washington, D.C., and at the United Nations in New York and Geneva, to facilitate this work.

Publications: The monthly journal *Peacework* can be read at the AFSC website or subscribed to; a variety of other publications, mainly tied to peace and criminal justice issues, are also available online.

American Jewish World Service
45 West 36th Street
New York, NY 10018
(800) 889-7146
ajws@ajws.org
http://www.ajws.org

Founded in 1985, the American Jewish World Service has a mission to alleviate poverty, hunger, and disease wherever they are found and regardless of race, religion, or nationality. It strengthens the bond of American Jews to that part of their heritage that "calls upon them to be of service to others, to pursue justice, and to help heal the world." In practical terms, the AJWS partners with local NGOs in projects involving education, health care, agriculture, and community-building. As just one example, AJWS supports a program in Haiti that makes literacy training available to the clients of a village banking program serving 10,000 Haitians.

Catholic Relief Services
209 West Fayette Street
Baltimore, MD 21201-3443
(401) 625-2220
Fax: 410-239-2983
webmaster@catholicrelief.org
http://www.catholicrelief.org

As with several other faith-based organizations, Catholic Relief Services (CRS) was begun during World War II. The first task it undertook was to help with the resettling of wartime refugees. During the 1950s, 1960s, and 1970s, CRS expanded its range of concern to the world as a whole. In 2000 it had 4,000 paid staff working in field offices and 300 more in its Baltimore headquarters. With an annual budget of roughly $250 million, it is able to assist, each year, around 45 million people in eighty-five countries. In 1999, just more than half of CRS's program expenses went toward what was called "emergency response": relief from natural disasters and from humanitarian crises such as those produced by violent conflict and massive disruption of people's livelihoods. Another quarter of the budget went to community health projects. Cameroon offers an example of a country in West Africa where there has been a CRS presence dating back to 1960. The CRS focus in Cameroon has evolved from food security to peace and justice. The agency perceives a serious problem of mismanagement and corruption in the country, resulting in a society of tension, mistrust, and great inequality in the distribution of wealth. Thus CRS and the Catholic Church are working to raise consciousness about corruption and the need for good governance. They have found partners in civil society for this and other efforts they are making in Cameroon.

Publications: CRS offers a wide range of issue-specific publications at their website. The topics range from recommendations on how the Bush administration ought to handle its new Millennium Challenge Account, to an assessment of the PRSPs that the World Bank and IMF now require borrowing countries to submit, to a handbook on school feeding programs. Since CRS is involved in microfinance, there are publications on that topic, too.

Food for the Poor
550 SW 12th Ave.
Dept. 9662
Deerfield Beach, FL 33442
(888) 765-5555
Fax: (954) 570-7654
donorservice@foodforthepoor.org
http://www.foodforthepoor.org

This rapidly growing Christian organization was founded in 1982 by Ferdinand Mahfood, a Catholic layman and businessman born in Jamaica. (He relinquished leadership of FFP in 2000.) Since then FFP has distributed more than $1 billion in assistance to countries in the Caribbean and Central America and has become the major international relief organization in the region. Three countries, Nicaragua, Jamaica, and Haiti, accounted for almost 60 percent of FFP aid distributions in 2002. FFP purchases medical supplies and equipment, books for schools, and the like in bulk. It also receives donated food surpluses from the U.S. government and other sources that are then distributed through churches, missions, and other charitable organizations.

Islamic Relief Worldwide
P.O. Box 6098
Burbank, CA 91510
(888) 479-4968
Fax: (818) 238-9521
info@irw.org
http://www.irw.org

This international relief and development NGO was started in the United Kingdom in 1984. It maintains fundraising offices in Europe and the United States and field offices in Asia, Africa, and the Balkan region of Europe. Its projects include relief to the displaced and to victims of civil and sectarian strife, as well as to orphans. It also engages in development projects, whether in water and sanitation, health and nutrition, or education. Some food distributions are tied to Islam's calendar of religious observances (Ramadan, the Eid).

Lutheran World Relief
700 Light Street
Baltimore, MD 21230
(800) LWR-LWR-2
lwr@lwr.org
http://www.lwr.org

It is estimated that World War II left one-fifth of the world's Lutherans homeless, mainly in Germany and Scandinavia. In 1945, American Lutherans began sending aid to those victims of the war; soon they widened the scope of their charity to all of Europe. In coming decades the assistance was widened further to include victims of civil strife, drought, hurricanes, and other disasters, all over the world. Currently LWR has programs aimed at improving harvests, health, and education in some fifty countries. In Latin America they focus their efforts on Central America (specifically, El Salvador, Honduras, Nicaragua) and the Andean region (Peru, Bolivia, Colombia), where they work with small farmers, indigenous families, and displaced and vulnerable populations. In Africa they are moving to a focus on four nations in East Africa (Kenya, Malawi, Tanzania, Uganda) and West Africa (Burkina Faso, Ghana, Mali, Niger). HIV/AIDS and food security have become central concerns of the Lutheran mission in Africa. They also have launched fair trade campaigns for coffee and cocoa bean producers. LWR not only works with the poor but also advocates on their behalf, "speaking truth to power" and challenging "not only the consequences of poverty and oppression but also the causes."

Mennonite Central Committee
21 South 12th St.
PO Box 500 Akron, PA 17501-0500
(717) 859-1151
mailbox@mcc.org
http://www.mcc.org

The North American Mennonite and Brethren in Christ churches sponsor the MCC, which calls itself a "relief, service, and peace agency." It began in 1920 as an organized effort by U.S. and Canadian Mennonites to assist hungry people in the Soviet Union. Today, while small in comparison with many other faith-based efforts, MCC has nearly 1,500 people working in fifty-eight countries on projects tied to health, agriculture, education, and disaster relief. In other countries, it generally partners with local churches, usually but not always Mennonite. (The Mennonite presence in Africa is growing: The Republic of Congo's Mennonite population is second only to that of the United States, and *ahead* of Canada's.) MCC generates funds from donations, "relief sales" of quilts, crafts, produce, livestock, and so forth, as well as revenues from thrift stores. It also gains funds from the operation of Ten Thousand Villages stores in North America; these stores purchase craft items at fair trade prices from developing countries.

Publications: The magazine *A Common Place* is published five times a year and can be received free. It has articles on the work of MCC in various parts of the world. *News and Views at the United Nations* is a bimonthly reflection on world events from the perspective of the office that the Mennonites maintain at the United Nations.

World Vision
P.O. Box 9716
Federal Way, WA 98063-9716
(253) 815-1000
http://www.worldvision.org

World Vision calls itself the "largest privately funded Christian relief and development organization in the world." It is a nondenominational NGO that was started in 1950 by Dr. Bob Pierce in an effort to aid Korean War orphans. Its child sponsorship program ("sponsor a child for $26 a month") highlights the child-focused approach that it takes and is perhaps the key to its fundraising success. In 2002, World Vision claimed to assist 85 million people in ninety-six countries. Its projects are both short-term—emergency relief—and long-term. The latter are aimed at sustainable development of communities, with locals helping determine which projects to prioritize, whether in agriculture, health, hygiene, or education. Where government policy excludes "public evangelism," World Vision complies; otherwise, Christian education is part of its activities.

Publications: The *WV Resources Newsletter* is published quarterly and is available free of charge. Both the newsletter and the selection of books available for purchase at the WV website have a strongly religious flavor.

Nonreligious Relief and Development

ACORD (London)
Dean Bradley House
52 Horseferry Road
London SW1 2AF
United Kingdom
http://www.acord.org.uk

This organization devotes itself to "challenging and changing the conditions that cause poverty and exclusion" in Africa. It has programs running in seventeen African countries, but, in an interesting example of institutional redirection, it recently decided to de-emphasize the delivery of services and instead focus on advocacy ("levering change"). ACORD will be involved in research, resource mobilization, alliance-building, and exerting influence on policies, practices, and attitudes as it tries to effect change in civil society, gender relations, livelihoods, and the continuing crisis of HIV/AIDS in Africa. ACORD receives funding from a galaxy of governments, UN agencies, and religious and charitable organizations. It has announced that it will be moving its headquarters from London to Africa in the future.

Action Against Hunger—USA
247 West 37th St., Suite 1201
New York, NY 1018
(212) 967-7800
Fax: (212) 967-5480
aah@aah-usa.org
http://www.aah-usa.org

Action Against Hunger—USA is one branch of the International Network of Action Against Hunger. French doctors, scientists, and writers set up the original branch in 1979, in Paris. The United States, Spain, and the United Kingdom followed in 1985, 1994, and 1995, respectively. A nonreligious, nonprofit international organization, Action Against Hunger has a mission, as its name suggests, of combating hunger worldwide. It intervenes in both natural and man-made crises that threaten to produce famine, but it also works at developing long-term food self-sufficiency through the distribution of seeds, tools, fishing equipment, and so forth, and through technical training programs for local residents. Active in forty countries, with an international staff of 400, Action Against Hunger receives financial support from both public and private sources. Its largest single donor is the U.S. government.

Publications: A few books are for sale at the aah-usa website, the most interesting (to a nonspecialist) being *The Geopolitics of Hunger 2000–01: Hunger and Power.* There are a few technical reports on the nutrition and mortality situations in several African locales, and the organization issues a bimonthly e-mail newsletter.

Africare
440 R Street, NW
Washington, DC 20001
(202) 462-3614
Fax: (202) 387-1034
development@africare.org
http://www.africare.org

Africare occupies a unique niche in the world of relief and development organizations, in that it directs virtually all of its efforts to the continent of Africa. In other ways, it is fairly typical of the many nongovernmental U.S. organizations trying to tackle poverty and disease in the developing world. It offers programs in the areas of food security, agriculture, health, HIV/AIDS, water resource development, education, and support of microenterprise. There are few nations in Africa that have not hosted an Africare-supported program since 1970, when the organization was founded. At present, twenty-six countries receive Africare assistance, mainly in the continent's southern and western regions.

Publications: The semiannual newsletter *Habari,* detailing Africare's challenges and accomplishments in Africa, can be read at the website.

American Refugee Committee International
430 Oak Grove Street, Suite 204
Minneapolis, MN 55403
(612) 872-7060
Fax: (612) 607-6499
info@archq.org
http://www.archq.org

The American Refugee Committee was founded in 1978 by a Chicago businessman. Its mission is simple: to work for "the survival, health, and well-being of refugees [and] displaced persons," with the goal of helping them eventually return home, if that is possible. ARC is a nonpolitical, nonsectarian organization whose beneficiaries are mainly women and children. The ARC is especially active in the Balkans, but it also works in several African countries torn by internal conflicts and in Thailand.

CARE
151 Ellis Street NE
Atlanta, GA 30303-2440
(404) 681-2552
Fax: (404) 589-2653
info@care.org
http://www.care.org

One of the best known and largest private humanitarian organizations in the United States—its budget is in the range of $400 million—CARE is also one of the oldest. It began in 1945 as the

Cooperative for American Remittances to Europe, with the purpose of sending relief supplies to that war-torn continent. As time passed, CARE's mission changed: in the 1950s it sent food to the hungry in developing countries; in the 1960s it began delivering health programs; in the 1970s it supported the famine-stricken in Africa, and so on. Today its priorities include education, HIV/AIDS, and emergency relief and preparedness. Of course the official name has changed: it is now Cooperative for Assistance and Relief Everywhere. CARE is actually an alliance of ten national organizations. The headquarters of CARE International is in Brussels, Belgium. The familiar CARE packages seen in early television appeals have long since disappeared; the organization has other ways to deliver its aid today. CARE gets about 57 percent of its revenue from the U.S. government.

Publications: There are online press releases, feature articles, and special reports at CARE's website.

Doctors without Borders (Medecins sans Frontieres)
6 East 39th Street, Eighth floor
New York, NY 10016
(212) 679-6800
doctors@newyork.msf.org
http://www.doctorswithoutborders.org

Known internationally by its French name and initials, MSF was founded in 1971 by a group of French doctors who believed it important not only to treat people in medical need without regard to national borders but also to bear witness to their suffering. Many kinds of professionals, from doctors and nurses to sanitation engineers and administrators, volunteer their time to work with MSF at the medical frontlines. They treat victims of natural and man-made disasters, vaccinate children, rehabilitate hospitals, and more. MSF often is in the headlines when it deals with short-term emergencies, but it also commits itself to longer-term efforts, working to combat chronic, endemic diseases and medically assisting populations that are marginalized or isolated. Winner of the 1999 Nobel Peace Prize, MSF takes both medicine and *advocacy* seriously. It engages in public education campaigns and speaks out against abuses of human rights in all kinds of forums.

Publications: MSF's high-impact website features news of current humanitarian crises. It also reports on both MSF activities in the field and MSF advocacy campaigns—for example, a campaign to improve global access to essential medicines, and a campaign for the development of drugs to treat "neglected" diseases (neglected diseases being those not heavily impacting rich nations). The website also offers curricular ideas for teachers.

The Hunger Project
15 East 26th Street
New York, NY 10010
(212) 251-9100
Fax: (212) 532-9785
info@thp.org
http://www.thp.org

Founded in 1977, The Hunger Project sees itself as a "strategic organization" working to end world hunger on a permanent basis. Mobilizing grassroots action and empowering women are two of its strategies. In place of traditional "relief and development" activities, The Hunger Project engages in efforts to change the assumptions and practices that impede development in poor nations. For example, it supports the National Girl Child Day (September 30) in Bangladesh as a way to alter preconceptions about the value of females in a culture that tends to favor males. In India, THP has established a prize to honor the best media reporting on women, and in Bolivia it provides partial funding for an indigenous-language radio station, including the training of "people's reporters" to go out into villages for news stories. THP has a quite modest budget but a stellar board of directors that includes Queen Noor of Jordan, former UN Secretary-General Javier Perez de Cuellar, and Nobel Laureate Amartya Sen.

Mercy Corps
3015 SW First Avenue
Portland, OR 97201
(503) 796-6800
Fax: (503) 796-6844
programs@mercycorps.org
http://www.mercycorps.org

The stated mission of Mercy Corps is to "alleviate suffering, poverty, and oppression by helping people around the world build safe and productive communities." Mercy Corps, not to be confused with the Catholic organization Mercy Volunteer Corps, started out in 1979 as Save the Refugees Fund. It is known for its rapid response capacity when natural and conflict-driven disasters strike, delivering food, medical supplies, clothing, agricultural equipment, seeds, and other materials. MC also makes microloans to encourage families to become self-supporting. And it tries to reconcile parties in conflict through "tension-reducing programming" that helps people "identify the root causes of conflict and find ways to overcome them." It is often called upon to implement its relief and reconciliation efforts simultaneously, and is recognized for being skilled at this. MC devotes most of its programming to crises abroad, but in the wake of the 9/11 events in the United States it devised a "Comfort for Kids" program aimed at helping low-income and immigrant children in New York City deal with the shock of those events. MC gets 45 to 50 percent of its funding from the U.S. government; its help reaches 5 million people every year in more than thirty countries. It has a particularly strong presence in central and south Asia, the Caucasus, and the Balkans.

Oxfam America
26 West Street
Boston, MA 02111
(800) 776-9326
Fax: (617) 728-2594
info@oxfamamerica.org
http://www.oxfamamerica.org

Oxfam was begun in 1942 as the Oxford Committee for Famine Relief, a British group advocating for aid to the victims of the Nazi occupation in Greece. From that simple start, Oxfam has grown to become perhaps the best-known international organization devoted to combating poverty and hunger. The parent entity is British, but it is affiliated to eleven other national Oxfams, in Ireland, Canada, Belgium, Germany, and the United States, among others. The full Oxfam network had more than 3,000 partner organizations in about a hundred countries in 2000. Oxfam advocates for specific policy changes that it deems necessary to improve the lot of the poor—for example, the reduction or elimination of U.S. subsidies on cotton production as a way to help Africa's cotton growers, and support for "fair trade" commodities like coffee. It sponsors school and community activities such as "Fast for a World Harvest" and "Hunger Banquet" as fundraising and consciousness-raising events.

Publications of Oxfam America: The quarterly *Oxfam Exchange* contains short articles on a wide variety of poverty-related topics, such as ethnic discrimination in Guatemala, community radio in Senegal, clearing landmines in Afghanistan, and pesticides in Cambodia—all topics from the spring 2003 issue. *Oxfam Updates* are occasional short reports on Oxfam-funded activities, while *Oxfam Briefing Papers* are more in depth. The *Annual Report* gives a good overview of the various activities in which Oxfam America participates.

Rotary International
One Rotary Center
1560 Sherman Ave.
Evanston, IL 60201
(847) 866-3000
Fax: (847) 328-8554
http://www.rotary.org

Only after one gets past the first three "objects of Rotary," in the official listing of the organization's purposes, does one arrive at "the advancement of international understanding, goodwill, and peace through a world fellowship of business and professional persons united in the ideal of service." What sets Rotary apart from many similar organizations is this *international* commitment. It has been manifested in several ways. Rotary added "International" to its title in 1922, at a time when Americans were not notably interested in the world beyond their shores. (There were already Rotary chapters on six continents, however.) Rotarians were well represented among the founding delegations of the United Nations in 1945, and other UN-Rotary linkages are too numerous to list. Surely the most meaningful demonstration of Rotary's commitment to global welfare began in 1985 with the announcement of a global antipolio initiative, to which Rotary pledged $120 million. Within three years the pledge had been doubled, and by 2005 it will reach a cumulative $500 million—the largest contribution of any single organization toward meeting the long-term costs of a global polio eradication campaign that now includes WHO, UNICEF, and the U.S. Centers for Disease Control.

Save the Children USA
54 Wilton Road
Westport, CT 06880

(800) 728-3843
twebster@savechildren.org
http://www.savethechildren.org

In 1919 an English activist, Eglantyne Jebb, established the Save the Children Fund to provide aid to children in Vienna who were suffering extreme deprivation after World War I. The U.S. branch of Save the Children grew out of a 1932 meeting of New Yorkers who were concerned about Depression conditions facing children in West Virginia. Save the Children USA continues to assist U.S. children (in nineteen states), but the organization broadened its mandate early on when it began individual sponsorships of European children in need during World War II. In the 1950s a further widening of activity involved new programs of community development, initially in Lebanon and Greece. Today, Save the Children USA is part of an international alliance of thirty Save the Children organizations; together, they work in more than a hundred countries. The U.S. branch operates in more than forty countries, offering emergency relief after natural or man-made disasters, creating literacy programs, especially for girls and women, supporting the health of children and their families, and even promoting small business development with microfinance resources. In a budget of more than $200 million, some 60 percent comes from government grants and contracts.

Publications: Information about Save the Children activities around the world may be found in the newsletter *Insights,* published twice a year and available online. The annual *State of the World's Mothers* can also be downloaded from the website; the theme of the 2003 report is "protecting women and children in war and conflict." One or two thematic reports also are placed on the website each year: *Children of Kabul: Discussions with Afghan Families* was posted in July 2003.

World Neighbors
4127 Northwest 122nd Street
Oklahoma City, OK 73120
(800) 242-6387
Fax: (405) 752-9393
info@wn.org
http://www.wn.org

Founded in 1951, World Neighbors is a "grassroots development organization" that works in eighteen countries of Asia, Africa, and Latin America. Its mission is to help individuals and communities find long-term solutions to their own problems of disease, poverty, and hunger. WN programs are aimed at improving community health, individual reproductive health, and sanitation, as well as making agriculture productive and sustainable. The emphasis is on achieving equitable development without a need for continuous aid. Projects are designed to last no more than ten years, after which trained local leaders can (in theory) sustain the ongoing progress. WN receives no funding from the government, only from individuals, foundations, and other private sources.

Publications: A substantial newsletter, *Neighbors,* is posted quarterly to the website, with many articles about the organization's far-flung activities.

Advocacy and Research

Bread for the World
50 F Street, NW, Suite 500
Washington, DC 20001
(202) 639-9400
Fax: (202) 639-9401
bread@bread.org
http://www.bread.org

In its literature, Bread for the World states that "churches and charities . . . can't do it all" when it comes to the relief of hunger, domestically and internationally. "The government must do its part to help." To *convince* government to do its part is the task BFW has taken on. With almost 50,000 members across the country, BFW has become a major antihunger lobbyist. A self-described "Christian movement," it engages in various educational and advocacy activities. It is known for its annual letter-writing campaign ("Offerings of Letters") directed to Congress in support of legislation it deems to be needed in the fight against hunger. BFW was begun in 1972 and has had only two presidents, both Lutheran ministers. Its funding comes almost entirely from individual donations. BFW's partner organization, Bread for the World Institute, is devoted to research and education on hunger issues.

Publications: As might be expected from an advocacy group, BFW maintains a lively website and offers numerous publications in their online "bookstore." The annual *Hunger Reports* of the BFW Institute delve into specific hunger issues. In 2003 the topic was agriculture in the global economy, and the message was that rich countries are hurting poor ones by continuing to massively subsidize their own farmers.

Center for Global Development
1776 Massachusetts Ave. NW
Washington, DC 20036
(202) 416-0700
Fax: (202) 416-0750
info@cgdev.org
http://www.cgdev.org

Founded in 2001, the Center for Global Development is a small, high-quality research institute focused on global poverty issues. It pays particular attention to the impact of policies adopted by the industrialized countries on the development prospects of poor countries. The CGD is dedicated to the reduction of global poverty and inequality. It is much too early to evaluate how much clout this organization will acquire in the policy-making circles it aspires to influence, but already it has done some interesting work. For example, it has constructed an "index of development commitment" that ranks twenty-one of the world's richest countries according to how helpful their policies regarding aid, trade barriers, greenhouse emissions, openness to immigrants, and so forth are to the five billion people living in poorer countries. Leading the list are The Netherlands and Denmark, while the United States and Japan rank lowest in their development commitment.

Publications: There are many *Working Papers* and *CGD Briefs* already posted to the website of this fledgling institution, all written by highly qualified experts.

Center for Globalization and Sustainable Development
The Earth Institute
2910 Broadway, MC 4501 Hogan Hall B-15
New York, NY 10025
(212) 854-8198
Fax: (212) 854-6309
http://www.earthinstitute.columbia.edu/cgsd

Headed by economist Jeffrey Sachs, who was hired away from Harvard in 2002 to direct it, the Earth Institute at Columbia

University calls itself "the world's leading academic center for the integrated study of Earth, its environment, and society." One of several centers housed under the Earth Institute rubric is the Center for Globalization and Sustainable Development. The CGSD engages in research and policy work relating to education, the environment, natural disasters, conflict resolution, and other issues facing the developing countries. A priority for the CGSD, as for all the research centers at the Earth Institute, is to keep the needs of the world's poor in view. One of its current projects involves the design of a national strategy to enable the Dominican Republic to meet its Millennium Development Goals by 2015.

Publications: The CGSD has not yet initiated any regular publication series, but at the Earth Institute website there is much information about the UN Millennium Project (directed by Jeffrey Sachs), including background papers on possible ways to meet the Millennium Development Goals.

Eurodad
Rue Dejoncker 46, B-1060
Brussels, Belgium
Fax: 32-2 544 0559
info@eurodad.org
http://www.eurodad.org

No humor is intended in the name of this organization, which is in fact a network of forty-eight development NGOs from fifteen European nations. The NGOs include Oxfam, KEPA (a Finnish umbrella organization of more than 200 development groups), CCFD (a French antihunger organization), the Coalition of the Flemish North South Movement in Belgium, and so on. The mission of Eurodad is to work for the eradication of poverty and the empowerment of the poor by advocating for lenient development finance policies. Eurodad wants to ease the debt burden of poor countries while enabling them to receive future assistance on fair terms. More broadly, it seeks fuller participation of civil society—and reduced influence for the IMF and World Bank—in setting economic policy in these countries.

Publications: The Eurodad website is a gold mine of information on all aspects of the debt issue, from both the borrowing and lending perspectives. There are *Reports* and *Updates* on debt arbitration, debt sustainability, development assistance, structural adjustment policies, the HIPC initiative, and much more—in presentations that are either descriptive or policy-*prescriptive* (after all, Eurodad favors some policies over others).

Food First/Institute for Food and Development Policy
398 60th Street
Oakland, CA 94608
(510) 654-4400
Fax: (510) 654-4551
foodfirst@foodfirst.org
http://www.foodfirst.org

In 1971, Frances Moore Lappé published *Diet for a Small Planet,* the thrust of which was that the world hunger problem could be solved if food (and land) were distributed more equitably, and— on a dietary level—if more grains were fed to people rather than to cattle. The book was an immediate best-seller and has re-mained in print for more than three decades. It was credited with helping to launch the vegetarian movement in the United States. In 1975, Lappé joined with Joseph Collins to found the Institute for Food and Development Policy, in Oakland, California. Food First, as it is popularly known, is a progressive "think tank" de-voted to research on food and globalization. It supports the right of all people to feed themselves, and more generally, the values of diversity, local knowledge, and community participation. It op-poses corporate or "industrial" agriculture and genetically modi-fied (GM) foods.

Publications: There are *Policy Briefs, Fact Sheets*, and *Backgrounder* papers available at a small charge from Food First, but they may be freely downloaded from their website; these deal with various aspects of food, agriculture, and hunger from a progressive per-spective.

Future Harvest Foundation
1225 Connecticut Avenue, NW, 4th Floor
Washington, DC 20036
(202) 223-1313
info@futureharvest.org
http://www.futureharvest.org

To know what the "mainstream," "official," "corporate," or "foundation-backed" position on world hunger is, one should look first to CGIAR and Future Harvest. CGIAR, the Consultative Group on International Agricultural Research, was started in

1971, grew steadily, and now comprises fifty-eight governments, foundations, and international organizations that jointly support the agricultural research carried out at sixteen research centers scattered around the world. The sixteen include the four original centers sponsored by the Ford and Rockefeller foundations: CIMMYT in Mexico, IRRI in the Philippines, CIAT in Colombia, and ITA in Nigeria. (CIMMYT and IRRI are generally recognized as the epicenters of the Green Revolution of the 1960s and 1970s.) In 1998 these sixteen food and environmental research centers created "Future Harvest" to be their educational and public-relations arm. Future Harvest takes the view that world hunger can be overcome, and several billion more people fed in coming decades, only if scientific advances in agriculture—of the kind being made at its research centers—continue to raise crop yields. Such increases in agricultural yields, according to this view, promote economic growth and reduce poverty. They can also reduce the violent conflicts that arise when people lack food security. And high-yield agriculture can even spare the environment by reducing the necessity for clearing virgin forests and tapping into unspoiled natural resources. The CGIAR/Future Harvest position is well funded and highly influential but strongly opposed by many environmentalists, organic-food proponents, and antiglobalization groups.

Publications: A wide range of resources, all quite up to date, may be found at the Future Harvest website. These include press releases, news features, and opinion pieces. (The "ambassadors" who write the opinion pieces and make speeches for Future Harvest include Oscar Arias, Norman Borlaug, Jimmy Carter, Archbishop Desmond Tutu, and Grameen-founder Muhammad Yunus.) "Feeding Minds, Fighting Hunger" is an educational package at the website, geared to primary, intermediate, and secondary levels of students.

Jubilee USA Network
222 East Capitol Street, NE
Washington, DC 20003
(202) 783-3566
Fax: (202) 546-4468
coord@j2000usa.org

As the last millennium was drawing to a close in the mid-1990s, a movement sprang up in the United States and many other countries seeking a general forgiveness of the foreign debt of the world's poorest countries. It gained the support of many activists, clerics, and celebrities, and in fact the World Bank adopted a program of partial debt relief (the HIPC initiative) in 1996, which was expanded in 1999. But all was not forgiven; a great deal of poor-country debt was carried into the new millennium. The U.S. organization that had been campaigning for debt cancellation, Jubilee 2000/USA, decided to continue its work under a new name, Jubilee USA Network. Its goal remains the abolition of debt, especially (1) the international debt of abjectly poor nations, and (2) debt that is "odious," that is, debt that was incurred by governments that did not have any democratic legitimacy and used the funds for corrupt purposes. Further, the network seeks debt abolition without strings attached by outsiders ("positive conditionality," in the accepted jargon). Dozens of organizations belong to the network, including the AFL-CIO, American Friends Service Committee (Quakers), Church World Service, Episcopal Church USA, Friends of the Earth, and Oxfam America. Individual members of the network are urged to join in an "action of the month," such as meeting with their congressional representatives, holding regional meetings, or writing op-ed pieces for local newspapers.

Publications: There are online reports, at the website, dealing with many aspects of international borrowing, lending, and debt. Many originate with either the UK branch of Jubilee, Catholic Relief Services Review, or the Center for Economic and Policy Research. Not surprisingly, given the makeup of the network, there are also "worship resources" for "Jubilee congregations."

RESULTS
440 First Street, NW
Suite 450
Washington, DC 20001
(202) 783-7100
Fax: (202) 783-2818
results@results.org
http://www.results.org

For about twenty years, the citizens' advocacy group RESULTS has worked to "create the political will to end hunger and the worst aspects of poverty" at home and abroad. Its approach resembles that of Bread for the World, namely, to be knowledgeable and politically savvy enough to lobby Congress effectively in support of legislation helpful to the poor. There are some 100 community chapters of RESULTS around the United States, each dedicated to domestic *and* global issues of poverty. Every month, grassroots volunteers around the country join in a conference call to hear experts discuss current issues and strategies to pursue in the coming month, and then they contact their representatives in Washington (or their staff). They also interact regularly with the news media. In 1997 the RESULTS Educational Trust convened the first Microcredit Summit in Washington, D.C., which set a goal of reaching 100 million of the world's poorest families with microcredit by 2005. RESULTS has six international partner organizations, in Australia, Canada, Germany, Japan, Mexico, and the United Kingdom.

Publications: A donation of $35 secures membership in RESULTS and a yearly subscription to the *RESULTS Quarterly Magazine,* although the current issue can be read online at no cost. A limited number of brochures and books related to hunger activism are also available at the website.

Transparency International—USA
1112 16th Street, NW
Suite 500
Washington, DC 20036
(202) 296-7730
Fax: (202) 296-8125
tiusa@transparency-usa.org
http://www.transparency-usa.org

Transparency International is an NGO devoted solely to reducing *corruption*—a serious impediment to economic growth and to the effectiveness of international aid. Founded in 1993, TI has grown dramatically in ten years. Its present structure is twofold: about ninety national chapters with a central secretariat located in Berlin. Each chapter tackles bribery, graft, and other forms of corruption within its own national boundaries, and information is shared by all chapters through the secretariat. At the secretariat level, TI tries to promote multilateral conventions and then monitors compliance with them by governments and corporations. At the chapter level, TI works to reform governance systems and increase access to information; it does not attempt to identify or pursue individual wrongdoings, arguing that that is the work of journalists.

Publications: TI has placed sourcebooks, tool kits, "good practice" guides, issue papers, and other resources on its website; its annual *Global Corruption Report* may also be downloaded. The vast quantity of materials at the website is disheartening testimony to the size of the problem being addressed.

WIEGO
Carr Center for Human Rights
Kennedy School of Government
Harvard University
79 John F. Kennedy Street
Cambridge, MA 02138
(617) 495-7639
Fax: (617) 496-2828
wiego@ksg.harvard.edu
http://www.wiego.org

For understandable reasons, Women in Informal Employment: Globalizing and Organizing is more commonly known as WIEGO. Founded in 1997, its mission is to improve the lot of women working in the informal sector of the economy. A self-evident principle on which WIEGO proceeds is that women workers must *organize* themselves in order to take advantage of the economic opportunities—and avoid the negative consequences—of globalization. WIEGO is a coalition of individuals and institutions. Strongly represented in WIEGO is another acronymic organization, SEWA, or the Self-Employed Women's Association, founded in 1971 and based in Ahmedabad, India. SEWA is a trade union for women with jobs like selling vegetables, hand-rolling cigarettes, and recycling trash; SEWA provides them with health insurance, small loans, and other services. WIEGO, on the other hand, is mainly involved in research and agenda-setting. It commissions research on a wide array of topics in order to identify policy priorities. Sometimes it follows up by convening workshops for grassroots activists, scholars, and policymakers.

Publications: The fact sheets and research papers at the WIEGO website are fairly current and cover such topics as "street vendors and urban policies" and social protections for informal workers. There is no WIEGO newsletter or journal.

World Hunger Year
505 Eighth Ave., Suite 2100
New York, NY 10018-6582
(212) 629-8850
Fax: (212) 465-9274
WHY@worldhungeryear.org
http://www.worldhungeryear.org

World Hunger Year was cofounded in 1975 by folksinger and social activist Harry Chapin and radio talk-show host Bill Ayres to advance long-term solutions to hunger and poverty, both in the United States and abroad. It began holding an annual twenty-four-hour "Hungerthon" that same year, to raise funds—and awareness—in the battle against hunger. Chapin's wife, Sandy, was instrumental in the creation of the 1978 Presidential Commission on World Hunger. A 1981 car crash took the life of Harry Chapin, but his family continues to be actively involved in the organization he founded. In 1991, WHY began its International Program, which advocates for food security, fair trade, microcredit, and other pro-poor causes. WHY gained agency recognition from the United Nations and started being represented at world summits related to justice and poverty. In 1994, WHY inaugurated a new educational program called Kids Can Make a Difference (KIDS). Its goal is to help young people of middle- and high-school age learn about the root causes of hunger and poverty and possible ways to address those problems. (Further information about KIDS, its newsletter, and a teacher's guide may be obtained from http://www.kidscanmakeadifference.org.)

Publications: Succinct presentations of this organization's views on topics related to hunger can be found in *WHY Speaks* articles at the website; the pieces are undated and seem to be posted on no particular schedule.

8

Selected Print and Nonprint Resources

For the student or citizen who wants information about some aspect of global poverty, there is no shortage of material available, and more is appearing all the time. In this chapter you will find a listing of books, journals, websites, and videos dealing with poverty. The select, annotated listing of books might serve as a starting point for research, if you have access to a good public or school library. Books are listed in three categories: (1) monographs, (2) publications of the United Nations and World Bank, and (3) a few reports by other agencies or NGOs. All of these titles are currently in print and may be ordered from a company like Amazon.com. Several may also be downloaded from agency websites or simply read online. A brief listing of periodicals that regularly feature articles about global poverty and are not overly technical comes next, followed by a list of useful websites. Only periodicals and websites that were not identified in the previous chapter are given here, and again this is but a sampling. Following the links to other print resources and websites should allow the researcher to generate enough information for almost any research project or personal interest. In the nonprint category, our focus is on videos. With so many currently available from various sources, it is fairly easy to draw the line at videos produced in 1998 or later (with a few exceptions). All of those reviewed here can be purchased or rented; those in the Life series can even be previewed online, though in very brief segments. Prices should be double-checked before ordering.

Monographs

Bales, Kevin. *Disposable People: New Slavery in the Global Economy.* Berkeley: University of California Press, 1999. 298 pages. ISBN 0520224639.

It sounds sensationalistic, but this book is carefully researched and soberly reported by the world's leading authority on modern-day slavery. By Bales's estimate there are 27 million people in the world subject to "total control . . . by another for the purpose of economic exploitation"—his definition of slavery. He presents five case studies of slavery, in Thailand, Brazil, Pakistan, India, and Mauritania. Slaves can be found making bricks, making charcoal, delivering water, tilling fields, or working as prostitutes. Bales gives concrete suggestions for action that we can take against the new slavery. See also Bales's *New Slavery: A Reference Handbook (2000)* in the ABC-CLIO series of reference handbooks.

Beckmann, David, and Arthur R. Simon. *Grace at the Table: Ending Hunger in God's World.* Paulist Press, 1999. 219 pages. ISBN 0-809-13866-2.

This is an excellent resource for people of Christian faith who want to get involved in the effort to end hunger, at home and abroad. It is packed with relevant information, and its question-and-answer format makes it highly readable. Beckmann is the current president, and Simon the founder, of Bread for the World, a Christian antihunger advocacy group based in Washington, D.C. Both are Lutheran ministers. Beckmann spent fifteen years as an economist at the World Bank.

Bello, Walden. *De-Globalization: Ideas for a New World Economy.* London: Zed, 2003. 144 pages. ISBN 1-842-77305-4.

Bello is a long-time critic of the global economy as dominated by transnational corporations, the IMF, the WTO, and the World Bank. His radical agenda for a "de-globalized" world economy therefore begins with reduced powers for those institutions, but also looks to strong measures of income and land redistribution within the developing nations, less reliance on foreign lending, and a reduced emphasis on export production. Bello is founder and director of Focus on the Global South, a research institute based in Bangkok; he also teaches at the University of the Philippines.

Bhalla, Surjit S. *Imagine There's No Country: Poverty, Inequality, and Growth in the Era of Globalization.* Washington, DC: Institute for International Economics, 2002. 248 pages. ISBN 0-88132-348-9.

Indian economist Surjit Bhalla challenges the conventional wisdom regarding the impact of globalization on the world's poor. He finds that the developing nations have experienced faster economic growth than the wealthy nations from 1950 to 2000, with the result that their relative and absolute poverty has declined—substantially. Global income inequality has also been reduced. These assertions are more positive than the World Bank's assessment. Only time will tell who is right. The book is technically demanding but deserving of close study.

Davis, Mike. *Late Victorian Holocausts: El Niño Famines and the Making of the Third World.* New York: Verso, 2001. 464 pages. ISBN 1-85984-739-0.

In this fascinating and well-researched work of Marxian "political ecology," Davis boldly argues that the modern inequality between the Third World and the First had its origins in a set of subsistence crises occurring in the late nineteenth century. In India and China those crises were the result of climatological forces—droughts or floods induced by El Niño—combined with an exploitative colonial policy and the imperatives of an expanding world trade. The text is complemented by black and white photographs and maps.

De Rivero, Oswaldo. *The Myth of Development: The Non-Viable Economies of the 21st Century.* New York: Zed, 2001. 211 pages. ISBN 1-85649-949-9.

De Rivero, a former Peruvian diplomat, presents a grim if not brutal view of what globalization now offers the world's poor nations. Most of them are not proceeding along a development path that will take them to the level of the modern industrialized economies. As laggards in the "global Darwinian jungle," these "quasi nation-states" should opt for an agenda of survival rather than progress. This book belongs to a series, Global Issues in a Changing World, that are jointly issued by several publishing houses and NGOs.

De Soto, Hernando. *The Mystery of Capital: Why Capitalism Triumphs in the West and Fails Everywhere Else.* New York: Basic Books, 2003 (reissue). 288 pages. ISBN 0-465-01615-4.

This book offers an intriguing new approach to explaining the economic backwardness of many countries. De Soto, a Peruvian economist, observes that poor people everywhere have assets, sometimes quite sizable, which, in the absence of established systems of property registration, remain "dead capital." Only when land and other forms of property can be legally titled does the dead capital become living, with new possibilities for credit, insurance, transfer, and consolidation. Numerous examples are given of the cumbersome, multiyear process required to register assets like land or a house in Peru, Haiti, Egypt, and the Philippines. De Soto's promarket views are receiving substantial attention in some quarters.

De Waal, Alex. *Famine Crimes: Politics & the Disaster Relief Industry in Africa.* Bloomington: Indiana University Press, 1997. 238 pages. ISBN 0-253-21158-1.

Sadly, famines have continued to occur in recent times, although more often in Africa than in Asia, where the most famous famines of the past occurred. De Waal, who is codirector of Justice Africa and a long-time student of African affairs, draws some telling contrasts between Asia and Africa in terms of the origins and persistence of famines. Through case studies of famine occurrences in Somalia, Sudan, Ethiopia, and Zaire, de Waal traces the joint responsibility of African governments, international financial institutions, and—perhaps most appalling—relief agencies themselves, for the persistence of starvation in a resource-rich continent.

Dixon, John, and David Macarov (eds.). *Poverty: A Persistent Global Reality.* London: Routledge, 1998. 272 pages. ISBN 0-415-14682-8.

Dixon, a senior official with the FAO, and Macarov, an emeritus professor of social work at Hebrew University, invited academic experts to address poverty as experienced in ten nations around the world. In each case, there is an attempt to contextualize poverty socially and historically, suggest some of its leading causes, determine how extensive it is, and describe the antipoverty strategies and policies that have been tried. The countries are Australia, Canada, Hong Kong (now a part of China), Ireland, Malta, The Netherlands, the Philippines, the United Kingdom, the United States, and Zimbabwe.

Easterly, William. *The Elusive Quest for Growth: Economists' Adventures and Misadventures in the Tropics.* Cambridge: MIT Press, 2001.

This widely read and reviewed book goes after many of the sacred cows of development orthodoxy. Its author, until recently a senior adviser in the World Bank, shares the conviction of nearly everyone that economic growth is the key to lifting billions of people out of poverty. But he dismisses the standard prescriptions for growth—foreign aid, population programs, debt forgiveness, education investments—as largely ineffective, and he has plenty of anecdotes to support his skepticism. What Easterly favors instead is institutional change that will create the kinds of incentives needed to promote progrowth behavior throughout the economy. Particularly important is the elimination of corruption in the developing countries.

Ellwood, Wayne. *The No-Nonsense Guide to Globalization.* New York: Verso, 2001. 143 pages. ISBN 1-85984-336-0.

The No-Nonsense series includes titles on international migration, climate change, and various other topics, all published by *The New Internationalist*, a progressive magazine based in Toronto. This particular guide takes the approach that globalization has much potential for good that has so far not been realized, partly because of actions and inaction by the Bretton Woods "trio" of IMF, World Bank, and GATT. Poverty gets less direct attention here than the misdeeds of global corporate giants.

Farmer, Paul. *Pathologies of Power: Health, Human Rights, and the New War on the Poor.* Berkeley: University of California Press, 2003. 419 pages. ISBN 0-520-23550-9.

A tireless and dedicated physician who works with some of the world's most desperately ill populations, in Haiti, Mexico, and Russia, Paul Farmer is also an anthropologist and a human rights activist. In this book he makes the case that when poverty and fatal diseases are the end results of "structural violence," that is, extreme inequalities of wealth and power maintained by force, human rights are violated. An important and passionate book.

Farmer's previous book, *Infections and Inequalities: The Modern Plagues* (1999), covers some of the same ground and is now available in an updated paperback edition.

Action against Hunger. *The Geopolitics of Hunger 2000–01: Hunger & Power.* Boulder, CO: L. Rienner, 2001. 354 pages. ISBN 1-555-87901-2.

This book offers a broad overview of food-security issues around the world. It avoids overly general, Malthusian-type warnings and theories, putting the focus instead on case studies (Honduras, Sierra Leone, Congo, Rwanda, Kosovo, etc.) of food supply disruptions resulting either from natural causes or political manipulation. An entire section is devoted to ethical and practical issues pertaining to humanitarian food aid. Action Against Hunger, the NGO that produced this edited volume, has been working to combat hunger on five continents since 1979.

George, Vic, and Paul Wilding. *Globalization and Human Welfare.* New York: Palgrave, 2002. 231 pages. ISBN 0333915674.

Written in a textbooklike format by two British professors of social policy, this book explores the nature of globalization and then assesses its impact, first on the advanced industrial countries and then on the developing ones. It concludes with a stimulating discussion of what a "global social policy" might look like.

Hollander, Jack M. *The Real Environmental Crisis: Why Poverty, Not Affluence, Is the Environment's Number One Enemy.* Berkeley: University of California Press, 2003. 237 pages. ISBN 0-520-23788-9.

Conventional wisdom has it that the environment is just as threatened, if not *more* threatened, by global affluence as by global poverty. First World consumers are depicted as resource hogs who ravage and pollute their environment. Hollander, a professor emeritus at the University of California, disputes this view. It is the poor, he suggests, who most threaten the environment by the way in which their poverty forces them to live. Logically, then, it is global poverty we should be addressing most urgently if we are ever to reach environmental sustainability. Hollander's thesis is controversial, yet he has admirers across the ideological spectrum.

Isbister, John. *Promises Not Kept: The Betrayal of Social Change in the Third World.* 6th ed. Bloomfield, CT: Kumarian Press, 2003. 272 pages. ISBN 1-56549-173-4.

Isbister, an economics professor and long-serving (until 1999) provost at the University of California, Santa Cruz, has kept this widely used college textbook up-to-date. It covers the basic topics—the extent of world poverty, explanations of underdevelopment, imperialism, nationalism, economic development in its theoretical and historical dimensions—and adds two unique chapters on foreign policy and "justice in an age of globalization." End-of-chapter notes give valuable suggestions for further reading.

Landes, David S. *The Wealth and Poverty of Nations: Why Some Are So Rich and Some So Poor.* New York: W. W. Norton, 1999. 658 pages. ISBN 0-393-31888-5.

Few modern historians have been intrepid enough to tackle the great question, Why are some nations rich and others poor? David Landes, a Harvard history professor, accepts the challenge. This is a sweeping account of the way in which the West managed to achieve technological and industrial supremacy over other areas, China, for example, which at one time seemed more likely to prevail in the global sweepstakes. Landes courts controversy by laying heavy emphasis on cultural traits—thrift, patience, curiosity, tenacity—rather than impersonal factors like climate, geography, or natural resource endowments, as keys to Europe's success. His superbly written book will be provoking rebuttals for years to come.

Lappé, Frances Moore, Joseph Collins, and Peter Rosset. *World Hunger: Twelve Myths.* Oakland, CA: Food First Books, 1998. 224 pages. ISBN 0-802-13591-9.

This is a completely revised version of the little booklet that started out as *ten* myths in 1979. It presents anew the case that world hunger results not from an inadequate capacity to grow the food that is needed but from the export-promoting policies forced upon developing nations by the international financial institutions. More production of cash crops for export means fewer acres devoted to the traditional subsistence crops.

Mandle, Jay R. *Globalization and the Poor.* Cambridge: Cambridge University Press, 2003. 160 pages. ISBN 0-521-89352-6.

Mandle gives a balanced assessment of the gains and losses from globalization, both for the developing countries and for those already developed. In his view, the critics of expanding global trade underestimate its benefits, whether in reduced poverty rates in countries like China and India, or in lower prices that consumers are able to pay for goods imported from such countries. Defenders of globalization, on the other hand, tend to ignore the real costs associated with it. With the right "adjustments," Mandle believes, trade can be beneficial to both sides.

Marris, Robin. *Ending Poverty.* New York: Thames and Hudson, 1999. 120 pages. ISBN 0-500-28114-9.

Marris, an emeritus professor of economics at London University, analyzes the problem of world poverty using a First-Second-Third World framework. He relates poverty to population, education, the environment, and aid, and does not ignore the existence of poverty in the *developed* countries. Concisely written and surprisingly comprehensive for such a short book.

McGovern, George. *The Third Freedom: Ending Hunger in Our Time.* New York: Simon and Schuster, 2001. 173 pages. ISBN 0-684-85334-5.

As ambassador to the UN agencies on food and agriculture since 1998, former senator McGovern has deepened his already considerable knowledge of the world food situation. One result is this book, which proposes a universal school lunch program and a universal WIC program like that of the United States. (WIC provides supplemental nutrition for women, infants, and children.) McGovern makes a strong case that ending hunger is both ethical and practical.

Pinstrup-Andersen, Per, and Ebbe Schioler. *Seeds of Contention: World Hunger and the Global Controversy over GM Crops.* Baltimore: Johns Hopkins University Press, 2001. 164 pages. ISBN 0-801-86826-2.

Pinstrip-Andersen, until recently the director-general of the International Food Policy Research Institute, and Schioler, a research and development consultant, have written a relatively positive assessment of the potential of genetically modified crops to ease the plight of the world's hungry and malnourished. They do not claim that GM is a panacea but believe that there are ways to increase the benefits and reduce the risks of GM agriculture. Pinstrup-Andersen is the 2001 winner of the prestigious World Food Prize.

Sen, Amartya K. *Poverty and Famines: An Essay on Entitlement and Deprivation.* Oxford: Clarendon Press, 1981. 416 pages. ISBN 0-198-28463-2.

This study by the 1998 Nobel laureate in economics has become a modern classic. Where most people have seen famines simply as the result of crop failures or other disruptions of food supply, Sen sees them more broadly as the outcome of inadequate "entitlements" to food, that is, income or other claims. He applies this simple logic to several historical episodes, including the great Bengal famine of 1943 and the famine that hit the Sahel in 1968–1973.

Singer, Peter. *One World: The Ethics of Globalization.* New Haven, CT: Yale University Press, 2002. 208 pages. ISBN 0-30009-686-0.

For those who want to ponder the question of what obligation the rich nations have toward the poor ones, and what the implications are for international aid and trade, this is the place to start. Singer is one of the most renowned (and controversial) philosophers of our time, in part because he is such a clear, consistent thinker. His arguments always stimulate debate.

Soros, George. *George Soros on Globalization.* New York: Public Affairs, 2002. 191 pages. ISBN 1-58648-125-8.

Soros, the well-known international financier and philanthropist, celebrates the society-opening effects of globalization but not its systematic underprovision of social goods, such as education and health programs. Foreign aid, in his view, needs to be greatly increased. Because that has proved politically difficult, he proposes instead a complex yet intriguing IMF-based scheme that would lift aid levels substantially.

Stiglitz, Joseph E. *Globalization and Its Discontents.* New York: W. W. Norton, 2002. 282 pages. ISBN 0-393-05124-2.

This book, by a Nobel Prize–winning economist who held a top position in the World Bank, goes after the IMF, criticizing it for the harsh medicine it often prescribes to developing nations when they ask for assistance. That medicine is part of what is known as the "Washington Consensus." Stiglitz is a smart enough economist to know exactly when, where, and why the Washington Consensus guidelines work against the interests of people in the developing countries.

Streeten, Paul P. *Globalisation: Threat or Opportunity?* Herndon, VA: Copenhagen Business School Press, 2001. 190 pages. ISBN 8-76300-084-9.

Although not primarily about poverty, this book by a respected figure in international economic policy does deal with the issue of foreign aid, as well as with international migration and the "brain drain" phenomenon. Streeten is said to have influenced Robert McNamara to turn the World Bank toward a new focus on poverty reduction. His mastery of issues related to development and globalization is unsurpassed.

Vaux, Tony. *The Selfish Altruist: Relief Work in Famine and War.* Sterling, VA: Earthscan Publications, 2001. 230 pages. ISBN 1-85383-776-8.

This is a disarmingly honest account, by a long-time Oxfam employee, of the conflicting motives that drive an international relief worker. Chapters explore such themes as "impartiality and self-respect," "vulnerability and power," and "pride and principle." Each chapter is keyed to a particular relief effort with which Vaux was involved: Kosovo, Ethiopia, Sudan, Mozambique, Afghanistan, Somalia, and so on. Anyone considering a career in the international humanitarian field would do well to peruse this book.

Watkins, Kevin. *The Oxfam Education Report.* Oxford: Oxfam Publications, 2001. 403 pages. ISBN 0-85598-428-7.

For anyone who sees education as a development issue—and everyone should—this is an indispensable resource. Thoroughly researched and lucidly written, it covers a wide range of topics: international targets that have been set for education and the progress toward meeting them, the role of education in human development, inequalities in educational opportunity, structural barriers that limit access to education for poor children, and some innovative partnerships between national governments and NGOs. The first goal, Watkins makes clear, is to achieve universal primary education.

Whaites, Alan (ed). *Masters of Their Own Development? PRSPs and the Prospects for the Poor.* World Vision International, 2002. 137 pages. ISBN 1-887983-40-6.

World Vision, the world's largest privately funded Christian relief organization, undertook this review of the 1998 Poverty Reduction Strategy Papers (PRSP) approach by the IMF and World Bank to Third World lending. It looked specifically at the PRSP process as it played out in Senegal, Ethiopia, Cambodia, and several Latin American countries. The general conclusion: PRSPs may be a marginal improvement on what came before, but greater debt reductions are what is truly needed by these poor countries.

UN and World Bank Publications

United Nations Children's Fund (UNICEF). *The State of the World's Children 2003.* New York: UNICEF, 2002. 136 pages. ISBN 92-806-3784-5.

This annual report from UNICEF does not focus on poverty specifically—the 2002 report had a leadership theme; the 2003 report features child participation—but there is almost inevitably material that relates to child poverty. Consider this: Most babies this year and for the next half-century will be born in developing countries. They will grow up under conditions of material deprivation. The 2003 report, like its predecessors, has statistical tables at the back that document child welfare in a number of dimensions—health, nutrition, education, mortality, and so forth. The report may be read online at the UNICEF website.

United Nations Conference on Trade and Development (UNCTAD). *The Least Developed Countries Report 2002: Escaping the Poverty Trap.* New York: United Nations, 2002. 285 pages. ISBN 92-1112562-6.

This volume focuses on the forty-nine countries deemed by the United Nations to be "least developed" in the world on the basis of low per capita GDP, weak human assets, and high economic vulnerability. A common characteristic among the LDCs is a heavy reliance on primary commodity exports, as opposed to exports of manufactured goods. Also, the great majority of the LDCs are in sub-Saharan Africa. The "poverty trap" concept is exhaustively explored as it applies to these countries, and recommendations are made for policy changes within and toward them.

United Nations Development Programme (UNDP). *Human Development Report 2003.* New York: Oxford University Press, 2003. 367 pages. ISBN 0-195-21988-0.

Each year since 1990 the United Nations has issued an annual *Human Development Report* on a development-related theme. In 2002 the theme was *Deepening Democracy in a Fragmented World,* while in 2003 it was *Millennium Development Goals: A Compact among Nations to End Human Poverty.* The Human Development Index, which measures human welfare, country by country, on the basis of several noneconomic variables in addition to per capita GDP (an approach pioneered by economist Amartya Sen), is presented here. So, too, are the Human Poverty Index, the "gender empowerment measure," and a number of other statistical series descriptive of health conditions, education, demography, economic performance, and the structure of trade. Almost half the book consists of text, with graphs and boxed mini-essays on nearly every page.

United Nations Population Fund (UNFPA). *The State of World Population 2002: People, Poverty and Possibilities.* New York: United Nations, 2002. 84 pages. ISBN 0-89714-650-6.

It is an unfortunate fact of our global political economy that the poorest, least developed nations have the highest rates of fertility. (The richest nations are shrinking in population.) For many years, the UNFPA has been making the case that overly rapid population growth results from inequitable gender relations and inadequate family planning programs. When those two things are attended to—and when girls get educated—family sizes grow smaller and economic growth tends to speed up. The 2002 edition of the *State of World Population* connects these arguments to the Millennium Development Goals and to the urgency of the HIV/AIDS epidemic. The annual report has never been more compelling.

World Bank. *African Poverty at the Millennium: Causes, Complexities, and Challenges.* Washington, DC: The World Bank, 2001. 139 pages. ISBN 0-8213-4867-1.

This report, prepared by Howard White and Tony Killick, portrays a continent falling behind not only the developed world but also the rest of the developing world, as it struggles with problems of climate, disease, corruption, civil strife, gender inequality, and a wide range of other factors that contribute to poverty. Two central messages emerge: Economic growth is key to the reduction of poverty in Africa, and national policies must be set at the national level because each country is unique. Graphs, tables, and a 6-page bibliography complement the text.

World Bank. *Attacking Extreme Poverty: Learning from the Experience of the International Movement ATD Fourth World.* Washington, DC: The World Bank, 2001. 136 pages. ISBN 0-8213-4939-2.

This volume, edited by Quentin Wodon, is unlike most World Bank publications in that it contains no tables of data and no graphs. Instead, it offers seven essays on the moral, institutional, and legal aspects of *extreme* poverty. Emphasis is placed on respecting the dignity of the poorest and on making public and private institutions more responsive to their needs.

World Bank. *Globalization, Growth, and Poverty: Building an Inclusive World Economy.* Washington, DC: The World Bank, and New York: Oxford University Press, 2002. 174 pages. ISBN 082135048X.

This policy research report, written by two World Bank economists, Paul Collier and David Dollar, paints a fairly bright picture of the impact globalization since 1980 has had on world poverty. The developing countries opening themselves most to trade and investment—China, India, Vietnam, and Uganda, for example—have had growth rates in excess of what the *rich* countries experienced. With rising wage rates, their numbers of poor have declined. But 2 billion people live in developing countries that are engaging less actively in world trade. They experienced negative growth during the 1990s and risk becoming marginalized. The authors give a number of recommendations for broadening the positive impacts of globalization.

World Bank. *Voices of the Poor.* Series edited by Deepa Narayan.
New York: Oxford University Press, 2000–2002.
Vol. 1: Can Anyone Hear Us? 343 pages, ISBN 0195216016.
Vol. II: Crying out for Change. 314 pages, ISBN 0195216024.
Vol. III: From Many Lands. 509 pages, ISBN 0195216032.

The *Voices of the Poor* series is premised on the view that, as the
World Bank says, "The poor are the true poverty experts." Based
on interviews conducted individually or in groups with some
60,000 people in sixty countries on five continents, the voices in
these three volumes give real immediacy to the lived experience
of the world's poor. Each volume features chapters keyed to
particular topics (for example, the struggle for livelihoods) or, in
Vol. III, to the concerns of people in particular countries, and
then a concluding chapter reflective of what the poor have said.
Many passages are brief, eloquent, and moving. An Egyptian father says: "Lack of work worries me. My children were hungry,
and I told them the rice is cooking, until they fell asleep from
hunger." Nearly all of this material can be accessed at the World
Bank's website.

World Bank. *World Development Indicators 2003.* Washington,
DC: The World Bank, 2003. 416 pages. ISBN 0821354221.

Published annually, the *WDI* is an indispensable compendium of
economic and social statistics for most countries in the world.
There are six sections in the 2003 edition: World View, People,
Environment, Economy, States and Markets, and Global Links.
Each section opens with a short essay, often referring back to a
recent international goal-setting conference, and then presents a
series of statistical tables. The World View section documents the
progress nations are making, or not making, toward meeting the
Millennium Development Goals, as set in 2000. While the tables
throughout are presented alphabetically by country, most have a
short summary table appended with group results for "low income" countries, "middle income" countries, and "high income"
countries, and some geographical breakdowns within those categories. The sheer magnitude of information contained in this
single volume is staggering: 600 tables for 152 countries. There is
a CD-ROM version of *WDI* available from the World Bank at con-
siderably higher cost. Its coverage is more extensive, with more
variables, more countries covered, and data going back to 1960;
it also has a custom-graphing feature. An online subscription to

the *WDI* database is also available, at individual ($100 per year) and institutional rates.

World Bank. *World Development Report 2003: Sustainable Development in a Dynamic World: Transforming Institutions, Growth, and Quality of Life.* New York: Oxford University Press, 2002. 271 pages. ISBN 0821351508.

Each year the World Bank issues a *World Development Report* of about 300 pages on a particular theme, such as health, infrastructure, labor, or the transition economies. For 2003 the theme is sustainable development. (A draft version of the report was posted on the Internet ahead of the 2002 Johannesburg summit on the same topic.) This volume tackles the question of how it will be possible simultaneously to reduce poverty for hundreds of millions in the developing world while preserving the quality of the environment globally as we move through the first half of this century. Some difficult issues of distribution, conflict, and competing objectives are raised. Toward the back of this and all the *Development Reports* is an abbreviated set of tables (less comprehensive than the *World Development Indicators*) covering the basic economic, demographic, and educational statistics for each country. In 2004 the topic of the *Development Report* will be "making services work for the poor." Still in print is the valuable 2000/2001 report on the theme *Attacking Poverty.*

Other Agency/NGO Reports

Bread for the World. *Agriculture in the Global Economy: Hunger 2003.* Washington, DC: Bread for the World Institute, 2003. 164 pages. ISBN 1-884361-11-0.

In its thirteenth annual report, Bread for the World highlights the disconnect between rich-nation pledges to help cut global poverty in half by 2015 and continued massive subsidies by those same nations to their own farmers. The subsidies effectively harm and discourage growers in the developing world who must compete against a stacked deck. Current subsidies amount to more than $300 billion, or *six* times the amount of official development assistance flowing to the developing countries. The report further argues that there are more effective ways to improve the well-being of rural America than to continue the crop subsidies.

Transparency International. *Global Corruption Report 2003.* London: Profile Books Limited, 2003. 352 pages. ISBN 1861974760.

Journalists, economists, and other observers of the development process now agree that corruption is among the worst enemies of economic progress, and that combating poverty goes hand in hand with combating corruption. Since its founding in 1983, Transparency International has been the world's leading NGO dedicated to fighting corruption. In 2001 they began publishing their annual *Global Corruption Report,* a handy reference work for anyone interested in the issue. The *GCR* ranks every country by a "Corruption Perceptions Index" (Finland is seen as the least corrupt, Bangladesh as the most), and it reports on regional trends. It identifies what actions are being taken, and what challenges remain.

World Health Organization. *The World Health Report 2002: Reducing Risks, Promoting Healthy Life.* Geneva: World Health Organization. 250 pages. ISBN 9241562072.

The 2002 *World Health Report,* the result of a huge research effort by WHO, suggests that worldwide life expectancy could be increased by five to ten years if people and governments took the right steps to reduce health risks. Gro Brundtland, the director-general of WHO until her term ended in mid-2003, pursued a major antitobacco initiative. Smoking is a highly unhealthful behavior that shortens lives in both the developed and developing nations. But iron deficiency, unsafe water, and underweight are problems more specific to *poor* countries, and unsafe sex is also taking a higher toll there.

Journals

Africa Recovery. This quarterly magazine, from the UN Department of Public Information, has readable articles about individual countries as well as the continent as a whole, with a main focus on development issues. Subscription: $20. Web address: http://www.africarecovery.org.

Development Policy Review. One of the top journals in the field of development, *DPR* is published bimonthly for the Overseas Development Institute, the leading British "think tank" on development issues. Articles are scholarly—suitable for college level and higher. Subscription: $53. Web address: http://www. odi.org.uk/publications/dpr.

developments: The International Development Magazine. This quarterly magazine is produced by the UK Department for International Development (DFID). Each issue opens with a section of three or four articles devoted to a particular development challenge. Accessible to students from high-school age through college. Subscription: free. Web address: http://www.developments. org.uk.

Finance & Development. Published quarterly by the IMF, this magazine deals with a number of issues that connect to poverty and development, including inflation and deflation, financial crises, and trade policy. Written to an upper-level high school, college, and general audience.

Subscription: $20 (air mail) or free (surface mail or online). Web address: http://www.imf.org/external/pubs/ft/fandd/fdinfo. htm#subscribe.

Forced Migration Review. Sometimes a cause and sometimes an effect of poverty, forced migration is a humanitarian crisis of our time. *FMR* is the in-house journal of the Refugee Studies Centre at Oxford University. Articles are highly readable and informative. Subscription: $25. Web address: http://www.fmreview. org.

Foreign Affairs. The venerable bimonthly journal of the Council on Foreign Relations frequently has articles touching upon world poverty. For example, the March–April 2003 issue carried G. Sperling and T. Hart, "A Better Way to Fight Global Poverty: Broadening the Millennium Challenge Account." Subscription: $32. Web address: http://www.foreignaffairs.org.

Gender and Development. Everyone agrees that gender is a key dimension of development theory and policy, and this journal, published by Oxfam GB, devotes itself to that proposition with articles that are accessible (to college-level readers), book reviews, interviews, and conference information. Subscription: $71. Web address: http://www.tandf.co.uk/journals/carfax/13552074.html.

Hunger Notes. Covering the hunger issue as seen both in the United States and abroad, this "online publication" from the non-profit World Hunger Education Service is updated irregularly. It features numerous links to other sites with information on poverty, hunger, and malnutrition, as well as to press articles (mainly in the *Washington Post*) on these topics. Subscription: free. Web address: http://www.worldhunger.org.

id21 insights. Funded by Great Britain's DFID but written to a higher level than *developments* (see above), this quarterly publication builds each issue around a theme—for example, globalization and employment, urban poverty, or educational gender gaps—and supports it with articles summarizing research done recently at UK institutions. Suitable for college and professional readers. Subscription: free. Web address: http://www. id21. org/insights.

Journal of Development Studies. This British-based academic journal has been at the forefront of development studies since its inception in 1964. Articles tend to be interdisciplinary and at the cutting edge of their subject. Suitable for college and professional readers. Subscription: $90. Web address: http://www. frankcass. com/jnls/jds.htm.

Oxford Development Studies. Formerly *Oxford Agrarian Studies,* this journal carries academic articles from a variety of disciplines, such as economics, history, anthropology, and sociology. Many take a critical stance toward accepted development theories and policies. Suitable for college and professional readers. Subscription: $79. Web address: http://www.tandf.co.uk/journals/car-fax/13600818.html.

Population and Development Review. For those who see connections between population growth and poverty—in a tradition that traces back to Malthus in the eighteenth century—this is the best journal for staying updated on the latest evidence one way or the other. College level. Subscription: $40. Web address: http:// www.popcouncil.org/pdr/default.asp.

Websites

http://apps.fao.org/default.htm. For the most comprehensive data relating to world food production and trade, the website maintained by the Food and Agriculture Organization of the United Nations is acknowledged to be the best. A CD-ROM version of the data series can also be obtained (for $600).

http://www.adb.org/Poverty/Forum/default.htm. The Asian Development Bank held its first international "poverty forum" in 2001, and this website was one outcome. (The next will be held in 2004.) Its many links to data, papers, and presentations make this site a strong foundation for research on Asian poverty.

http://www.chronicpoverty.org/index.html. The Chronic Poverty Research Centre was established in 2000 to pull together the resources of universities, research institutes, and NGOs in Britain to study, and find solutions for, chronic poverty. Most of the papers presented at an international conference on this topic in spring, 2003, are available online. One section of this impressive website is devoted to chronic *child* poverty.

http://www.eldis.org/. This extraordinarily useful "gateway to development information," with links to databases, key documents, e-mail news services, and other resources, would be a logical starting point for a research project on any aspect of world poverty. It is core-funded by the development agencies of Norway, Denmark, and Sweden.

http://www.feedingminds.org/default.htm. "Feeding minds, fighting hunger" calls itself an international classroom for exploring issues of malnutrition and food insecurity, with project ideas for students from primary through secondary school level. It is sponsored by the FAO.

http://www.globalisation.gov.uk/. In December 2000, Britain's government issued a widely discussed white paper entitled "Eliminating World Poverty: Making Globalisation Work for the Poor." The entire paper can be downloaded from this website, along with all of the background papers and various other supporting materials.

http://www.itdg.org/. In 1966, E. F. Schumacher published what was to become a highly influential tract, *Small Is Beautiful*, advocating a shift away from megascale, environmentally destructive technologies. This website of the Intermediate Technology Development Group, based in Britain, shows how Schumacher's belief in the poverty-reducing power of small-scale technologies continues to be heeded.

http://www.paris21.org/betterworld/home.htm. This website, officially titled "2000: A Better World for All," provides charts, tables, and text to summarize the Millennium Development Goals, as established in the fall of 2000. A good starting point for research on the MDGs.

http://www.propoortourism.org.uk/. This interesting British website is devoted to the idea and practice of tourism that is "pro-poor"—that is, makes the maximum contribution to reducing poverty in destination countries.

http://www.reliefweb.int. Sponsored by the UN Office for the Coordination of Humanitarian Affairs (OCHA), this site is a resource for international relief workers and policy-makers. Go to it for current information on natural disasters and what are called "complex" (human-caused) emergencies around the world.

http://www.thehungersite.com. Commercially sponsored, this website provides you with a chance to "give free food" just by clicking your mouse. A world map shows which countries are most likely to have people starving (every three seconds a country goes black—emblematic of the latest death).

http://www.worldbank.org/poverty. In any given year, the World Bank probably issues more words and numbers about global poverty than any other organization. "PovertyNet" is your road map to that mountain of information. Much more than merely data, the site offers definitions, methods of calculation, readings, and Q and A on poverty and inequality. Well organized and indispensable.

Videos

For the ordinary person living in a rich country, world poverty can seem a very remote problem—something one reads about in a weekly news magazine or glimpses in a brief TV news segment. The mainstream media do not pay much attention to *domestic* poverty, much less to poverty in dusty foreign locales, making exceptions only for major conflicts, famines, and highly destructive natural disasters. Fortunately, though, anyone who really wants to know something about the problems and prospects of the world's poorest inhabitants has a ready resource: educational videos. The term may sound vaguely medicinal, but in fact the quality of most of the videos listed below is so high that viewers with any curiosity at all about the rest of the world should be drawn in and given something to ponder. Most of these videos would enliven a community discussion group or a classroom session, and rental fees are generally reasonable.

A welcome recent development is the "Life" series of videos produced by the Television Trust for the Environment (TVE), a nonprofit film-producing company begun in 1984 and headquartered in the United Kingdom. Additional funding for the series comes from several European governments, some private foundations, the ILO, the United Nations, the European Commission, and the World Health Organization. These are award-winning productions, generally 24 to 27 minutes long, that have all been shown on BBC World. Each focuses on a particular aspect of globalization as it affects poverty and social development in poor regions of the world. For each individual video there is additional information and a full-text transcript available online at http://www.tve.org/lifeonline/archive, opening up possibilities for further engaging students who have Internet access. Three separate series have been produced so far, and all remain available for rental or purchase—a total of sixty-two videos! The U.S. distributor is Bullfrog Films. Every video listed below with Bullfrog as the source is in the "Life" series.

Note: A few of the films are available in DVD format. When that is the case, the purchase price is $20 to $30 higher than for the video version.

Because They're Worth It
Date: 2000
Length: 24 minutes
Price: $195 (purchase), $45 (rental)
Source: Bullfrog Films
P.O. Box 149
Oley, PA 19547
(800) 543-3764
http://www.bullfrogfilms.com

The microcredit idea first put forward by Muhammad Yunus, the Bangladeshi economist, has taken hold around the globe. This video looks at its application to China—specifically, to a remote province near the mountainous border with Burma. Poor women are taking out loans to purchase pigs, set up greenhouses for raising vegetables, open small restaurants, and so forth. The Social Development Program for Poor Areas, or SPPA, provides benefits beyond the financial: Women learn from each other, gain status within their families, and acquire better health and diet information. And 90 percent of the loans are repaid. Suitable for grades 7 to 12, college, and adults.

Bolivian Blues
Date: 2000
Length: 24 minutes
Price: $195 (purchase), $45 (rental)
Source: Bullfrog Films
P.O. Box 149
Oley, PA 19547
(800) 543-3764
http://www.bullfrogfilms.com

If any country needs a new approach to development, it is Bolivia. Two-thirds of its people live on less than $1 a day; one-fifth of Bolivian children are malnourished. This video looks at the new dialogue-based approach to national development adopted in 1997 by the government of Bolivia, which coincided with the World Bank's introduction of its "comprehensive development framework," or CDF, in that country. Mixed results are reported in education, provision of water, and replacement of coca-growing by substitute crops. Some tough questions the video seems to raise are these: How can an economy with severe geographic liabilities (Bolivia is landlocked) make economic headway? How can deep-rooted structures of inequality be tackled? And how do you make democracy effective at all levels? Suitable for grades 9 to 12, college, and adults.

City Life
Date: 2001
Length: 26 minutes
Price: $195 (purchase), $45 (rental)
Source: Bullfrog Films
P.O. Box 149
Oley, PA 19547
(800) 543-3764
http://www.bullfrogfilms.com

More and more of the world's people—and its poor—are urban dwellers. "City Life" gives an overview of the social and environmental challenges faced by "megacities" such as Brazil's Sao Paolo. A fifty-five-year-old psychiatrist and mother of three, Marta Suplicy, is the dynamic new mayor of that city. She has a clear sense of the problems that need to be addressed and is filmed visiting a women's shelter, a *favela* (shantytown), a school, and a hospital, everywhere displaying the qualities of optimism and empathy that have made her the "people's mayor." A theme of the video is the stark contrast between the "glamour zone," where those integrated into the global economy live and work, and the "war zone," where the isolated and excluded feel like refugees in their own country. Suitable for grades 7 to 12, college, and adults.

Coat of Many Countries
Date: 2000
Length: 54 minutes
Price: $395 (purchase), $75 (rental)
Source: Filmakers Library
124 East 40th Street, Suite 901
New York, NY 10016
(212) 808-4980
http://www.filmakers.com

This jaunty video is a sort of globalization version of "This is the house that Jack built"—tracing all the steps in the production of a men's suit, from the raising of Australian sheep for wool to the stitching together of the suit components in a provincial Russian factory. Stops along the way include a textile factory in the Punjab of India, where workers earn wages of $2.75 per day, a Chinese factory where women sew shoulder pads, a South Korean plant where suit linings are manufactured, a Canadian button producer in Montreal, and Hamburg, Germany, where all the parts of the suit are gathered for trucking eastward into the low-wage remnants of the Soviet empire. The message conveyed in the video—graphically and effectively—is that globalization means a relentless push to find lower costs of production, wherever they may be. Whether this will lift wages (and standards of living) is the big question. As the affable Canadian menswear dealer puts it, "Are we exploiting or helping the labor market" in those far-off corners of the "global village" where workers are getting $2 to $3 a day to turn out suit components for the North American market? Suitable for audiences from high-school age upward.

The Debt Police
Date: 2000
Length: 24 minutes
Price: $195 (purchase), $45 (rental)
Source: Bullfrog Films
P.O. Box 149
Oley, PA 19547
(800) 543-3764
http://www.bullfrogfilms.com

Will debt relief for developing countries, as urged by the Jubilee 2000 movement and many others, really bring tangible benefits to the poor? That is the question raised in this well-focused video, with Uganda as the case study. The problem, of course, is that nothing can guarantee that debt reductions will not find their way straight into the pockets—or Swiss bank accounts—of corrupt government officials. The video spotlights an organization, Uganda Debt Network, that is trying to monitor and fight corruption, as well as the newly created Poverty Action Fund, into which savings from debt relief are funneled for use in Ugandan antipoverty efforts. A professor at Johns Hopkins explicitly questions whether any of this really works; he argues that there is no substitute for economic and civil liberties. Suitable for grades 7 to 12, college, and adults.

Educating Lucia
Date: 2000
Length: 24 minutes
Price: $195 (purchase), $45 (rental)
Source: Bullfrog Films
P.O. Box 149
Oley, PA 19547
(800) 543-3764
http://www.bullfrogfilms.com

Who can doubt that children who get no chance to complete a primary school education will have an uphill struggle to overcome poverty as adults? This video drives the message home by focusing on the situation in Africa. Lucia, a twelve-year-old girl in Zimbabwe, attends a primary school and has hopes of going on to secondary school as well. But Lucia and her two sisters are AIDS orphans, and their grandmother cannot afford to send more than one of them to school. In Benin, the video introduces us to two more girls, both left with relatives because their families could not afford to raise them. One is lucky enough to go to school, the other is not. Key messages here: Girls have less opportunity for schooling than boys (by parental choice); many African families make huge sacrifices to give their children an education; and the children themselves know the difference school can make to their future. Suitable for grades 7 to 12, college, and adults.

A Fistful of Rice
Date: 2001
Length: 27 minutes
Price: $195 (purchase), $45 (rental)
Source: Bullfrog Films
P.O. Box 149
Oley, PA 19547
(800) 543-3764
http://www.bullfrogfilms.com

Children throughout the developing world are at risk for protein energy malnutrition, or PEM. A poor diet and infection together lead to PEM, which in turn can lead to stunting, slow physical development, poor mental development, or death. This video considers the case of Nepal, a country in which nine in ten children show some form of malnutrition. Girls are more likely to suffer PEM than boys because often, under prevailing customs, they get less food and care. Much of the problem is rooted in early marriage and childbearing. Women who are under twenty when they give birth are likely to produce small, sickly babies, yet early marriage is very common in Nepal. The picture is fairly grim and does not appear to be improving. (Political instability makes matters worse.) Suitable for college and adult audiences.

Free Trade Slaves
Date: 1999
Length: 56 minutes
Price: $89.95
Source: Films for the Humanities & Sciences
P.O. Box 2053
Princeton, NJ 08543-2053
(800) 257-5126
Fax: (609) 275-3767

The title sounds overheated, but the situations described in this video are appalling. Free trade zones have been cropping up all over the world since the 1960s, for a simple reason: They bring in foreign investment and create jobs in low-income countries. Businesses locating in these zones want to pay the "bottom dollar" in wages, they want no labor unions, and they often operate under the most lax of environmental rules. Big U.S. corporations are involved, as well as many Asian-based companies. The video looks at the *maquiladoras* along the U.S.-Mexican border, similar zones in El Salvador and Sri Lanka, and a massive new free trade zone being built in northern Morocco. The women interviewed tell wrenching stories of forced labor, intimidation, and birth defects tied to pollution from manufacturing plants. Viewers are challenged to make a connection between the brand-name clothes they buy in the store at a low price and the working conditions under which those items were produced. Hard-hitting and thought-provoking. Suitable for high school and above.

Geraldo Off-Line
Date: 2000
Length: 23 minutes
Price: $195 (purchase), $45 (rental)
Source: Bullfrog Films
P.O. Box 149

Oley, PA 19547
(800) 543-3764
http://www.bullfrogfilms.com

Some might call it gimmicky, but the approach this video takes to making sense of job loss in a globalized economy does capture one's attention. Geraldo Da Souza has been employed at a Ford factory in Brazil for six years when he suddenly gets laid off, along with 2,000 other workers. He can't figure out why, but a U.S. investigative journalist, Jon Alpert, agrees to travel far and wide, interviewing people who might shed light on why folks like Geraldo lose their jobs. The gimmick is that the two will periodically communicate by Internet to share their thoughts and experiences. That is the concept (or gimmick), and it works well. The answer to why Geraldo got laid off is found in the 1997 Asian and 1998 Russian financial crises, which triggered capital flight out of emerging markets like Brazil and forced the Brazilian government to hike interest rates. That in turn reduced demand for Ford cars and, indirectly, Ford workers like Geraldo. Sound economics is rarely packaged this engagingly. Suitable for grades 9 to 12, college, and adults.

The Global Dimension: The Risks of Globalization
Date: 2000
Length: 25 minutes
Price: $129.95
Source: Films for the Humanities & Sciences
P.O. Box 2053
Princeton, NJ 08543-2053
(800) 257-5126
Fax: (609) 275-3767

This video does not deliver on its title—it barely scratches the surface of the "risks of globalization"—but how *could* it, in less than half an hour? What it does convey are a couple of important messages: that developing countries must strive to keep up with advancing technology, and that they must be open to new forms of cooperation with the industrialized countries, in trade, business, and education. In Quito, Ecuador, we see a program sponsored by a Canadian NGO that allows street children to spend one day a week becoming computer-literate. Another innovative program, called "Tools for Development," arranges for Canadian companies to donate used machinery to microentrepreneurs in

Peru. And in Costa Rica, coffee growers form cooperatives to grow and sell high-quality, fair-trade coffee beans to a firm in Germany. Suitable for high school level and above.

Lines in the Dust
Date: 2001
Length: 27 minutes
Price: $195 (purchase), $45 (rental)
Source: Bullfrog Films
P.O. Box 149
Oley, PA 19547
(800) 543-3764
http://www.bullfrogfilms.com

This film explains how an innovative approach to literacy called REFLECT can put adults on the path to literacy and numeracy while also getting them to rethink age-old gender roles. REFLECT uses no textbooks, no printed materials of any kind, only space on the ground where participants can draw grids with a stick and place tokens that stand for men, women, and working activities. In a northern Ghana village, we see men and women participating in the program together—an unusual thing for a Muslim community. Women learn how to speak in public for the first time. Men discover that they can share in the heavy labors traditionally performed by women without losing status. When the scene shifts to eastern India, we find the REFLECT program again having the effect of giving women more confidence and more of a voice in decision-making. A whole community finds itself empowered by the program to resist the privatization of their communal resources. It is remarkable that such a short film can raise so many issues—gender, power, the role of the market, indigenous rights—without ever becoming dry or academic. Suitable for grades 7–12, college, and adults.

Lost Generations
Date: 2000
Length: 24 minutes
Price: $195 (purchase), $45 (rental)
Source: Bullfrog Films
P.O. Box 149
Oley, PA 19547
(800) 543-3764
http://www.bullfrogfilms.com

Videos on world poverty seem to fall into one of two categories, either problems-with-solutions or just *problems*. This video belongs to the latter category. The problem of early marriage for women (girls) is clearly identified and documented. The country in focus is India. And the most obvious solution to the problem— a change in the law and social customs toward a later age at marriage—is not going to come soon enough for millions of Indian girls ("lost generations"). Not only are these child brides denied the chance to develop to their full potential, but they face heightened mortality risks in bearing children at a young age. Since they are often poor and undernourished, there is a high risk that their babies will be underweight. It's a grim situation, but at http://www.tve.org/lifeonline, the website for videos in the TVE-produced "Life" series, one can find plenty of information that leads in the direction of progress on this issue. Suitable for grades 9 to 12, college, and adults.

The Miller's Tale: Bread Is Life
Date: 2001
Length: 27 minutes
Price: $195 (purchase), $45 (rental)
Source: Bullfrog Films
P.O. Box 149
Oley, PA 19547
(800) 543-3764
http://www.bullfrogfilms.com

Iron deficiency anemia affects more than 3 billion people worldwide, mainly in poor countries and disproportionately in the Middle East. It is especially hard on children, who do not develop as they should, either physically or mentally, and on women. Rates of maternal mortality, miscarriage, and stillbirth are much higher for anemic women. This film describes the problem and a solution now being adopted in Egypt and Yemen: fortification of flour. There are social and cultural problems to be overcome— bread is a sacred food, not to be tampered with lightly—yet something that costs only $2 per person per lifetime and brings such crucial health benefits certainly looks like a step in the right direction. Suitable for grades 7–12, college, adults.

My Mother Built This House
Date: 2001
Length: 27 minutes

Price: $195 (purchase), $45 (rental)
Source: Bullfrog Films
P.O. Box 149
Oley, PA 19547
(800) 543-3764
http://www.bullfrogfilms.com

Poverty around the world is usually assessed in terms of per capita income, malnutrition, and other such indices. Yet for the poor themselves nothing is more critical on a day-to-day basis than the quality of their *housing*—whether they have a roof over their head (that doesn't leak), indoor plumbing, and a sense of personal security. In South Africa, as virtually everywhere in the Third World, millions on the urban outskirts live in shantytowns. This video looks at the work the Homeless People's Federation is doing in providing decent housing for those who have been living in shacks. The federation gives its members, mainly women, a place to save, to borrow, to organize with others, and to obtain government funding—and it helps them put "sweat equity" into housing that transforms the quality of their lives. As with the other videos in the "City Life" series, there is a webpage available with much additional information on this topic. Suitable for grades 7 to 12, college, and adults.

Sixteen Decisions
Date: 2000
Length: 59 minutes
Price: $250 (purchase), $95 (rental)
Source: University of California Extension
Center for Media and Independent Learning
1995 University Ave.
Berkeley, CA 94720
(510) 642-0460
http://ucmedia.berkeley.edu

From its title, this video promises to be about the Grameen Bank, a Bangladesh microlending institution that has become world renowned and much imitated. The women who borrow small sums from Grameen—and more than nine out of ten borrowers *are* women—recite the "sixteen decisions" at each weekly meeting of their borrowing group. These decisions, or resolutions, have to do with helping one another, keeping up their houses, building and using pit latrines, keeping their family sizes small, getting their children educated, and so on. But the video is not primarily about the Grameen concept, or even the sixteen decisions. Rather, it is a kind of meditation on what it means to be poor, young, and female in a country that places a limited value on women. Viewers will not soon forget Selena, the eighteen-year-old subject of the film, for whom the Grameen Bank offers a way not only to improve her family's financial status but also to expand her social network and lift her self-esteem. Muhammad Yunus, the genial founder of Grameen, offers some on-camera insights. Suitable for college and adult audiences.

Stop the Traffick
Date: 2001
Length: 27 minutes
Price: $195 (purchase), $45 (rental)
Source: Bullfrog Films
P.O. Box 149
Oley, PA 19547
(800) 543-3764
http://www.bullfrogfilms.com

One of the most wrenching features of poverty in many parts of the world is trafficking in children, the subject of this film. Rural parents are often so impoverished, with so many children to support, that they are willing to "sell" (or take out a "loan" on) a daughter in the belief that she will become a household servant in the city—when in fact she will be forced to become a prostitute, or "sex worker." That is the case with the twelve-year-old Cambodian child at the center of this film. The facts and figures relating to the Cambodian situation are presented in a matter-of-fact tone that suggests journalistic objectivity even as it heightens the viewer's outrage. The film shows how the government is making efforts, along with the ILO and other groups, to halt this trade and to rescue and rehabilitate its victims. Suitable for college level and adults.

These Girls Are Missing
Date: 1996
Length: 60 minutes
Price: $295 (purchase), $75 (rental)
Source: Filmakers Library
124 East 40th Street, Suite 901
New York, NY 10016

(212) 808-4980
http://www.filmakers.com

Subtitled "The Gender Gap in Africa's Schools," this video asks
why it is that girls are seen in much lower numbers than boys in
the classrooms of rural Africa. There is no simple answer, but
much of the explanation lies in traditional attitudes toward gender and resistance to anything that would alter traditional gender
roles. Some of these attitudes are: Boys are smarter; girls act su-
perior when they go to school, they get pregnant at school, they
never finish school, they should be more at home to do household
chores, and when educated they refuse to marry. Featuring several school-age girls in Malawi and Guinea, the video proceeds at
a leisurely pace, with only the lightest narration. It offers no easy
answers, only some very good questions. Suitable for college and
adult audiences.

T-shirt Travels
Date: 2001
Length: 56 minutes
Price: $350 (purchase), $75 (rental)
Source: Filmakers Library
124 East 40th Street, Suite 901
New York, NY 10016
(212) 808-4980
http://www.filmakers.com

The subtitle of this video reads: "The Story of Second-Hand
Clothes and Third World Debt." It turns out that some important
economic truths about Africa can be illuminated through looking
at the flow of second-hand U.S. clothing into African markets.
The video focuses on a young man, Luka, whose buying and selling of such clothes give him enough profit to support his mother,
siblings, and cousins in a remote Zambian town—but barely.
What we also learn is that Zambia once had a thriving textile and
clothing industry of its own that fell victim to free-trade policies
imposed on the country by the IMF in the 1970s. Textile companies were bankrupted and thousands of workers were thrown out
of work. The video offers a fairly simplistic and one-sided view of
how Zambia got into its current economic troubles (with not a
word about corruption) and leaves the viewer wondering what
policy changes could offer the country a less bleak future than it
now faces. A lively discussion could be provoked by asking the

audience, after the closing credits, "Okay, now what?" Suitable for college classes and adults.

Up at Dawn
Date: 2001
Length: 50 minutes
Price: $295 (purchase), $75 (rental)
Source: Filmakers Library
124 East 40th Street, Suite 901
New York, NY 10016
(212) 808-4980
http://www.filmakers.com

Child labor is a common phenomenon in the developing world, one that is coming under increasing scrutiny in international forums. This video, subtitled "The Working Children of Egypt," offers some insight into the problem. Two million school-age children in Egypt work, and they represent 11 percent of the country's labor force. Here they are seen in several institutional settings in which they appear to be well treated and contented, though clearly scrubbed and coached for the camera. One of the handicaps under which the filmmakers labored was that a government "minder" accompanied them at all times, in Cairo and outside the city, thus limiting their access to the full range of child labor activities. In the end, "Up at Dawn" is as much about cross-cultural and political sensitivities as it is about child labor in the Third World. Suitable for high school, college, and adult audiences.

The Women's Bank of Bangladesh
Date: 1996
Length: 47 minutes
Price: $149.95
Source: Films for the Humanities & Sciences
P.O. Box 2053
Princeton, NJ 08543-2053
(800) 257-5126
Fax: (609) 275-3767

This is one of the best videos available on the topic of the Grameen Bank. Grameen is Professor Muhammad Yunus's powerful innovation whereby very poor, landless Bangladeshi women have been able to borrow small sums of money at interest rates well below what moneylenders would charge. The funds enable them to purchase needed raw materials for craft work, or chickens whose eggs can be sold, or bulk rice that can be resold in smaller amounts, and so forth. The video features half a dozen women telling their stories of what Grameen has done for them. It has given them a path out of poverty but also out of the isolation that many women experience in traditional societies. There is no denying the fact that more conservative versions of Islam are challenged, even threatened, by Grameen, and those objections are freely voiced here. (A moneylender is also given the opportunity to vent his anger at the way in which his former customers have deserted him for Grameen, with its lower interest charges.) There is no formal narration beyond Professor Yunus expounding the basic facts about Grameen. Suitable for high school, college, and adults.

Women in the Struggle against Poverty
Date: 1995
Length: 29 minutes
Price: $149.95 (purchase), $75 (rental)
Source: Films for the Humanities & Sciences
P.O. Box 2053
Princeton, NJ 08543-2053
(800) 257-5126
Fax: (609) 275-3767

This is a very positive introduction to the idea of women in traditional societies taking the initiative to start businesses, find new gender roles, and improve their families' prospects. It focuses on Sanwara Begum, a woman in rural Bangladesh who tells us that she was once so poor that she had only a single sari to wear. After getting a microcredit loan, she was able to add to her livestock, build up her savings, buy more land, buy her husband a rickshaw, and even employ two workers to help her. The Grameen "village banking" concept is presented, and other examples are given of women making the transition to greater autonomy and improved livelihoods. The message is clear, easy (for Westerners) to accept, and even inspiring. But when a few scenes are shown of angry "Muslim fanatics" objecting to women engaging in activities outside the home, the video's spell seems to be broken. How deeply rooted, in fact, *is* the trend toward modernization in Bangladesh? Suitable for high school audiences and older.

The World Bank: The Great Experiment
Date: 1997
Length: 2 videos, 50 minutes each
Price: $249.95
Source: Films for the Humanities & Sciences
P.O. Box 2053
Princeton, NJ 08543-2053
(800) 257-5126
Fax: (609) 275-3767

Critics of globalization have made punching bags of the World Bank and the IMF. Given those institutions' awesome financial power and the voting strength of the rich nations in their decision-making, it could hardly have been otherwise. This two-part video puts us in a front-row seat as the World Bank goes ten rounds with the tenacious representatives of a developing country, Uganda. (The time frame is 1995–1996.) The Ugandan government wants loans, and it wants to use the proceeds as it sees fit. The Bank is willing to lend but with strings attached: It wants its funds going to social projects like primary schools rather than to roads, power plants, or the defense budget. Teams of negotiators shuttle back and forth as the parties try to reach an accommodation. One gets a very good sense of the human interactions between the two sides—the elaborate courtesies and good humor— as well as some of the frictions *within* each side. (The Ugandans are not completely united in their budget priorities, and the World Bank negotiators have to contend with an IMF team pursuing an agenda different from their own.) This would be a very effective video to show in a development policy class. It manages the improbable feat of humanizing bureaucrats, economists, and finance ministers! Perhaps the most compelling figure in the video is Brian Falconer, the World Bank's "Res Rep" or "Resident Representative" in Kampala, a sort of Bretton Woods proconsul who could have walked right out of a Grahame Greene novel. Suitable for college and adult classes.

You Can't Eat Potential: Breaking Africa's Cycle of Poverty
Date: 1996
Length: 56 minutes
Price: $395 (purchase), $75 (rental)
Source: Filmakers Library
124 East 40th Street, Suite 901

New York, NY 10016
(212) 808-4980
http://www.filmakers.com

This video raises important questions about agriculture in sub-Saharan Africa—its current state, the food prospects for the continent if nothing changes, and a few of the possible paths toward more self-sufficiency in food production. The strongest parts of the film depict the actual experiences of farmers who follow traditional practices, versus those who have accepted new methods of farming (in the Green Revolution mode). It is persuasively argued that African soils are so badly depleted of essential nutrients that there remains hardly any alternative to using chemical additives, which, for the foreseeable future, will have to be imported. The video is unable, in fifty-six minutes, to deliver a fully fleshed-out analysis of how Africa can "break the cycle of poverty." It touches upon IMF structural adjustment policies but leaves the viewer uncertain whether those policies have been positive or negative, on balance, in their effects on African development. It also refers to population growth, rural-to-urban migration, urban unemployment, and even gender relations—more topics than can be woven together in a one-hour video. Most suitable for college and adult audiences.

Glossary

absolute poverty A way of conceptualizing poverty that relies on objective measures of deprivation, such as caloric intake, access to clean water, education, and life expectancy; often contrasted with relative poverty. Also, a particularly low level of money income—see **extreme poverty**.

bilateral aid Economic aid provided by one country to another—for example, funding from the U.S. Agency for International Development that finances the construction of a school in Liberia.

Bretton Woods institutions The World Bank and the International Monetary Fund (IMF), created at the 1944 conference held at Bretton Woods, New Hampshire.

child mortality A widely cited social indicator that is high in most poor countries, low in most rich ones. It refers to the mortality rate of children under the age of five. One of the Millennium Development Goals is to reduce the child mortality rate by two-thirds between 1990 and 2015.

civil society The nongovernmental organizations and groups in a country that give its people the means to express and organize themselves outside the political sphere—for example, through religious, fraternal, labor, and academic organizations. There is a growing appreciation for the role of civil society in the formulation of national policies to reduce poverty.

commodity exports The type of exports, whether cocoa, coffee, cotton, or copper, on which poor countries have long relied. World prices for most of these commodities have been unstable and trending downward for decades; the impact on the export earnings of poor countries has been devastating.

concessional loans Loans made to developing countries on favorable terms, such as below-market interest rates or grace periods during which no principal or interest payments need be made.

conditionality A term used to characterize certain agreements made between borrowing nations and international financial institutions (e.g., the IMF) by which the borrower agrees to certain conditions, such as reducing its fiscal deficit or removing price controls.

country-owned A term favored by the United Nations and World Bank to describe strategies for economic development and poverty reduction that are formulated by developing countries themselves, not imposed by outside agencies (such as the World Bank).

country-specific poverty line An income line that a country establishes, using any criteria it chooses, for the purpose of counting the number who are below and above it in order to estimate the extent (and trend) of national poverty. See **international poverty line**.

debt service The total of all payments a country must make each year on its external debts, whether interest or principal. For poor countries, debt service can reach crippling proportions, using up scarce foreign exchange earnings that might have gone to more productive purposes.

developed country A country that has industrialized its economy and modernized its society, thereby achieving a high per capita GDP and high levels of health, life expectancy, education, and labor productivity; in short, a rich country.

developing country A country that has not yet experienced enough economic growth to be called "developed"; per capita GDP, along with many other indicators of human well-being, is much lower than what is seen in the rich, developed countries.

development economics A field within economics that aims for an understanding of how economies are able to make a transition from low standards of living to higher ones. No consensus has yet emerged on how exactly this can be managed, although it is clear that development involves political and social factors as well as economic ones.

economic growth A pattern of rising per capita GDP that lays the foundation for eliminating poverty over time. Poverty impacts, however, can be minimal if the benefits of economic growth are disproportionately reaped by the wealthy, as happens in many developing countries.

economies in transition The economies of formerly Soviet-dominated countries that have been making the difficult transition from central planning to a market orientation, often experiencing high rates of poverty in the process.

export-led growth Economic growth that is initiated and/or sustained by strong sales of goods in foreign markets. The great success stories of the mid to late twentieth century—Japan, South Korea, Taiwan, Singapore—were of this kind. China's impressive current pace of economic growth and poverty reduction also relies heavily on production for export.

extreme poverty A condition of deprivation experienced by those with incomes so low that they are unable to afford the basic requirements of food, clothing, and shelter; also known as absolute poverty. The most widely accepted measure of extreme poverty is the World Bank's $1-a-day standard.

G8 Eight large industrialized countries that meet regularly to set goals concerning world trade and other economic issues. The eight are the United States, Japan, Great Britain, Germany, France, Italy, Canada, and Russia. Before Russia joined the group in 1997, it was the G7.

G77 A group of developing countries that began in 1964 as 77 and in time grew to more than 100; the G77 promotes the interests of less developed countries in world forums and is, at least symbolically, a counterweight to the G8.

gender equality A goal now accepted by virtually all governments and articulated in nearly every international declaration or agreement but still far from being achieved. It refers to equal treatment under the law, equal access to education, equal opportunities for political participation, and so forth. When countries are ranked on a "gender empowerment measure," even the top-rated nation, Iceland, falls short of complete equality (*Human Development Report 2003*, p. 314).

gender gap The difference between male and female rates of literacy, poverty, labor force participation, or any other socioeconomic indicator. One of the Millennium Development Goals calls for the elimination of the gender gap in primary and secondary schooling by 2015, and preferably much sooner.

globalization A complex process of increasing international communication and economic integration that is affecting societies everywhere in profound, sometimes destabilizing ways. Critics contend that globalization works more to the advantage of the developed than the developing countries; advocates argue that trade is the key to lifting developing nations out of poverty.

Grameen Bank A microcredit institution, founded by the Bangladeshi economist Muhammad Yunus in the 1970s, that has served as a model for many similar efforts around the world. From the beginning, Grameen lent primarily to poor rural women; its aims are to reduce poverty and to empower women.

gross domestic product (GDP) The most widely accepted measure of total economic activity in a country, encompassing the output of consumer goods and services, whether produced for the private or public sector, capital goods, and output produced for export (minus goods and services imported). Production of capital goods, such as factories, equipment, and infrastructure, plays a crucial role in economic development.

gross domestic product per capita A country's GDP divided by its population. This is the economist's preferred index of economic performance and is used by the World Bank to categorize countries as low income, lower-middle income, upper-middle income, or high income. It does not take into account how equally or unequally the GDP is divided across the population.

Highly Indebted Poor Countries (HIPC) initiative A program run by the World Bank and the IMF under which poor countries with heavy foreign debts may qualify to have their debt service burdens eased and even have their debt principal reduced or eliminated. Begun in 1996, the program was "enhanced" in 1999 and promises to offer tens of billions of dollars of debt relief over time.

HIV Human immunodeficiency virus, the virus that leads to AIDS. Along with TB and malaria, HIV/AIDS takes a huge toll in lives and health, especially in developing areas. Two-thirds of the global HIV-infected population live in Africa.

Human Development Index A measure of socioeconomic well-being that takes into account not only monetary income but also the life expectancy and educational attainment of the population; introduced in the 1990 *Human Development Report* of the UN Development Programme and updated annually.

Human Poverty Index A measure of socioeconomic deprivation based on mortality rates, illiteracy rates, lack of access to clean water, and percentage of children who are underweight; it is updated annually and published in the *Human Development Report*.

hunger A problem affecting much of the developing world and not unknown in the developed world. The UN's Food and Agriculture Organization, in a 2003 report, puts the global number of hungry at 840 million. One of the Millennium Development Goals is to reduce the number of hungry in the world by half between 1990 and 2015—a goal not likely to be met.

infant mortality rate One of the most commonly reported social indicators. It is the rate of death among infants up to age one, expressed per 1,000 live births.

infrastructure The built-up physical capital that undergirds an economy, whether in the form of roads, bridges, dams, canals, power grids, schools, or hospitals.

International Monetary Fund (IMF) The international short-term lending institution cocreated with the World Bank in 1944. Although World Bank loans are intended to promote long-term economic development, IMF loans are meant to help borrowing nations stabilize their currencies and their balance of payments.

international poverty line   A per capita real income level below which a person living anywhere in the world is considered to have insufficient income to cover basic needs. The two best known international poverty lines are the $1-a-day and $2-a-day lines established by the World Bank on the basis of U.S. dollars of 1985 purchasing power.

Jubilee 2000 campaign   A global campaign of the 1990s, also known as Drop the Debt, which was directed at major debt relief for the world's poorest and most indebted nations. Although it fell short of its ultimate objective, the campaign may have contributed to the creation of the HIPC initiative (see above). Successor organizations include Jubilee USA Network, Jubilee Research, and Jubilee South.

Least Developed Countries (LDCs)   A group of forty-nine countries that meet specific criteria of low per capita income, economic vulnerability, and weak human assets. These are among the poorest countries in the world; a majority of them are located in sub-Saharan Africa.

literacy   An often-cited index of social development. High rates of literacy are considered a prerequisite for advancing from low-productivity, agrarian types of economic activity to more urban, knowledge-based activities that offer higher incomes.

malnutrition   A medical condition brought on by a diet insufficient in calories, protein, or micronutrients such as iron, vitamin A, and iodine. Malnutrition can cause stunting in children, and, in all age groups, an increased susceptibility to infection and higher mortality. Poverty is the root cause of malnutrition.

maternal mortality   A social indicator on which developed and developing countries differ widely. It measures the rate of mortality for women due to pregnancy or childbirth in relation to the total number of live births in a year. A Millennium Development Goal is to improve maternal health enough to achieve a three-quarter reduction in maternal mortality between 1990 and 2015.

microcredit   Small-scale lending to individual farmers, entrepreneurs, or craft-workers in a system wherein funds are continually being repaid and re-lent. Participants are generally too poor to qualify for an ordinary bank loan. See Grameen Bank.

Millennium Development Goals (MDGs)   A set of eight long-range goals adopted by the Millennium Summit in New York in the fall of 2000. The main goal is a 50 percent reduction in extreme poverty and hunger between 1990 and 2015; other goals call for improvements in the environment, education, gender equality, child mortality, maternal health, and control of deadly diseases.

multilateral aid   Economic assistance from the rich countries to the poor, delivered through agencies such as the World Bank, regional development banks, and the United Nations.

NEPAD The New Partnership for Africa's Development, a plan worked out by African governments and formally adopted in 2001, that aims to halt the marginalization of Africa in the world economy, quicken the pace of economic development, and reduce poverty. It is a response to the widespread belief in Africa and elsewhere that a continent in crisis cannot be allowed to drift, without a vision of something better for its future.

nongovernmental organization (NGO) Any of the myriad nonprofit organizations *not* connected to a government that work to achieve social and economic goals in the developing world. Some examples are Oxfam, Catholic Relief Services, Save the Children, and Bread for the World.

North A term sometimes used to denote the developed countries. Most of the world's richest nations are located in the Northern Hemisphere. Compare the **South**.

odious debt Foreign debt incurred by poor countries while ruled by undemocratic regimes, with the borrowed funds benefiting a favored few, not the majority of the people; some argue that such debt is illegitimate and can lawfully be repudiated by successor (democratic) regimes.

OECD The Organization for Economic Cooperation and Development, a group of wealthy market economies that are also democracies. It was formed in 1960 and now consists of thirty nations, mainly in Europe and North America but including Japan, South Korea, Australia, and New Zealand. They meet periodically to discuss economic and social policies.

Official Development Assistance (ODA) The most commonly cited measure of foreign aid, being the total of grants and loans made on concessional terms to poor countries by rich countries belonging to the OECD.

poverty gap A measure of the depth of poverty that takes into account how far below the poverty line people fall. If most of the "poor" have incomes just under the poverty line, the "gap" is much less than if most of the poor have incomes below *half* of the poverty line. Data on poverty gaps are published annually in the World Bank's *World Development Indicators*.

Poverty Reduction Strategy Paper (PRSP) A document that poor countries must prepare as part of an application for debt relief under the HIPC program; the PRSP emerges from a consultative process involving government, civil society, NGOs, and other international partners, and it details the steps to be taken by government to reduce poverty over the long run.

poverty trap A self-defeating circumstance that condemns a poor country or region to continued poverty. For example, if incomes are so low that people have no capacity to save, then funding cannot be generated for the investments that might raise incomes and allow for saving to take place.

privatization   The selling off to private investors of previously state-owned enterprises. Although it can cause short-term unemployment problems and higher prices for customers, privatization is believed to lead to a more efficient allocation of resources in the long run.

pro-poor growth   Economic growth that proceeds in a way that favors the poor; in recent years, development experts have called on developing nations to design and pursue strategies that deliver a substantial share of the fruits of economic growth to the poor.

Purchasing Power Parity (PPP)   A way of expressing a country's GDP or any other economic indicator in units that are comparable to U.S. currency; for example, if a country's per capita GDP is $5,000 in PPP terms, even though it may be earned in pesos or rupees, it means that, on average, individuals in that country have incomes that allow them to buy what can be bought for $5,000 in the United States.

regional development bank   Any of several multilateral financial institutions, such as the Inter-American Development Bank and the Asian Development Bank, that channel funds from richer countries to poorer ones through loans to (mainly) public entities. Such loans often finance infrastructure projects. The banks also offer technical assistance to developing nations.

relative poverty   A way of conceptualizing poverty that defines being poor as having less income than some arbitrary percentage of the total population—for example, having an income lower than 80 or 90 percent of the people in the country.

social indicators   Nonmonetary measures of well-being, such as child mortality, maternal mortality, and literacy rates.

South   A term sometimes used to denote the developing countries, the majority of which are located in the Southern Hemisphere. Compare the **North**.

sustainable development   Economic development that does not exploit natural resources at such a high rate, or pollute the air, land, and water to such a degree, as to threaten the prospects for continuing growth and development in the future.

Third World   A term not often used any more to refer to the developing (poor) countries; the First World consists of the wealthy industrialized nations of Europe, North America, and the Pacific region; the Second World was the set of countries dominated by the Soviet Union before its collapse.

tied aid   Economic assistance funds that must be spent on goods or services of the donor country. Development experts consider tied aid much less desirable than untied aid, but given political realities, it is sometimes a case of tied aid or *no* aid.

United Nations Conference on Trade and Development (UNCTAD)
A UN agency that works to integrate developing countries into the world economy on terms favorable to them.

United Nations Development Programme (UNDP) A UN agency whose primary purpose is to encourage development among poorer nations. It sponsors health and educational initiatives, as well as basic infrastructure investments. The annual *Human Development Report* is issued by the UNDP.

United States Agency for International Development (USAID) The main conduit of technical and financial assistance from the United States to the developing countries.

Washington Consensus A set of doctrines, said to be promoted or enforced by the U.S. Treasury Department, the IMF, and the World Bank, including free trade, fiscal discipline, privatization, market determination of exchange rates, and unrestricted capital movements from one country to another.

World Bank A financial institution of great importance to the developing countries, with a primary mission of reducing and eliminating poverty. Formally known as the International Bank for Reconstruction and Development, the World Bank was created at the Bretton Woods conference in 1944. It is an indispensable source of international poverty data, much of it posted on the website http://www.worldbank.org/data/.

World Trade Organization (WTO) The successor to GATT, or the General Agreement on Tariffs and Trade, as the "traffic cop" for global trade. It is the organization that sponsors negotiations on liberalizing trade and investment among nations, and it adjudicates disputes on trade-related issues such as tariffs, quotas, subsidies, and intellectual property. WTO activities are fiercely protested by various groups opposed to globalization in its current form.

Index

281

About the Author

Geoffrey Gilbert is professor of economics at Hobart and William Smith Colleges, Geneva, NY. His published works include ABC-CLIO's *World Population: A Reference Handbook.*